# AFTER QUEER STUDIES

*After Queer Studies* maps the literary influences that facilitated queer theory's academic emergence and charts how they continue to shape its evolution as a critical practice. Exploring the interdisciplinary origins of queer studies, this volume argues for the prominent role that literary studies has played in establishing the concepts, methods, and questions of contemporary queer theory. It shows how queer studies has had an impact on many trending concerns in literary studies, such as the affective turn, the question of the subject, and the significance of social categories like race, class, and sexual differences. Bridging between queer studies' legacies and its horizons, this collection initiates new discussion on the irreducible changes that queer studies has introduced in the concepts, methods, and modes of literary interpretation and cultural practices.

TYLER BRADWAY is author of *Queer Experimental Literature: The Affective Politics of Bad Reading* (2017). He is the editor of "Lively Words: The Politics and Poetics of Experimental Writing," a forthcoming special issue of *College Literature*, and his essays have appeared or are forthcoming in *GLQ, Mosaic, Stanford Arcade, American Literature in Transition 1980–1990*, and *The Comics of Alison Bechdel: From the Outside In*.

E. L. MCCALLUM authored *Unmaking The Making of Americans: Toward an Aesthetic Ontology* (2018) and *Object Lessons: How to Do Things with Fetishism* (1999), coedited with Mikko Tuhkanen *The Cambridge History of Gay and Lesbian Literature* (2014), and *Queer Times, Queer Becomings* (2011). Her essays have appeared in *camera obscura, Postmodern Culture, Poetics Today*, and *differences*, as well as edited collections (including *The Cambridge Companion to the Modern Gothic, Primary Stein*, and MLA's *Approaches to Teaching William Faulkner*). She recently won the Paul Varg Alumni Award for Faculty, recognizing outstanding teaching and scholarly achievement at Michigan State.

# AFTER SERIES

This series focuses on the legacy of several iconic figures, and key themes, in the origins and development of literary theory. Each book in the series attempts to isolate the influence, legacy and the impact of thinkers. Each figure addressed not only bequeathed specific concepts and doctrines to literary study, but they effectively opened up new critical landscapes for research. It is this legacy that this series tries to capture, with every book being designed specifically for use in literature departments. Throughout each book the concept of "After" is used in 3 ways: After in the sense of trying to define what is quintessential about each figure: "What has each figure introduced into the world of literary studies, criticism and interpretation?' After in a purely chronological sense: 'What comes after each figure?', 'What has his/her influence and legacy been?" and "How have they changed the landscape of literary studies?" Lastly, After in a practical sense: "How have their respective critical legacies impacted on an understanding of literary texts?" Each book is a collaborative volume with an international cast of critics and their level is suited for recommended reading on courses.

# AFTER QUEER STUDIES

*Literature, Theory and Sexuality in the 21st Century*

EDITED BY

## TYLER BRADWAY
*SUNY Cortland*


## E. L. MCCALLUM
*Michigan State University*

CAMBRIDGE
UNIVERSITY PRESS

# CAMBRIDGE
## UNIVERSITY PRESS

University Printing House, Cambridge CB2 8BS, United Kingdom

One Liberty Plaza, 20th Floor, New York, NY 10006, USA

477 Williamstown Road, Port Melbourne, VIC 3207, Australia

314–321, 3rd Floor, Plot 3, Splendor Forum, Jasola District Centre, New Delhi – 110025, India

79 Anson Road, #06–04/06, Singapore 079906

Cambridge University Press is part of the University of Cambridge.

It furthers the University's mission by disseminating knowledge in the pursuit of
education, learning, and research at the highest international levels of excellence.

www.cambridge.org
Information on this title: www.cambridge.org/9781108498036
DOI: 10.1017/9781108627832

© Cambridge University Press 2019

First published 2019

Printed and bound in Great Britain by Clays Ltd, Elcograf S.p.A.

*A catalogue record for this publication is available from the British Library.*

*Library of Congress Cataloging-in-Publication Data*
NAMES: Bradway, Tyler, 1983– editor. | McCallum, E. L. (Ellen Lee), 1966– editor.
TITLE: After queer studies : literature, theory, sexuality in 21st century / edited by Tyler Bradway,
SUNY Cortland, E.L. McCallum, Michigan State University.
DESCRIPTION: Cambridge, United Kingdom ; New York, NY : Cambridge University Press, 2018. |
Series: After series | Includes bibliographical references and index.
IDENTIFIERS: LCCN 2018035160 | ISBN 9781108498036 (hardback) |
ISBN 9781108739733 (pbk.)
SUBJECTS: LCSH: Homosexuality in literature. | Queer theory. | Sexual orientation in literature.
CLASSIFICATION: LCC PN56.H57 A383 2018 | DDC 809/.93353–dc23
LC record available at https://lccn.loc.gov/2018035160

ISBN 978-1-108-49803-6 Hardback
ISBN 978-1-108-73973-3 Paperback

# Contents

# Notes on Contributors

MATT BRIM is Associate Professor of Queer Studies at the College of Staten Island, City University of New York (CUNY). He is the coeditor of *Imagining Queer Methods* with Amin Ghaziani (2019) and the author of *James Baldwin and the Queer Imagination* (2014), as well as an open-access study guide for the HIV/AIDS activist documentary film *United in Anger: A History of ACT UP*. His current book project is titled *Poor Queer Studies* (forthcoming in 2020). His work has appeared in the *Journal of Homosexuality*, *WSQ: Women's Studies Quarterly*, and the *Journal of Modern Literature*.

ANDRÉ CARRINGTON is Associate Professor of African American Literature at Drexel University. His first book, *Speculative Blackness* (2016), interrogates the cultural politics of race in the fantastic genres through studies of print, visual, and online texts. His writing also appears in the journals *American Literature*, *Lateral*, and *Souls* and the Eisner Award-winning anthology *The Blacker the Ink*. With cartoonist Jennifer Camper, he cofounded the Queers & Comics international conference in 2015, and with Abigail De Kosnik, he is coeditor of "Fans of Color/ Fandoms of Color," a special issue of *Transformative Works & Cultures*.

STEPHEN GUY-BRAY is Professor of English at the University of British Columbia. He specializes in Renaissance poetry and queer theory. He has published three monographs, two coedited collections, and numerous articles and book chapters, chiefly on Renaissance literature. He is currently working on a study of the queerness of representation.

SHARON PATRICIA HOLLAND is the Townsend Ludington Term Distinguished Endowed Professor in American Studies at the University of North Carolina at Chapel Hill. She is a graduate of Princeton University (1986) and holds a PhD in English and African American Studies from the University of Michigan, Ann Arbor (1992). She is the author of

*Raising the Dead: Readings of Death and (Black) Subjectivity* (2000), which won the Lora Romero First Book Prize from the American Studies Association (ASA) in 2002. She is also coauthor of a collection of transatlantic Afro-Native criticism with Professor Tiya Miles (American Culture, UM, Ann Arbor) entitled *Crossing Waters/ Crossing Worlds: The African Diaspora in Indian Country* (2006). Professor Holland is also responsible for the publication of a feminist classic entitled *The Queen is in the Garbage* by Lila Karp (2007). She is the author of *The Erotic Life of Racism* (2012), a theoretical project that explores the intersection of critical race, feminist, and queer theory. She is also at work on the final draft of another book project entitled simply, "little black girl." You can see her work on food, writing, and all things equestrian on her blog, http://theprofessorstable.wordpress.com//. She is currently at work on a new project, "Vocabularies of Vulnerability: hum.animal.blackness," an investigation of the human/animal distinction and the place of discourse on blackness within that discussion. She is the editor of *South: A Scholarly Journal* (formerly *Southern Literary Journal*), https://southjournal.org.

RICHARD A. KAYE is Associate Professor of English at Hunter College and the Graduate Center of the CUNY. He is the author of *The Flirt's Tragedy: Desire without End in Victorian and Edwardian Fiction* (2002) and is the editor of the Broadview edition of Alan Dale's 1889 novel *A Marriage Below Zero* (2017). He is editing a collection of essays on Oscar Wilde's *The Picture of Dorian Gray* and is completing a book entitled "Voluptuous Immobility: St. Sebastian and the Decadent Imagination."

AMBER JAMILLA MUSSER is Associate Professor of American Studies at George Washington University. She writes about the intersection of aesthetics, race, and sexuality. She is the author of *Sensational Flesh: Race, Power, and Masochism* (2014) and *Sensual Excess: Queer Femininity and Brown Jouissance* (2018).

KEVIN OHI is Professor of English at Boston College. The recipient of fellowships from the National Humanities Center, the Guggenheim Foundation, and the Cornell Society for the Humanities, he is the author of *Innocence and Rapture: The Erotic Child in Pater, Wilde, James, and Nabokov* (2005), *Henry James and the Queerness of Style* (2011), and *Dead Letters Sent: Queer Literary Transmission* (2016). He is currently completing a book entitled "Inceptions."

RICARDO ORTIZ is Chair and Associate Professor of US Latinx Literature in the English Department at Georgetown University, where he is also affiliated faculty in the Programs in American Studies and Comparative Literature, as well as the Center for Latin American Studies. Professor Ortiz's first book, *Cultural Erotics in Cuban America* (2007), won Honorable Mention for the 2008 Alan Bray Prize of the Modern Language Association and his article "Revolution's Other Histories" was joint winner of the Crompton-Knoll Award from the MLA in 1999. Professor Ortiz has published on queer Latinx topics in multiple venues, including the volume *The Queer Sixties* and journals including *The Journal of Homosexuality, Social Text, Contemporary Literature*, and *GLQ*.

NICK SALVATO is Professor and Chair of Performing and Media Arts at Cornell University. He is the author of *Uncloseting Drama: American Modernism and Queer Performance* (2010), *Knots Landing* (2015), and *Obstruction* (2016). His essays have appeared in numerous venues including *Camera Obscura, Critical Inquiry, Criticism, Discourse, TDR: The Drama Review*, and *Theatre Journal*.

DANA SEITLER is Associate Professor of English and Director of the Centre for Sexual Diversity Studies at the University of Toronto. Her research interests include late nineteenth- and early twentieth-century American literature and culture, queer theory and sexuality studies, feminist theory, science studies, aesthetic philosophy, and visual culture. She is the author of *Atavistic Tendencies: The Culture of Science in American Modernity* (2008). Her second book, *Reading Sideways: The Queer Politics of Art in Modern American Fiction*, is forthcoming in winter 2019. Her current project, *I'm Dying To! Ecstasy, Withdrawal, Biopolitics*, focuses on the aesthetics of refusal, renunciation, and pleasure in American literature and culture. She has published articles in many scholarly journals, including *American Quarterly, American Literature, Genre, Cultural Critique, GLQ, Criticism*, and *A/SAP*, and is the recipient of several research grants and awards from the Mellon Foundation, the Connaught Fund, the Jackman Humanities Institute, and the Social Sciences and Humanities Research Council of Canada.

REBEKAH SHELDON is Assistant Professor of English at Indiana University and the author of *The Child to Come: Life after the Human Condition* (2016). She is currently at work on a new project on the history and theory of queer occultism.

# Acknowledgments

The editors would like to thank all of the authors in this volume for their commitment to this project and for their contributions to tracing the entwined pasts and futures of queer literary studies. We're grateful to the anonymous readers for their invaluable insight into the intersections of queer and literary studies. We want to thank Sarah Panuska for her keen editorial assistance, Scott Sheldon for preparing the index, and Amy Mower for ushering the manuscript into production. We thank Ray Ryan, our editor at Cambridge University Press, for supporting this project from its inception and for encouraging our work throughout every stage of its development. Finally, we wish to express our debt to the countless writers, thinkers, and scholars of queer studies that came before, whose work continues to inspire the hope for a queerer future to come.

# Introduction
## Thinking Sideways, or an Untoward Genealogy of Queer Reading

### E. L. McCallum and Tyler Bradway

Queer studies' inception is canonically marked by two philosophical books: Michel Foucault's *The History of Sexuality: An Introduction, Vol. 1* (1976) and Judith Butler's *Gender Trouble* (1990).[1] Foucault recounts how a "Victorian" view of sexuality rose to predominance in Europe and North America. Its defining formation is confinement: in the home, within a monogamous heterosexual couple, legitimized by the state and religious authorities through marriage. Forms of sexual practice other than heterosexually monogamous domestic reproduction, not to mention the pleasures and cultural understandings that emerge from such alternative engagements, were considered illegitimate or worse. Yet, humans being who they are – pleasure-seekers who emerge from an infantile polymorphous perversity – many stray from this ideal.

Through this model, which Foucault termed the "repressive hypothesis," sexuality came to be aligned with privacy, secrecy, and purely utilitarian – reproductive – aims. Yet Foucault demonstrated that sexuality is nonetheless imbricated with public, political, and social spheres. In other words, Western understandings and experiences of sexuality are fundamentally bound up with the liberal nation-state and the dominance of the bourgeoisie. This social, economic, and political formation of the liberal capitalist nation-state emerged from the Enlightenment (a period roughly from the middle of the seventeenth century to end of the eighteenth century) and came to full fruition in the period Foucault nominates "Victorian" – the nineteenth century. While the Victorian era shaped much of the thinking in our contemporary world, its "repressive hypothesis" also generated counteractions. Foucault showed that repression produced sexuality rather than simply contained it, and sketched how sexuality's perverse pleasures might be deployed by other forms of power. Thus, as political, scientific, and economic forms evolve – from liberalism to neoliberalism, from colonial capitalism to globalization, from national governments to multinational corporations, from industrial power to bio-power – so too do forms of sexuality evolve. New norms emerge to regulate sexuality even as some communities experiment with how their bodies and pleasures may contest those norms.

Commonly understood as an expression of our innermost self, sexuality turns out to be implanted from outside of us. Butler's *Gender Trouble* develops this Foucauldian insight. Butler integrated Foucault's social con-structionism with the psychoanalytic model of how the subject comes to be and the deconstructive model of how language works. Rather than being a static or absolute essence, identity is a performance that we are compelled to repeat; its performance gains meaning within social dis-course, in reference to other performances going on simultaneously.

Butler builds on Sigmund Freud, who, despite Foucault's criticisms, also complicated heteronormativity's repressive hypothesis. Butler trans-poses Freud's notion of melancholia to describe how heterosexuality and gender identity emerge from the twin taboos of homosexuality and incest. Melancholia, Freud suggests, is a perverse reaction to the loss of a desired object. In melancholia, someone has become unavailable to our desire and attachment. When we absorb the prohibitions against incest and homo-sexuality, Butler argued, the same-sex parent becomes lost to us. Thus, we internalize that person inside our minds. We *become* them, perhaps only unconsciously, taking on the characteristics of the same-sex parent to preserve our forbidden love for them.

Becoming that lost object of desire is not a one-time event, nor is it merely psychological. Rather, identity has to be asserted in the social world. Here Butler drew on philosophers J. L. Austin and Jacques Derrida, who showed that language does not have an anchored meaning that refers to things outside of itself. Words, phrases, sentences act in the world, and their meaning relies on contexts that make their actions felicitous or effective. A promise, a bet, a marriage vow – these are what Austin called performative speech acts. Performative speech acts only take place in language and under the right circumstances; there is always a risk of failure. You can name a child "Sue," but if Sue comes to understand that his name does not align with his gender, then he may want to change it. Or, he may, as in Johnny Cash's song, redefine how others understand the name "Sue." Butler argues that identity itself is in this sense performative: an action that requires constant reassertion and interpretation within language. It can succeed – and will succeed to the degree that it is socially intelligible – but our performative expression always risks failure and incoherence.

As we strive to assert an identity that others recognize as coherent, we inevitably fail to perform that identity perfectly. One is never as feminine, straight, Black, or middle-class as the ideal. In part, this is because we are never simply performing one identity but are operating at the intersection of many: gender, race, class, ethnicity, nationality, sexuality, disability, among so many others. We might be fluent in certain gestures, habits, and ways of speaking, but not all of these fluencies match the ones preferred by dominant culture. Indeed, our identity performances may not be compatible with one another, producing disturbances in one's social intelligibility that might be called . . . queer. As José Esteban Muñoz observes, "We can √ understand queerness itself as being filled with the intention to be lost. Queerness is illegible and therefore lost in relation to the straight minds' mapping of space. . . [O]ne's queerness will always render one lost to a world of heterosexual imperatives, codes, and laws."[2] To queer is to distance oneself from norms, and to embrace that distance.

Yet while queer is a glitch in the matrix – a disturbance in how smoothly one's cultural or social intelligibility operates – it can also be a skillful subversion of intelligibility. Through irony, parody, camp, and other deployments of language, some people *queer* identities and other social practices. Queer marks an opportunity for reinterpretation. In this sense, queer is not an identity, a thing, or an entity but an *activity*. Queer names a √ practice, an approach, a way of relating. Scholars and activists seized on the term "queer" as a way to describe not fitting in, not being fully intelligible to mainstream demands for comportment, and even to question those demands for normativity in our desires, pleasures, bodies. As queer, we may be able to articulate how we are not fitting in – to confess to or fear, for instance, being too much of a sissy compared to masculine norms. Or we might resist specifying our queerness – as some people do in affirming nonbinary gender fluidity. While queer offers elasticity, it always hinges on √ bodies, pleasures, relations, or desires at cross-purposes with heteronormativity. It is a mode of thinking, but also a mode of recognizing the unconscious commitments we find ourselves in because of our desires. In fact, a crucial lesson of queer is that thinking – which might seem to be disembodied – is inherently a bodily practice.

Insofar as queer is a mode of thinking, it is a mode of thinking sideways, of turning around a question in unexpected ways.[3] When we reflect on that sideways thinking, we have theory. Theory is a second-order mode of investigation: if literature is creative expression in the world, literary theory is *about* literature's creative expression; in other words, it reflects on how literature works. Queer studies looks at a range of ways of being queer – in this volume, specifically literary ways – while queer theory hinges on how we think about queer. Queer theory is thus inseparable from queer studies. Indeed, Ramzi Fawaz and Shanté Paradigm Smalls have noted the irony that the major scholarly texts of queer theory tend to be more widely read than the actual literary works queer theorists analyze.[4]

Although the term emerged in the 1990s, queer theory predates its canonical inception in Foucault and Butler. Two movements define this convergence: feminism and gay liberation. In the feminist stream, Cherríe Moraga and Gloria Anzaldúa's 1981 anthology *This Bridge Called My Back* marks a watershed moment in the thinking of feminism, race, class, and sexuality.[5] Another landmark essay, Gayle Rubin's "Thinking Sex" (1984), joins the ongoing conversation in the radical feminist philosophy of the 1970s and 1980s, exemplified by Adrienne Rich, Audre Lorde, and Marilyn Frye, to reconsider what "counts" as sexuality and how sexuality can be wielded against people in oppressive ways.[6] Similarly, Anzaldúa's *Borderlands | La Frontera: The New Mestiza* (1987) explored the intersectional limits of identity through a Chicanx feminist lens we now recognize as queer, because it reflects on the unintelligibility of being in the world in relation to various communities – within her family and her community of origin on the Texas border, within the white-dominated academy, and among a non-hispanophone Latinx/Chicanx feminist community in the San Francisco Bay area, among others.[7] Importantly, Anzaldúa's experimentations with form subverted the norms of serious philosophical writing, anticipating the intimacy of literature and theory in queer studies.

Parallel to the feminist movement, and contemporaneous with Foucault, writers such as Dennis Altman, Guy Hocquenghem, and Leo Bersani grappled with the possibilities of gay liberation in the 1970s and 1980s, presciently laying groundwork for the emergence of queer theory in the 1990s. John D'Emilio's important essay "Capitalism and Gay Identity" appeared in 1983, charting a path for future intersections of queer and Marxist theory.[8] D'Emilio tied the emergence of urban homosexual enclaves to socioeconomic changes, such as the ability of individuals to support themselves financially rather than rely on family. D'Emilio's work connects the social formation of individualism to the development of gay liberation, instigated by the 1969 Stonewall rebellion. He provides a Marxist view of sexuality to counter the psychoanalytic model predominant in the mid-twentieth century.

Feminism and gay liberation shared some common intellectual roots in psychoanalytic theory's radical reconsideration of gender and sexuality as polymorphously perverse, not fixed from birth. Both also launched important critiques of psychoanalytic institutions and discourses, which often imposed and naturalized oppressive sexual norms. Feminist and gay liberationist scholars were also influenced by post-structuralist theory – thinkers like Derrida, Foucault, and Roland Barthes – who gained ascendancy in US intellectual circles in the 1980s. Arguably, the convergence of these two strands – feminism and gay liberation – can be seen in the appearance of *Gender Trouble* and its significant intervention in the feminist debates around essentialism and social constructionism.

Yet queer theory's seemingly ivory-tower thinking was deeply embedded in activist movements. Indeed, Butler's conceptions of desire and loss were particularly resonant in gay and lesbian communities devastated by the AIDS epidemic in the 1980s. From the identification of the earliest victims of the epidemic in 1981 through the mid-1990s, HIV/AIDS was a death sentence. Only in 1995, when the FDA approved the first protease inhibitors, was HIV+ transformed into a chronic, but not unmanageable, condition. This era is marked by the catastrophic loss of lovers and friends, but it is also a moment of radical mobilization. "Silence = Death" became a rallying cry in a nation where the President refused to discuss AIDS publicly until 1985, and where normative institutions – the government and the medical-industrial establishment – failed to intervene in the crisis. HIV+ people and their allies responded to this silence in a powerful explosion of creative work – prose, drama, poetry, essay, art, performance, film, and television. The untimeliness of AIDS deaths – among a population that was just coming into its own socially, politically, artistically, and professionally – exacerbated the sense of urgency felt by queer communities. The scholarly profession was not without its losses: John Boswell, author of *Christianity, Social Tolerance, and Homosexuality*, a pioneering treatise on gay history;[9] Craig Owens, noted art scholar and editor of *Art in America*; Essex Hemphill, African-American poet and essayist; and Foucault himself. AIDS casts a shadow over the development of queer studies that cannot be forgotten; indeed, the crisis crystallized the political and performative stakes of coming out, reading queerly, and queering identity.

We have been tracing a certain origin story without tracing the origin itself. The etymology of the term "queer" shows, rather fittingly, that its origins are somewhat obscure. Origins are suspect in queer studies, for they reinscribe a sense of propriety, lineage, norms; as Robert McRuer notes, "Any myth of origin suggests a linear (or might we say 'straight') path of development and implies a pure and singular starting point."[10] The origin is often mistaken for authority, when really an origin just encapsulates a few potentialities of a term. Yet if we understand an origin as a trajectory, rather than a beginning or essence, it can be useful to chart queer's "before" as we turn to its "after." Of queer's etymology, the OED notes:

> Origin uncertain; perhaps (or perhaps even cognate with) German *quer* transverse, oblique, crosswise, at right angles, obstructive, (of things) going wrong (now rare), (of a person) peculiar (now obsolete in this sense), (of a glance) directed sideways, especially in a surreptitious or hostile manner (now rare), (of opinion and behaviour) at odds with others (see thwart *adv.*), but the semantic correspondence is not exact.[11]

We cite this origin story because of its vivid spatial designation for queer: "transverse, oblique, obstructive," which resonates with our description of queer theory as thinking sideways. The dictionary now acknowledges queer as a formerly derogatory term for homosexual that denoted an "identity that does not correspond to established ideas of sexuality and gender, especially heterosexual norms." Yet, recalling Austin and Butler, the simplicity of this definition should become complicated by how the term is used. Because it puts identity into question, queer undoes subjects and objects – their limits, relations, formations, and modes of operation. For this reason, queer comes to be used in seemingly undisciplined ways. Eve Kosofsky Sedgwick describes queer as "the open mesh of possibilities, gaps, overlaps, dissonances and resonances, lapses and excesses of meaning when the constituent elements of anyone's gender, of anyone's sexuality aren't made (or can't be made) to signify monolithically."[12] Although she acknowledges that queer sometimes serves "to denote, almost simply, same-sex sexual object choice, lesbian or gay, whether or not it is organized around multiple criss-crossings of definitional lines," Sedgwick also locates in queer "experimental linguistic, epistemological, representational, political adventures." The vast range between simple "same-sex object choice" and experimental "adventures" captures the inherent slipperiness in defining "queer" as well as the opportunities such slipperiness affords.

Queer's slipperiness bears on the "after" in our title. Recently, queer literary studies has become particularly focused on queering temporality, a move that troubles the linear genealogy we have presented thus far. We see this turn in Lee Edelman's influential polemic *No Future* (2004) as well as Jack Halberstam's *In a Queer Time and Place* (2005), Muñoz's *Cruising Utopia* (2009), Valerie Rohy's *Anachronism and Its Others* (2009), Elizabeth Freeman's *Time Binds* (2010), Peter Coviello's *Tomorrow's Parties* (2013), and Juana María Rodríguez's *Sexual Futures, Queer Gestures, and Other Latina Longings* (2014).[13] Despite their differences, these works evince queer studies' ongoing reconceptualization of past, present, and future – as well as of the modes of periodization, genealogy, history, linearity, and causality that we use to think about queer time.

Alongside the temporal turn, queer studies has begun to ask: Whither queer studies now? In their pathbreaking issue of *Social Text*, "What's Queer about Queer Studies Now?" (2005), David L. Eng, Halberstam, and Muñoz answered this question by contextualizing queer theory alongside the War on Terror, US imperialism, neoliberalism, and "queer liberalism," which forsakes the radicalism of the AIDS era and embraces assimilation to existing norms of the state, exemplified by the marriage equality movement.[14] Insisting on its political and social relevance, Eng, Halberstam, and Muñoz called for queer theory to adopt a "politics of epistemological humility" (15). By humbly approaching the question of "what a desirably queer world might look like?" queer theory becomes more ethically and politically responsive to global forms of otherness that continue to be marginalized. While Eng, Halberstam, and Muñoz looked ahead, others looked back to reflect on the disciplinary legacies of queer theory, including Janet Halley and Andrew Parker's "After Sex? On Writing since Queer Theory," a 2007 special issue of *SAQ* (expanded and published as a book in 2011), Michael Warner's essay "Queer and Then?" (2012), and Matt Brim and Amin Ghaziani's "Queer Methods" (2016), a special issue of *Women's Studies Quarterly*.[15] In Brim and Ghaziani's words, our moment is marked by a "reframing [of] the endlessly rehearsed question '*what* is queer theory?' as the nascent '*how* is queer theory done?'"[16]

As our title suggests, we see genealogy itself as a promisingly queer method – a way of thinking queer as well as thinking queerly. In this respect, our book resonates with recent work by scholars such as Rohy, David M. Halperin, and Kevin Ohi, who focus on the passage or transmission of queer knowledge and culture.[17] Rohy critiques the homophobic fantasy of how homosexuals and their cultures reproduce – "through seduction, influence, recruitment, pedagogy, predation, and contagion" – offering an insightful perspective from which to reflect on how queer studies has an "after." Rohy argues that such homophobic fantasies led lesbian and gay advocates to counter such fears by appealing to biological determinism – that we are "born this way," as Lady Gaga says. Yet even the question – *what causes homosexuality?* – is a pernicious one, whose insistence on being asked presumes that finding a cause is necessary – as if homosexuality is in need of explanation. Such investigations share a retrospective form that produces the origin as an effect of their investigations.

Queer theory teaches us to be suspicious of backward glances that look for causes, so any genealogy of queer studies – even the limited and partial one posed above – is itself rather a perverse move.

Instead of looking for a beginning or end, the "after" of queer studies might be thought through *Nachträglichkeit*, a concept Freud used to describe deferred realization. The term literally means "afterwardsness," and although it stems from Freud's earliest work, *Studies in Hysteria* (1895), the term only came to full fruition in Freud's case study of the Wolf Man (1918), where the subject belatedly realizes that his parents' seeming violence, which he witnessed as a toddler, was actually sexual congress.[18] Later in the twentieth century, French psychoanalysts Jean Laplanche and Jean-Bertrand Pontalis and then queer theorist Leo Bersani located this concept at the core of sexual development. A belated realization often seems to emphasize an impotent or tragic sense of "too late!" – especially as it is used in classical melodrama, like the films of Douglas Sirk. Yet *Nachträglichkeit* can also bestow power. As Laplanche and Pontalis observe, the term is "frequently used by Freud in connection with his view of psychical temporality and causality: experiences, impressions, and memory traces may be revised at a later date to fit in with fresh experiences or with the attainment of a new stage of development. They may in that event be endowed not only with a new meaning but also with psychical effectiveness."[19] What now is possible?

The afterglow of *Nachträglichkeit*'s illumination clarifies how we understand the "after" of queer studies as an empowering new stage of development in the field. Our provisional genealogical emphasis on "after" initiates a new discussion on the influences of queer theory, or, rather, what we can only now realize as the catalysts that queer studies has set in motion. If queer theory is a lapidary moment at the end of the twentieth century, it is timely now to trace some of the changes that it initiated in the field of literary studies. We may find that, as Muñoz has admonished us, "we are not yet queer."[20] For this very reason, *After Queer Studies* weaves its retrospective reflections alongside a consideration of queer thinking and analysis that remains urgently to be done.

The "after" of our title, then, might be understood less as a look backward than a queer mode of looking forward. Of course, the stories we tell about a future often rely on a reproduction of the past and an investment in the persistence of social order itself. Even as it claims to imagine a radical break from the past, reproductive futurism, as Edelman argues, denies difference. By contrast, a desire to think a future for queer studies does not stem from a denial of radical difference. We do not imagine a grand telos for queer studies, nor do we assume its unchanged persistence into the future. Rather, we reckon strange, circuitous, prolifer- ✓ ating, and looping temporalities will generate friction and stimulate new potentialities, which may or may not continue under the signifier "queer."

Precisely because queer is a problem of legibility and interpretation, *After Queer Studies* centers on literary studies, for this is the discipline that has tackled the queerness of reading, writing, and language. Moreover, / literature has been an archive for queer theorizing from the start. Despite ✓ its predominately philosophical and psychoanalytical roots, in its formative years queer studies was driven largely by literary scholars. Even when landmark collections like Michael Warner's *Fear of a Queer Planet* appear in non-literary journals (in 1990 as a volume of the journal *Social Text*), queer thinking remains marked by Warner's training as an early American literature scholar.[21] Similarly, Bersani's first book was a study of Marcel Proust.[22] Sedgwick's foundational contribution to the field, *Between Men: English Literature and Male Homosocial Desire* (1985), was deeply engaged in literary analysis, while her more widely read and field-defining texts, *Epistemology of the Closet* (1990) and *Tendencies* (1993), both exhibit polished skills in close reading born of a deeply literary approach to texts.[23] Moreover, her paradigm-shifting essay on paranoid reading and reparative reading in queer and literary criticism initially appeared as an introduction to the anthology *Novel Gazing: Queer Readings in Fiction* (1997), which itself grew out of "Queerer than Fiction," a 1996 special issue of *Studies in* ◁ *the Novel.*[24] In this important essay, Sedgwick gave queer scholars a new ✓ matrix for articulating how affect motivates compelling new interpretive methods and aims. Although the very distinction of paranoid and repara- tive emerged from Sedgwick's work on shame, sexuality, and psychoanaly- sis, its literary context is often forgotten.

If the intimacy of queer and literary studies has been overlooked – perhaps because it seemed unremarkable or given – so too has the central- ity of literature to queer theory and queer communities alike. D. A. Miller elegantly charts this relation in *Jane Austen, or the Secret of Style.*[25] Sedgwick likewise describes a childhood attachment by queers to "a few cultural objects, objects of high or popular culture or both, objects whose meaning seemed mysterious, excessive, or oblique in relation to the codes most readily available to us" (*Tendencies* 3). These objects become a "prime resource for survival." Reparative work, as Sedgwick notes, fears that "the culture surrounding it is inadequate or inimical to its nurture; it wants to assemble and confer plenitude on an object that will then have resources to offer an inchoate self."[26] This affective dynamic might also be said to underlie the desires that many LGBTQ readers bring to literature. Indeed, there is a profound need for marginalized readers to discover selves reflected in a world that otherwise denies their very existence. At the same time, seeking this identification may fuel a hope, or demand, that literature should accurately, clearly, and positively represent queer lives and experiences. While queer studies by no means discounts the power or value of such representations, it extends its destabilization of identity to literary meaning. As Ohi argues, literature's failures to cohere – its ruptures in meaning, its thwarted moments of understanding – *are* the place where it preserves and transmits queerness as potentiality. By defining queerness in terms of a depersonalized, desubjectivized negativity, Ohi follows in the anti-identitarian tradition inaugurated by Bersani. However, in an important twist, Ohi reframes "queer theory as a mode of literary reading" and identifies close reading as a queer mode to "access the potentiality of a literary work – not to settle it, once and for all, in a meaning that masters it, but to rewrite it, perpetually."[27] In short, queer turns to literature not for legible reflections of a self but for moments when the self becomes ecstatically illegible.

In a related move, we do not assume a coherent or privileged identity for "literature." Our chapters move from William Shakespeare, James Baldwin, Audre Lorde, and Henry James to queer commix, camp performance, and science fiction. This movement is, itself, a queer one – not simply because of the disruption of the boundaries between high and low culture but also because queer reading has historically been marked by its capacious attachment to and appreciation of a range of aesthetic forms. As Sedgwick notes, queer readers "have invented for themselves, in the spontaneity of great need, the tools for a formalist apprehension of other less prestigious, more ubiquitous kinds of text: genre movies, advertising, comic strips" (*Tendencies* 4). *After Queer Studies* questions the "spontaneity" of this invention by acknowledging the historical forces that gave rise to the practices we now think of as "queer reading" as well as the role that literature plays in soliciting queer interpretative practices from its readers. Still, Sedgwick's observation underlines the importance of *form* – as an aesthetic and social concept – for queer readers. After all, we need only to think of how drag aesthetics, Jamesian and Steinian sentences, or the lines in Assyrian sculpture (to name just a few examples) have galvanized queer thinking.

The refusal to choose between aesthetics and politics is precisely why queer studies is so crucially oriented around literary studies. In "Queer Form: Aesthetics, Race, and the Violences of the Social," Kadji Amin, Amber Jamilla Musser, and Roy Pérez call for a new thinking of the queer as enmeshed within – and indeed, activated and enabled by – the structures of aesthetic form, social inequality, and conceptual categorization within which the work of engaged artists takes shape. *Form informs* ✓ *queerness*, and queerness is best understood as a series of *relations* to form, relations not limited to binary and adversarial models of resistance and opposition.[28]

A relational approach to queerness and form opens up new possibilities for staging a rapprochement between aesthetics and politics. Indeed, as their work suggests, queer thinking needs to account for the political and social work that artists are *already* doing within form. To do so, we must understand the aesthetic, like queerness, as enmeshed within and responsive to the violences of the social world. We must have a richly intersectional notion of how aesthetic form crosses with the axes of gender, sexuality, racialization, class, and other modes of power. *After Queer Studies* thus attends to the transversals that link queerness, form, and social power, taking our cue from the relations that queer literature provokes, imagines, and demands. In its latest turn, queer theory deliberates the social implications of formal and aesthetic innovation that literature constantly strives for in its engagements with the world.

Reading might be one idiom for queerness's engagement with the entwinement of aesthetics and politics. Hence, our chapters do not stage reading or reader relations only, or even primarily, in terms of the binary choice between paranoid or reparative reading. Sedgwick's heuristic was initially significant for thinking about the affective motivations that inspire queer reading, putting a name to a previously unnamed cluster of affects that undergird critical theory. Yet she also called for an openness ✓ to weak modes of theory that do not work toward mastery but operate within the liminal "middle ranges of agency" (*Touching* 13). Refusing a grand alternative to the repressive hypothesis, Sedgwick's turn to reparation carved out a less oppositional approach for queer reading. Such potentiality serves not as an end in itself, nor does it counter arguments for queer negativity, asociality, and nonrelation. In this vein, our chapters exemplify queer studies' increasingly agnostic openness to – and curiosity about – the interleavings of queerness and form that may yet arise beyond the repressive hypothesis. If they contain a common methodological commitment, however, it is an insistence on the indissociability of queerness with the social, historical, and aesthetic forms that conditions its emergence, a commitment that grounds their proliferating relationality to a range of forms (high and low, canonical and marginal, popular and unpopular, etc.).

"Studies," the final word in our title, might seem to require no remark, given that "queer studies" nominates a disciplinary field. Yet if queer is an activity – a way of thinking sideways – then it raises profound questions about methodology, about *how we study* the object of literature. Indeed, as the 2013 "Queer Method" conference attests, queer theorists now find themselves reflecting on the "disciplinary effects and affiliations of queer studies."[29] Such a reflection cannot be divorced from the overwhelming loss of prestige suffered by the humanities, particularly the literary and philosophical approaches that we have traced in our genealogy. Indicative of this moment of uncertainty and experimentation, our authors do not presume or argue for one single methodology; rather, each stakes a claim about the methods of queer theorizing they see as most relevant to their cultural objects. Yet we are struck by a twinned persistence of and resistance to the human that arises across the collection, even within single essays. On the one hand, an investment in the subjective, experiential, and affective dimensions of literature persists, despite calls to move beyond the "subject." On the other hand, our authors ask, as Dana Luciano and Mel Chen urge, "has the queer ever been human?"[30] This question confronts the impersonal negativity of sexuality, the monstrous potentiality of inhuman forces, and the social exclusions wrought in the name of the human. We hope these crosscurrents resonate with one another, testifying to the ongoing dexterity of literary studies to think queer and, perhaps more importantly, that their friction suggests traces of queer studies that are not yet legible – readable only through their restless, unstable movements.

Part I, "Reading Queer Literary History," expands the questions about genealogy and method from this introduction. At the risk of seeming to invoke an origin, we open with Stephen Guy-Bray's chapter "Shakespearean Sexualities," but we do so to disrupt an originary gesture for queer literary history. Guy-Bray confronts the questions readers must ask after queer studies: Is a "queer" text one that represents same-sex desire, one written by an author whose biography indicates same-sex erotic attraction, or one that has to be read against the grain to expose its queerness? Guy-Bray replies by urging readers to presume *all* texts as queer. If this stance is made possible by queer theory, Guy-Bray demonstrates how early modern representations of sexuality prefigure and even exceed contemporary notions of queerness. In this respect, the literary archive preserves a future for queer readings to come. Dana Seitler's chapter, "Write, Paint, Dance, Sex," rethinks queer literature as a style – a texture, syntax, or tone. As Seitler argues, style enables readers to understand the "literariness of queerness" but also the "relationship between literature and the social world, between aesthetics and politics." Her chapter sweeps through the canon of American literature – from Melville, Hawthorne, and Whitman, to Stein, Hurston, and Crane – tracing how style forges a nexus between the erotic, the aesthetic, and the social. Seitler's location of dance as a mode of queer style resonates with Ricardo Ortiz's chapter, "Queer Latinx Studies and Queer Latinx Literature 'After' Queer Theory." Ortiz positions queer literary studies after the 2016 Pulse dance club massacre, the deadliest incident of violence against LGBTQ people in the United States, which specifically targeted queer Latinx people. Ortiz links this brutal moment to a long history of systemic violence suffered by and combated among queer Latinx communities. Tracing an intellectual genealogy of *queer latinidad*, Ortiz unravels fixed distinctions between literature and theory, noting that they "quite often manifest simultaneously in the same discursive, writerly act." Not only does Ortiz demonstrate the importance of deft movements among literature and theory to queer studies, but he unpacks the fraught relationships that queers of color have had to the genre of "queer theory," which has often marginalized non-white thinkers and their interests.

Part II, "Reading Queer Writers," turns to four authors – Oscar Wilde, James Baldwin, Henry James, and Audre Lorde – whose literature has consistently grounded the scholarship that has become queer studies. These chapters demonstrate that reading a queer writer demands complex thinking about literature's relationship to authorial biography and historical context. Richard A. Kaye's chapter, "Oscar Wilde and George Bernard Shaw in Queer Time," juxtaposes Irish writers Wilde and Shaw, contrasting their opposed views of sexual transgression. By taking us into their contemporary moment to defamiliarize our own, Kaye demonstrates the untimeliness that marks the reading of queer writers. Indeed, his essay reveals how their debate over the place of sexuality within the political sphere anticipates and gives rise to contemporary debates around queer liberalism. In "After Queer Baldwin," Matt Brim similarly demonstrates the historical and conceptual influence of Baldwin's literature on the emergence of queer of color critique. Baldwin was a pivotal figure both for articulating queer theory prior to its emergence in the 1990s and an interlocutor for later queer theorists of color. If black queer studies finds itself now decentering Baldwin, Brim argues that this is a salutary move that signals a vital expansion of the cultural archive for black queer thought. Moving from the social back to the textual, Kevin Ohi's chapter, "Revision, Origin, and the Courage of Truth" directly confronts the perennial problem of conceiving the relationship between literature and biography that plagues the reading of queer writers. In a striking move, Ohi questions queer studies' allergy to origins. Indeed, through a reading of James's prefaces, Ohi discovers a "perpetual return to potentiality in writing's search for its origins." In their refraction of the relationship between life and writing, James's prefaces confront the suspension and revision of meaning that conditions queerness and literature alike. Finally, addressing the gender of "origins," Amber Jamilla Musser's "All about Our Mothers" turns to Audre Lorde to ask what it means to think about a writer as a "mother" to queer theory. Musser asks why we can "embrace Lorde as a prototype, a mother, shall we say, of queer theory, but we have difficulty grappling with what she says about the mother?" By returning to Lorde's writing, Musser presses back against queer theory's resistance to the feminine and especially the maternal, arguing for a queer theory that contends with black women's experience of racism, capitalism, and colonialism.

Part III, "Reading Queerly," dives into cultural forms that have often failed to count as "literature" and yet have been central to the development of queer reading. At the same time, this section raises new questions about how an interpretative practice can "queer" a text. Nick Salvato's "Camp Performance and the Case of *Discotropic*" braids together these two concerns in its consideration of camp. Camp is an archive of performance as well as a style that playfully engages with mainstream culture. By looking to queer of color camp performances, Salvato pushes camp studies in a new direction. He contests the arch and ironic affect that typically defines white, gay, male camp, clearing room to consider negative affects, such as sadness and somberness, in camp performance. Through these affects, queer of color camp offers a mode for reflecting on the corporeality of trans and racialized subjectivities. Where Salvato sees a future for queer reading in an expanded archive, andré m. carrington argues for a new apprehension of its past. His chapter, "Reading in Juxtaposition," argues for the centrality of subcultural commix to the formation of queer subjectivities and communities. He contests narrow definitions of the genre, arguing for an acknowledgement of the queer entwinement of comics with other genres. Doing so displaces the marginalization of comics while also bringing into relief how comics have been bound up with queer stigmatization. Where carrington looks to the queerness of the superhero, Rebekah Sheldon turns to the monster, beginning with the Gothic vampire and moving toward more contemporary visions of monstrosity. Sheldon's "Reading for Transgression" positions queer studies within a broader nexus of feminist new materialism and ecocriticism, questioning the centrality of "trouble making" to conventional definitions of queer reading. Sheldon turns to the archive of speculative and weird fiction to rethink queerness as a monster that cannot be controlled or predicted, and that has little interest in the persistence of humanity. Finally, Sharon Patricia Holland also queers the human, focusing on the distinction between human and animal that arises in the racialization of black, white, and indigenous subjects. "Sovereignty" traces the intersecting margins of US imperialism and minority racialization through Toni Morrison's *A Mercy*, deforming the norms of whiteness that prevail in animal studies, American studies, and queer studies. Her chapter makes a powerful case for the endurance of queer theory's thinking sideways, exemplifying queer theory's interrogation of its own norms and its assumption that the question of who "we" are is a question of relationality at the limits of the social.

As we have argued, "queer" arises through the nexus of feminism, gay liberation, and the confrontation with the AIDS's epidemic's radical dehumanization of subjects who had just begun to claim their place in the social world. By ending with the limits of the human and of life itself, we hope to provoke a compelling set of questions as to what queer studies may be after now.

### Notes

1 Michel Foucault, *The History of Sexuality: An Introduction, Vol. 1* (New York: Vintage, [1976] 1990); Judith Butler, *Gender Trouble: Feminism and the Subversion of Identity* (New York: Routledge, 1990).

2 See José Esteban Muñoz, *Cruising Utopia: The Then and There of Queer Futurity* (New York: New York University Press, 2009), 72–73.

3 We are indebted to Kathryn Bond Stockton for this idea of queer as sideways. See Kathryn Bond Stockton, *The Queer Child, or Growing Sideways in the Twentieth Century* (Durham: Duke University Press, 2009). Freud's idea of perversion – etymologically a turning from, per- [from] –vers [turn] – is also influential here, since perversions were sexual acts that deviated in either aim or object from heterosexual copulation (that is, reproductive sexuality). See Sigmund Freud, *Three Essays on the Theory of Sexuality* (New York: Basic, 2000).

4 On this irony and the contemporary import of rethinking queer reading, see their recent special issue: "Queers Read This! LGBTQ Literature Now," ed. Ramzi Fawaz and Shanté Paradigm Smalls, *GLQ* vol. 24, no. 2–3 (2018).

5 Cherríe Moraga and Gloria Anzaldúa, *This Bridge Called My Back: Writings by Radical Women of Color*, 4th ed. (Albany: SUNY Press, [1981] 2015).

6 Gayle Rubin, "Thinking Sex: Notes for a Radical Theory of the Politics of Sexuality," in *Deviations: A Gayle Rubin Reader* (Durham: Duke University Press, 2011), 137–81.

7  Gloria Anzaldúa, *Borderlands/The New Mestiza: La Frontera* (San Francisco: Aunt Lute Books, 1987).

8  John D'Emilio, "Capitalism and Gay Identity," in *Powers of Desire: The Politics of Sexuality*, ed. Ann Snitow, Christine Stansell, and Sharon Thompson (New York: Monthly Review Press, 1983), 100–13.

9  John Boswell, *Christianity, Social Tolerance, and Homosexuality: Gay People in Western Europe from the Beginning of the Christian Era to the Fourteenth Century* (Chicago: University of Chicago Press, 1980).

10  Robert McRuer, "Review of William B. Turner's *Genealogy of Queer Theory*," *National Women's Studies Association Journal* vol. 14, no. 2 (2002): 227.

11  "queer, adj.1." OED Online, January 2018, Oxford University Press.

12  Eve Kosofsky Sedgwick, *Tendencies* (Durham: Duke University Press, 1993), 8. All subsequent references appear parenthetically in the text.

13  Lee Edelman, *No Future: Queer Theory and the Death Drive* (Durham: Duke University Press, 2004); J. Jack Halberstam, *In a Queer Time and Place: Transgender Bodies, Subcultural Lives* (New York: New York University Press, 2005); Muñoz, *Cruising Utopia*; Valerie Rohy, *Anachronism and Its Others: Sexuality, Race, Temporality* (New York: SUNY Press, 2009); Elizabeth Freeman, *Time Binds: Queer Temporalities, Queer Histories* (Durham: Duke University Press, 2010); Peter Coviello, *Tomorrow's Parties: Sex and the Untimely in Nineteenth-Century America* (New York: New York University Press, 2013); Juana María Rodríguez, *Sexual Futures, Queer Gestures, and Other Latina Longings* (New York: New York University Press, 2014).

14  "What's Queer about Queer Studies Now?," a special issue of *Social Text*, ed. David L. Eng, J. Jack Halberstam, and José Esteban Muñoz, vol. 23, nos. 3–4 (2005). Subsequent references cited in text.

15  Janet Halley and Andrew Parker, *After Sex? On Writing since Queer Theory* (Durham: Duke University Press, 2011); Michael Warner, "Queer and Then," *The Chronicle of Higher Education*, January 1, 2012, www.chronicle.com/article/QueerThen-/130161; "Queer Methods," a special issue of *WSQ: Women's Studies Quarterly*, ed. Matt Brim and Amin Ghaziani, vol. 44, nos. 3–4 (2016).

16  Brim and Ghaziani, "Introduction: Queer Methods," 14.

17  Valerie Rohy, *Lost Causes: Narrative, Etiology, and Queer Theory* (Oxford: Oxford University Press, 2014); David Halperin, *How to Be Gay* (Cambridge, MA: Harvard University Press, 2012); Kevin Ohi, *Dead Letters Sent: Queer Literary Transmission* (Minneapolis: University of Minnesota Press, 2015).

18  Sigmund Freud, *The "Wolfman" and Other Cases*, trans. Louise Adey Huish (New York: Penguin 2003).

19  Leo Bersani, *Freudian Body: Psychoanalysis and Art* (New York: Columbia University Press, 1990); Jean Laplanche and Jean-Bertrand Pontalis, *The Language of Psychoanalysis* (London: Karnac Books, 1988), 111.

20  Muñoz, *Cruising Utopia*, 1.

21  Michael Warner, ed., *Fear of a Queer Planet: Queer Politics and Social Theory* (Minneapolis: University of Minnesota Press, 1993).

22 Leo Bersani, *Marcel Proust: The Fictions of Life and of Art* (Oxford: Oxford University Press, 1965).

23 Eve Kosofsky Sedgwick, *Between Men: Literature and Male Homosocial Desire* (Columbia: Columbia University Press, 1985); Eve Kosofsky Sedgwick, *Epistemology of the Closet* (Berkeley: University of California Press, 1990).

24 Eve Kosofsky Sedgwick "Paranoid Reading and Reparative Reading: Or, You're So Paranoid, You Probably Think This Introduction Is about You," in *Novel Gazing: Queer Readings in Fiction*, ed. Eve Kosofsky Sedgwick (Durham: Duke University Press, 1997), 1–37.

25 D. A. Miller, *Jane Austen, or the Secret of Style* (Princeton: Princeton University Press, 2003).

26 Eve Kosofsky Sedgwick, *Touching Feeling: Affect, Pedagogy, Performativity* (Durham: Duke University Press, 2003), 149. Subsequent references appear parenthetically in the text.

27 Ohi, *Dead Letters Sent*, 219, 29.

28 Kadji Amin, Amber Jamilla Musser, and Roy Pérez, "Queer Form: Aesthetics, Race, and the Violences of the Social," *ASAP / Journal* vol. 2, no. 2 (2017): 228, original emphasis.

29 "Queer Method," http://queermethod.tumblr.com/.

30 Dana Luciano and Mel Y. Chen, *GLQ: A Journal of Gay and Lesbian Studies* vol. 21, nos. 2–3 (2015): 186.

# Reading Queer Literary History

PART I

# Reading Queer Literary History

# CHAPTER I

# Shakespearean Sexualities

## Stephen Guy-Bray

The title for this essay could lead in several directions, perhaps most obviously either towards a discussion of Shakespeare's own sexuality or a discussion of the sexualities of the characters of his plays. While neither of these is my concern here, I want to consider for a moment these avenues of inquiry. Queer theory began as gay and lesbian studies, and (in the field of English literature, at least) these studies tended to be rooted in the biographies of writers and their characters. Shakespeare was an especially productive source for this kind of research. Interpreted as autobiographical, the sonnets have often been taken to give us a glimpse of a bisexual man, one who moves over the course of the sequence from desiring a man to desiring a woman and whose romantic problems crucially come from the personalities of his love objects and not from any inner torment over what we would now call his sexual orientation. Predictably, this view of Shakespeare as a bisexual has met with opposition, and even today some conservative critics continue desperately to assert that the love sonnets to the man, which take up most of the sequence, are purely platonic; at the same time, there appears to be no end to the appetite for middlebrow fictional depictions of a strictly heterosexual Shakespeare.

While discussions of the relationship between the male–male love in the sonnets and Shakespeare's own life may now seem somewhat out of date (although they continue to be written), discussions of the sexualities of Shakespeare's characters persist. With the possible exception of Achilles and Patroclus in *Troilus and Cressida*, there are no unmistakably homoerotic relationships in Shakespeare's plays. There are, however, a number of intense same-sex relationships that often appear either sexual or romantic or both: Antonio and Sebastian in *Twelfth Night* and Helena and Hermia in *A Midsummer Night's Dream* are only two of the most obvious examples, and many others could be cited, both in Shakespeare's works and in the works of his contemporaries. To many people, these relationships seem unmistakably romantic, and they are often presented this way in staging, but it could be said in each case that the two characters are just friends, a statement often accompanied by the accusation that critics or directors who see anything romantic in these friendships are "reading too much into it" or "being anachronistic." Such a view might seem risibly conservative, and yet it still has a certain currency.

Because of this, before I look at examples of what we can see as queer relationships in Renaissance texts I feel the need to deal with one of the most prevalent of these objections. One that will be familiar to people working in many periods is the demand for legal-quality proof: in other words, at the same time that queer scholars work on literature from periods in which anything like homosexuality was a crime, and often a capital crime, they are expected to find clear and unambiguous admissions of this crime. This is a very bad way to think; that it still has any currency is due to the implicit feeling that homosexuality is a crime and that both authors and their characters must benefit from the presumption that they are "innocent until proven guilty." By the very nature of Renaissance texts and contexts, we are not going to find texts that meet the legal standards of proof; nor should we have to. A popular slogan of the (much more recent) past was "Don't presume I'm straight," and I propose that we adopt this admirable slogan as our motto, assuming that all texts are queer unless proved otherwise. This attitude is no less rigorous than the presumption of heterosexuality, and it is long overdue.

In what follows, I shall do a brief and tendentious survey of early work in the field of Renaissance gay and lesbian studies. Although much of this work now appears somewhat old-fashioned, I want to pay tribute to it and also to give some sense of what scholars do now in what is in many ways a very different field. The most obvious change has probably been the move from looking at the biographies of writers or providing inventories of characters who have strong same-sex attachments to looking at the ways in which queerness is figured and represented in Renaissance texts. Another way to describe this shift – which we could summarize as the move from "gay and lesbian" to "queer" – is to say that most critics in the field have moved from seeing the work they do as based in social history to seeing the work they do as based in critical theory, and especially in those kinds of theory that are psychoanalytically or linguistically based. It is not my intention to suggest that this change has been uncontroversial: a number of critics over the last few years have called for a return to historicist work and, even, a return to work with demonstrable gay and lesbian content as opposed, for instance, to work that deals with the queerness of textuality. I note this development, but I shall not discuss it further.

## Gay and Lesbian to Queer

One of the most important books for early work in Renaissance gay and lesbian studies was Alan Bray's *Homosexuality in Renaissance England,* which appeared in 1982.[1] Although cautious and suspicious of literary texts, Bray made a number of useful points. For one, he paid attention to the names that Renaissance English people gave to same-sex activities. He also drew attention to the literary use of classical Greek and Roman precedents and ideas of male friendship as covers for same-sex love of various kinds. As well, he did painstaking archival research and demonstrated that although there were laws against sodomy and although it was publicly condemned quite often, there were very few prosecutions for sodomy in this period. Bray's conclusion was that sodomy was prosecuted chiefly when it was part of a larger threat to order – when it was part of a mixing of races or classes, for example. Perhaps most productive was his comment that "What sodomy and buggery represented ... was ... the disorder in sexual relations that, in principle at least, could break out anywhere."[2] Although Bray seems not to have known it, this association also appears in the notes to Edmund Spenser's *Shepheardes Calender,* first published in 1579, when the commentator refers to "some savour of disorderly love, which the learned call pæderastice."[3] One of the insights of much recent queer work on Renaissance literature (and in this respect the scholars are only catching up to Renaissance writers) is just how varied a category "disorderly love" can be.

I have mentioned Bray partly because his work has been so influential in the study of same-sex love in the English Renaissance, but also because of this association of sodomy with disorder, a connection that now seems to prepare the way for the queer studies that would eventually replace gay and lesbian studies. As Bray shows, while to us sodomy means anal sex, in the Renaissance the word was used to refer to a number of offences, including not only bestiality but also such nonsexual acts as holding heretical opinions. Bray did not explore the implications of this confusion of categories – this, at least, is how it looks to us – but looking back at the field from the present day we can see how Renaissance sodomy looks like queerness as Lee Edelman has defined it, something that troubles identities rather than something that is an identity in itself.[4] Rather than being anachronistic the word "queer" is a more suitable term for Shakespearean sexuality than we have thought. Insofar as it is a term that does not characterize all gay people but does characterize some straight people, queerness is more fluid and thus more suitable in the context of Renaissance literature, in which there often appears to be no firm distinction between kinds of sexual or emotional attachment.

In English, queer Renaissance studies became a recognized discipline in the 1990s, producing a large number of essay collections, monographs, and articles. Perhaps the most important volume in the early period of what we can now see as a shift from lesbian and gay studies to queer studies was *Queering the Renaissance*, which was edited by Jonathan Goldberg and appeared in 1994.[5] Goldberg was already one of the best Renaissance critics: two years earlier he had published *Sodometries: Renaissance Texts, Modern Sexualities*, a work that argued forcefully for the continued value and relevance of Renaissance literary study.[6] *Queering the Renaissance* was a wide-ranging book that dealt with both famous and lesser-known literary texts (not all of them English), as well as with authors not usually considered literary, such as Erasmus and Bacon. The best-known contributor was Alan Bray, who wrote an important essay on the opposition between male friendship and sodomy, but also on the connection between them. Male friendship was the most highly prized form of relationship in Renaissance England, but also potentially a cover for sodomy.

I do not have space to go over *Queering the Renaissance*, but I want to make the point that its essays established what are still the main avenues of investigation in the field. For instance, as well as work on queer sexuality, writers also looked at the queerness of textuality and at the imbrication of queerness in the discourses of history, theology, and philosophy: from this point on, queerness in Renaissance texts would be seen as something that inhered in textuality itself as well as being a question of subject matter or an author's biography. The collection also helped to move the discipline from one that was primarily concerned with relations between and among men to one that was also concerned with relations between and among women. Valerie Traub, one of the contributors to this volume, expanded her article into a groundbreaking book called *The Renaissance of Lesbianism*, and while many or perhaps most of the scholars working in this area still concentrate either on men or on women, the study of women, both as characters in texts and as producers of texts, is now central to queer Renaissance studies.[7]

## Renaissance Sex Theory

Up to this point, my essay has traced – partially and imperfectly – the beginnings of the discipline in which I and many others work: I consider this a necessary step. But rather than continue in this vein and produce a survey of work in the area, I want now to turn to the texts themselves. My precedent here is the remarkable collection called *Shakesqueer*, edited by Madhavi Menon, which includes essays on all of Shakespeare's texts (including the ones that have not survived).[8] In the introduction, Menon asks "can Shakespeare be regarded as a queer theorist, or is he always the object on which queer theory acts?"[9] Rather than wishing to queer Shakespeare, Menon wants us to recognize that queerness and queer theory are not, or not just, contemporary things that we bring to the texts of the past, but rather things that already exist in those texts. With this in mind, I turn now to three Renaissance texts that all demonstrate the queerness of the past and the extent to which Renaissance thinking about same-sex attachments of various kinds can be said to anticipate queer theory. These long-dead authors are not the inert subjects on which we perform our scholarship, but are rather our collaborators and even – especially in their awareness of the varieties of same-sex attachments – our teachers.

Although the Renaissance did not produce either a theory or a taxonomy of sexuality, it did produce a number of statements about the different kinds of emotional bonds that a man might encounter. These statements, found throughout Renaissance texts of all kinds, focus on friendship as the highest form of relationship possible. By friendship, I mean friendship between men: women were generally – if tacitly – thought incapable of the higher forms of friendship, although there were exceptions and I shall discuss one important example of female friendship later. By our standards, Renaissance discussions of friendship are highly rhetorical, passionate, extravagant – in a word, gay. Conservative critics have been at pains to point out that the extravagance of this discourse, which to us looks like the language of romantic love, cannot be taken as evidence of anything that we might call homosexuality. This is true, but obviously it cannot be used to rule out the existence of what we might call homosexuality either. An unprejudiced reader will observe that friendship is, then and now, a perfect cover for illicit love and sexuality. For this reason, in what follows I shall focus on the use of friendship discourse.

As I have suggested, there is no shortage of passages on friendship in Renaissance literature. For my purposes, the foundational discourse of male friendship comes at the beginning of the ninth canto of the fourth book of the *Faerie Queene*, which is the book devoted to friendship. The narrator begins by announcing the problem of weighing the various forms of love: "Hard is the Doubt, and difficult to deem, / When all three kinds of Love together meet" (IV.ix.1). He will go on to define these kinds –

> The dear Affection unto Kindred sweet,
> Or raging Fire of Love to Woman-kind,
> Or Zeal of Friends combin'd with Vertues meet
>                                         (IV.ix.1)

but I think it is significant that he assumes the three kinds will be known to his readers. The scheme cannot apply to women, however tempting it might be for us now to think of the "Fire of Love to Woman-kind" as evidence of lesbian-like sentiment.

In the next stanza, Spenser underlines that his ordering of the kinds of love should be taken as a narrative:

> For natural Affection soon doth cease,
> And quenched is with Cupid's greater Flame:
> But faithful Friendship doth them both suppress.
>                                         (IV.ix.2)

There is so much that should be strange to us here: love for one's family, although it is the only kind of love that Spenser calls natural, is presented as quickly ending, like an infatuation. The fact that it cedes to a man's love for a woman seems less strange, but friendship – between men – is stronger than both earlier kinds of love. One popular understanding of sexual development for the last hundred years has been that homosexuality is just a phase; here both heterosexuality and familial love are the phases. The highest and most worthwhile kind of love is the love of two male friends for each other. Still, it is important to remember that this male love does not replace the others entirely but is instead constructed upon them. The heterosexually organized family is the basis of society in this scheme, as it is the world in which we grew up; the difference is that the family is not the most valuable form of affective bonds: the male couple, rather than the heterosexual married couple, is the true microcosm of the government.

The coexistence of these various kinds of love is crucial to the Renaissance and the *Faerie Queene* illustrates this coexistence perfectly in the tableau that introduces the two main characters of Book IV:

> Two knightes, that lincked rode in louely wise,
> As if they secret counsels did partake;
> And each not farre behinde him had his make,
> To weete, two Ladies of most goodly hew,
> That twixt themselues did gentle purpose make.
>                                         (IV.ii.30)

The scene gives us two same-sex couples, but as Spenser says that each of the men is followed by his "make," he gives us two mixed-sex couples as well. Thus, what we now call homosexuality and what we now call heterosexuality are presented simultaneously, although the fact that the male couple is presented before either the female couple or the mixed-sex couple suggests – in keeping with Spenser's presentation of the kinds of love I discussed above – that the male homosocial bond is the most important bond of all.

The characters seeing these four people send a squire to find out who they are. He returns with a description that underlines our sense of the interconnection of the bonds among them:

> Two of the prowest Knights in Faery long;
> And these two Ladies their two louers deare,
> Couragious *Cambell*, and stout *Triamond*,
> With *Canacee* and *Cambine* linckt in louely bond.
>
> (IV.ii.31)

The first and third lines of this passage deal with the men; the second and fourth with the women. Only the phrase "their two louers deare" unambiguously connects the two pairs. A heteronormative reading of the poem would see the phrase "linckt in louely bond" as referring to two mixed-sex marriages, but I would argue that the phrase is ambiguous: grammatically, at least, it seems to refer to a connection between the women, or perhaps to a group marriage. The phrase could even suggest that the two men are "linckt" to the two women in a tetrad. And even if we read the phrase as indicating heterosexual couples, there is a further ambiguity: is Cambell married to Canacee or to Cambine?

The section of Book IV that I have been discussing is probably the oddest part of the oddest book in the *Faerie Queene*, itself a notably odd poem, but I would nevertheless argue that it is typical of much of what English Renaissance literature offers in the way of a discourse of sexuality. The traditional reading of the situation Spenser gives us is that we are reading about two heterosexual couples and that everything else is just – "just" – friendship; the kind of reading typical of the early days of gay and lesbian studies would be that although there are two heterosexual couples the truth of the situation is the homosexuality of each of the two same-sex couples. For me, these readings are partial (in both senses). It is important to consider that both the heterosexual and the homosexual readings might be accurate. What is more, we should also consider the possibility I mentioned above, which is that we should see all four characters as forming a tetrad that cannot necessarily be broken into smaller parts. At times, any one of these relationships might prevail; all are possible. Reading the tableau this way could lead us to a sense of relationships as irreducible to any straightforward binary between same-sex and mixed-sex bonds. Spenser's ability to see all these relationships as happily coexisting could serve as a model for contemporary queer theory.

## The Places of Male Friendship

One result of this kind of reading could be that our current (and essentially binary) system of sexuality is insufficiently detailed. For one thing, I feel that the focus on sexuality is unnecessarily limiting: should we really feel that the sexual content of a relationship (even if we could agree on what counts as sex, or sexual; and, as it turns out, we cannot agree) is the most important fact of a relationship? As well, the choices given us are only homo or hetero. The main problem here is that the former means same while the second does not mean other, but only the other of two: the term presupposes that there are only two genders. I have written elsewhere that what we need is a new system in which things are labeled either homo or allo – "allos" being the Greek adjective meaning other when there are three or more choices.[10] This system would not center sexuality and the differences between two people would be potentially infinite, just as they are in real life. A further benefit of this system is that the same relationship could be simultaneously homo and allo. This system would allow us to consider the importance to a relationship of such things as race or class, to name only two examples. Although this is a new taxonomy, my point here is that it is one that is more useful to describing Renaissance relationships as they are presented in texts than the taxonomy we now use. A system like that would allow us to see the queerness of the two marriages in the passage from Spenser and the normality of the two same-sex relationships simultaneously.

The Renaissance text that most famously and controversially investigates the overlap between friendship and sodomy with which Bray and others have been so concerned is Christopher Marlowe's *Edward II*. This play is also interesting as it is one of only a very few Renaissance texts that has almost without exception been understood to present what we now think of as homosexuality – partly, of course, because the historical Edward is understood to have had male lovers. The relationship in question is between Edward and Piers Gaveston. Although Gaveston was chosen by Edward I to be his son's companion, it is clear to (almost) everyone that the relationship between him and the younger Edward exceeded what are typically considered the limits of friendship. Indeed, as Stephen Orgel pointed out, this play provides "the only dramatic instance of a homosexual relationship presented in the terms in which the culture formally conceived it – as antisocial, seditious, ultimately disastrous."[11] While the other same-sex relationships in Renaissance plays that seem to a greater or lesser extent homoerotic to us do not appear to pose any problem to the status quo, the relationship between Edward and Gaveston is perceived by the majority of the play's other characters as a threat to the entire world of the play.

Interestingly, and perhaps counterintuitively to us now, it is not the sexual activity in itself that is the problem, as we see when the elder Mortimer advises his rebellious nephew to cease opposing the king:

> Thou seest by nature he is milde and calme,
> And seeing his minde so dotes on *Gaveston*,
> Let him without controulement have his will.[12]

He follows this advice with a list of famous soldiers and philosophers who had male favorites: Alexander, Hercules, Achilles, Cicero, and Socrates. Lists of pairs of male friends from the classical era are quite common in Renaissance literature, but this is the only example I can think of with a clearly erotic connotation: the elder Mortimer uses the word "minions" (I. iv.391), still at this point a word associated with the male lovers of the (recently deceased) French king Henry III. One way of describing this passage would be to say that Marlowe is queering one of the commonest and most foundational of literary tropes in his period; while Spenser's presentation, like the majority of Renaissance depictions of friendship, allows readers to understand a given friendship as Platonic or romantic or sexual, the elder Mortimer removes the uncertainty. Marlowe's refusal to consider that friendship means "just" friendship should be a model for contemporary scholars looking at the relationships of the past.

His nephew's response is instructive. Like his uncle, the younger Mortimer has no objection to sex between men as such:

> Unckle, his wanton humor greeves not me,
> But this I scorne, that one so baselie borne,
> Should by his soveraignes favour grow so pert,
> And riote it with the treasure of the realme.
>
> (I.iv.402–5)

Mortimer's problem is with Gaveston's access to the royal finances, rather than with his access to the royal body. His problem is also with Gaveston's mockery:

> Whiles other walke below, the king and he
> From out a window, laugh at such as we,
> And floute our traine, and jest at our attire:
> Unckle, tis this that makes me impatient.
>
> (I.iv.416–19)

This speech demonstrates Mortimer's petulance perfectly: the repetition of "Unckle," the rhymes, and the final ability to keep to the meter show his perturbation. I should add that the speech is also valuable as an early – and perhaps first – example of the fragility of the male heterosexual ego.

The aspect of this exchange that is especially instructive in the context of this essay is that it provides us with some sense of the status of sexual relations between men in the Renaissance. While the sex itself does not appear to cause problems, and while it can even be justified by the very serious and elevated classical precedents provided by the elder Mortimer, it cannot be allowed to disturb the status quo. Mortimer's anecdote, in which Edward and Gaveston are literally above Mortimer and the other peers ("such as we"), should direct our attention to the fact that Gaveston is also metaphorically above them. The king is inherently superior to the nobles, but that same hierarchy dictates that Gaveston should be below the nobles; in fact, Marlowe significantly lowers the status of the historical Gaveston precisely to emphasize this violation of protocol. The problem in the world of the play – a problem that eventually results in the violent death of all the men we could consider homosexual – is that Edward seeks to make Gaveston his consort. Their sexual and romantic connection is not itself the problem, despite the laws and the religious prohibitions against sodomy. In keeping with Bray's observation about prosecutions for sodomy, their connection only becomes a problem when it poses a threat to the social and political order, when it becomes disorderly.

## The Places of Female Friendship

As I have suggested, the discourse of friendship in the Renaissance could more accurately be called a discourse of male friendship. There are exceptions, however. In the middle of the seventeenth century, Katherine Philips wrote a number of poems celebrating friendship between women, addressed to a number of pseudonymous women.[13] The best known of these poems are the ones addressed to a woman whom Philips called Lucasia. Poems celebrating female friendship were very rare indeed at that time (they have never been particularly common), and for that reason alone Philips's works would be noteworthy, but they are also interesting for the large claims she made for these friendships. Although the discourse of male friendship frequently presented these friendships as the highest form of human relationship and although there was an acknowledgment that these male friendships were central to the society of the time, women's affairs in general were considered part of private life. Philips's poems are groundbreaking in their insistence on the importance of friendships between women; furthermore, she often presents female friendship as religious in nature, and sometimes as a religion in its own right. Her female friendships inhabit the public sphere.

The poem I want to look at here is called "Friendship's Mystery, To my Dearest Lucasia." The opening words – "Come, my *Lucasia*" – recall many amorous poems from the first half of the seventeenth century, in which a man summons his mistress (1). From this it might appear that Philips is going to queer seduction poetry, and she is, but she is also even more ambitious than this. At the time, the word "mystery" had a chiefly religious connotation, and it is this connotation that Philips highlights in the poem's first stanza:

> Come, my *Lucasia*, since we see
> That Miracles Mens faith do move,
> By wonders and by prodigy
> To the dull angry world let's prove
> There's a Religion in our Love.
>
> (1–5)

Philips intends to queer religion itself. She goes on to describe a religion, clearly modeled on seventeenth-century English Protestantism, that has at its center a female couple. In this first stanza, Philips says that just as the Christian god is a mystery that can only be understood by miracles that happen on earth, so the love between herself and Lucasia will be an example of this new gynocentric religion.

In the second stanza, Philips proves adept at using the dominant tropes and metaphors of the Christian discourse of her time and at employing them in the service of same-sex love. Neatly incorporating the debates between predestination and free will, for instance, she describes herself and Lucasia as "design'd t'agree, / That Fate no liberty destroyes" (6–7) and that

> our Election is as free
> as Angels, who with greedy choice
> Are yet determin'd to their joyes.
>
> (8–10)

The paradoxes here – for instance, the two women agree, which suggests free will, but are "design'd" to do so, which suggests predetermination – are both the paradoxes common to religious language and the paradoxes typical of the erotic poetry of the seventeenth century. Perhaps the most striking part of this stanza is its sexualized depiction of angels. While the two women agree, which is a relatively neutral verb, the angels are "determin'd to their joyes," a phrase which means both that they are intent on these joys (and the reference to their choice of them as "greedy" adds a strongly sexual note) and that they were created to partake in them. For readers now, the salient feature of these lines may be their insistence on this same-sex love as entirely natural and even intentional on God's part.

Philips returns to religious imagery in the poem's last stanza, but in the stanzas before the conclusion she focuses on more specifically romantic imagery of the sort that is now probably most familiar to us from the poetry of John Donne. I do not cite Donne merely as an example of a famous poet of the earlier part of the century, however, but also because I believe that in these stanzas Philips consciously uses and revises Donne. For instance, she writes of their union that "Here Mixture is Addition grown" (12), using the language of science to suggest that her bond with Lucasia results in something that is greater than either of them singly. Perhaps the most striking of the images in these stanzas is her statement that "we whose Minds are so much one, / Never, yet ever, are alone" (14–15). Here, the relationship between the two women is described in terms of union, of two people becoming one. This trope is a commonplace, found in poetry both good and bad throughout history, but what is unusual is her development of the trope. I think she has in mind the lines from Donne's "The Exstasie" in which the union of the two lovers is said to eliminate "the defects of Lonelinesse" typical of singleness.[14] Philips goes further than Donne in not getting rid of loneliness. Instead, she sees a true bond between people as one in which solitude, so often valorized in English Renaissance poetry, and society can coexist.

In the fifth stanza, Philips expands on this theme of union and she does so partly by returning to Donne:

> We are our selves but by rebound,
> And all out Titles shuffled so,
> Both Princes and both Subjects too.
> (23–5)

Instead of the two selves that become one, which is the usual language of love poetry, the two selves, which are also the one self that is two, only exist "by rebound": to know each other is to know one's self and oneself and, we could even say, oneselves. There is no loss of identity in this union, but rather a fuller knowledge of a fuller identity. When Philips says that the women are "Both Princes and both Subjects too," she alludes to Donne's poem "The Sunne Rising," in which the speaker celebrates his perfect union with his beloved by saying "She's all States, and all Princes, I, / Nothing else is" (21–2). Donne's vision is attractive in that it presents the couple as entire and complete in itself, but it clearly presents the woman as subordinate, and even as inanimate. Philips transforms this image into one of perfect mutuality and equality.

Using Philips's poem as my final example allows me to end this essay on a happy note. Philips queers both the dominant tropes of erotic poetry and the dominant tropes of religious language in order to describe a perfect union, ending in a fusion that is at once sacred and orgasmic (keeping in mind the contemporary use of "to die" as a synonym for "to have an orgasm"): describing their hearts as "mutual Victims" (26) in a religious ritual in which they are at once "Altars, Priests, and Off'rings" (28), she ends by saying "each Heart which thus kindly dies, / Grows deathless by the Sacrifice" (29–30). Philips's extraordinary celebration of her mutual love for another woman is undeniably daring, but as was the case with the numerous celebrations of male friendship in Renaissance literature, she never quite oversteps the bounds. In an era of great repression and officially sanctioned opposition to homoeroticism, writers were still able to find ways to talk about same-sex love. While Marlowe's *Edward II* shows the cost of exceeding the discursive limits of same-sex attachment, both Spenser and, more explicitly and more fervently, Philips celebrate these attachments in ways that never become transgressive. The writers of the English Renaissance showed a queer resourcefulness that is typical of queerness to the present day, but that queer Renaissance studies has only begun to discuss.

### Notes

1 Alan Bray, *Homosexuality in Renaissance England* (London: Gay Men's Press, 1982).

2 Ibid., 25.

3 Edmund Spenser, "Januarye," in *The Shepheardes Calender, Poetical Works*, ed. J. C. Smith and E. de Selincourt (Oxford: Oxford University Press, 1912), n. to line 59. Quotations from Spenser are to this book and will appear parenthetically in the text.

4 See Lee Edelman, *No Future: Queer Theory and the Death Drive* (Durham: Duke University Press, 2004), 1–31.

5 Jonathan Goldberg, ed., *Queering the Renaissance* (Durham: Duke University Press, 1994).

6 Jonathan Goldberg, *Sodometries: Renaissance Texts, Modern Sexualities* (Stanford: Stanford University Press, 1992).

7 Valerie Traub, *The Renaissance of Lesbianism in Early Modern England* (New York: Cambridge University Press, 2002).

8 Madhavi Menon, ed., *Shakesqueer: A Queer Companion to the Works of William Shakespeare* (Durham: Duke University Press, 2011).

9 Ibid., 5. For a similar approach to a later author, see William F. Edmiston, *Sade: Queer Theorist* (Oxford: Voltaire Foundation, 2013).

10 Stephen Guy-Bray, "Same Difference: Homo and Allo in Lyly's *Euphues*," in *Prose Fiction and Early Modern Sexualities in England, 1570–1640*, ed. Constance C. Relihan and Goran V. Stanivuković (New York: Palgrave Macmillan, 2003), 113–27.

11 Stephen Orgel, "Nobody's Perfect: Or Why Did the English Stage Take Boys for Women?," *South Atlantic Quarterly* vol. 88 (1989): 12.

12 Christopher Marlowe, *Edward II*, in *The Complete Works of Christopher Marlowe, Volume II*, ed. Fredson Bowers (Cambridge: Cambridge University Press, 2008), I.iv.388–90. Quotations from *Edward II* are from this book and will appear parenthetically in the text.

13 Katherine Philips, *Poems by the Incomparable, Mrs. K. P.* (London: Richard Marriott, 1664.). Quotations are from this book and will appear parenthetically in the text. I am quoting from one of the very first editions of her poems because there is, still, no contemporary scholarly edition of her works.

14 John Donne, "The Exstasie," in *The Complete English Poems of John Donne*, ed. C. A. Patrides (London: J. M. Dent, 1985), 44. Quotations from Donne are from this book and will appear parenthetically in the text.

# CHAPTER 2

# Write, Paint, Dance, Sex
## Queer Styles/American Fictions

### Dana Seitler

Susie Asado. Sweet sweet sweet sweet tea. Susie Asado. Enunciate it slowly and let the S's roll off your tongue. And again. Susie Asado. Sweet sweet sweet sweet tea. Susie Asado. We could say that, for Gertrude Stein, sexuality is the letter S. In the poem *Susie Asado*, of which these are the first two lines, the verses unfold like an S coiling around the tongue.[1] The poem, itself shaped like the letter S, curves in and out and around like a form of sensory realism. Yes, Stein was fascinated by Matisse, Picasso, and other modernist experiments with Cubism, fragmentation, and collage. But this poem, and her work in general, evoke more of what sexuality feels like than many detailed realist descriptions do. Sexuality, Stein reminds us, is not an essence, a content, an identification, or a singular noun; it is more like the simultaneity of a shape, a sound, a taste, a visual and haptic experience, a melody, a dance, a shifting aesthetic practice – ineffable, tangible, both. Embracing Stein's embrace of the letter S, sexuality is, we could say, a style.

Inspired by the rhythm and movement of a flamenco dancer Stein had seen perform in Spain, "Susie Asado" and its companion piece "Preciosilla," both published in 1914, have a lot to tell us about queer style, about what it means to paint with words, about the sexiness of sound, about the erotics of organic and inorganic life worlds that Dana Luciano and Mel Chen have variously described as the queerness of "the non-human fold" and the affordances of "trans/material attachments."[2] Stein produces any number of superimposed verbal planes to create a space of perception not as a form of organized consciousness or logical sequence but as an overlap of patterns and images, sounds and rhythms, textures and grains, what Stein herself describes as "a continuous present and using everything and beginning again."[3]

Thus "Preciosilla": "Lily wet lily wet while. This is so pink so pink in stammer, a long bean which shows bows is collected by a single curly shady, shady get, get set wet bet."[4] The invagination of language Stein performs is less a rendering of a lily as reducible to a clitoris (the long bean), surrounded by pubic hair (the curly shady), in the act of coming (get set wet bet), than it is a demonstration of the *clitoral*, of or pertaining to a set of queer, specifically lesbian, sensations. The poem makes use of the play of language as a vehicle for estranging us from and bringing us closer to the erotic variability of words. Simultaneously a deliberate transgression of the boundaries of the human – lilies becoming bodies becoming arousal – and a queer meditation on how words, natural objects, and bodies rub on, and against, each other, thus generating new forms, these poems encapsulate some of the tactics of queer studies in general – a practice that Stein designates in her coinage of the verb "to exstate" in "Preciosilla": to extract language from itself, to make language ecstatic.

In "A Sketch of the Past," Virginia Woolf describes such heightened moments of pleasure as instances of affective comprehension that emerge to counter the emotional and social numbing of the modern world. The routine tasks we perform in everyday life are "not lived consciously," but instead are embedded in "a kind of nondescript cotton wool."[5] At other times though, both banal and extraordinary, we experience an intensity of feeling that can be understood through the language of aesthetics: "The whole world is a work of art; we are parts of the work of art. We are the words; we are the music; we are the thing itself" (72). For Woolf, our realization of our lives as a work of art is a moment when we catch a glimpse of and receive inspiration from our entanglement with the otherwise opaque and muted surfaces of everyday life.

And so, in Woolf's short story "Kew Gardens," we are privy to a view of desire from the perspective of a snail, itself situated in the lush corporeality of a summer garden, slowly sliming its way through "tongue-shaped leaves half way up and unfurling at the tip red or blue or yellow petals marked with spots of colour raised upon the surface."[6] A man and a woman walk by the garden where the snail moves, and the woman, Eleanor, is stirred to remember a startling kiss.

> Imagine six little girls sitting before their easels twenty years ago, down by the side of a lake, painting the water-lilies, the first red water-lilies I'd ever seen. And suddenly a kiss, there on the back of my neck. And my hand shook all the afternoon so that I couldn't paint. I took out my watch and marked the hour when I would allow myself to think of the kiss for five minutes only – it was so precious – the kiss of an old grey-haired woman with a wart on her nose, the mother of all my kisses all my life. (57)

What is queer about this moment is not reducible to the life-changing arousal one woman experiences when kissed by another, nor even to the ostensibly exceptional fact that the kiss was from an older, wart-nosed woman. Rather, it is that the kiss produces such significant agitation, is so exquisite and *catalytic*, that it seems to mark the origins of Eleanor's sexuality, a moment akin to what Lauren Berlant and Lee Edelman, in *Sex, or the Unbearable*, describe as "the subject's constitution by and attachment to varieties of being undone."[7] In "Kew Gardens," snails and humans and flowers and plants and lips on flesh merge into the shapes and colors of the natural world in such a way that also merges theme with style, where the content of desire is dissolved into and thereby made over by aesthetic form. In the story, Woolf treats words as painters treat paint, constructing a network of human interaction through associations of tone, color, and hue, offering us textures of language over plot. Objects, animals, people are transformed into interactive forms, and our knowledge of them as readers becomes dependent on the senses. Color words – the repetitions of red, blue, and yellow – open an optical space of perception and invite imaginative, rapturous response.

This is all to say that sexuality and its attendant forms of desire, love, relationality, and non-relationality (human and nonhuman both) can be considered along the lines of Stein's letter S and Woolf's color palette as a series of still unfolding styles, consisting of counterintuitive reading, temporal disjuncture, the performative, narrative interruption and suspension, non-closure, negativity, ambivalence, affective intensity, color, texture, syntax, and tone that make up the queer literary domain. Since its inception, queer studies has defined itself as a critical practice consisting of imaginative interpretative acts, ones intent on exploring how sexuality and sociality map onto one another, on enacting a reading practice of and for unpredictable impulses and methods that operate against normative and normativizing life narratives, and ultimately on working to expand the networks of kinship, feeling, friendship, love, and desire that can be thought and read in the first place. In this sense, queer methods of reading were never about marking a fixed sexual or erotic practice. Its methodological innovations have imagined and continue to imagine queer sex and sexuality in ways that eschew traditional narrative teleology and finite definition, redirecting historical, formalist, and political interest to the social energies of a text that unfold in different directions, what Arthur

Rimbaud legendarily describes as *"dans tous les sens"* (calling upon all senses, hinting at all meanings, going in all directions).[8]

## Interpretive Acts and Strategic Misreadings

To think about queer style is to pay attention to the literariness of queer narrative – its tones, textures, and literary techniques – but also to emphasize the relationship between literature and the social world, between aesthetics and politics. It is to approach queer literature from a different angle of vision than the space of fixed identity or objective historicity. Queer studies and its generation of queer readings of cultural texts can instead be understood along the lines of what, in a different context, Ariella Azoulay calls "potential history" in which "the reconstruction of unrealized possibilities, practices, and dreams that motivated and directed the actions of various actors in the past" becomes possible.[9] In the context of queer temporality, this is akin to what Elizabeth Freeman refers to as "erotohistoriography" – "the centrality of pleasure, especially sexual pleasure, in queer practices of encountering and documenting the past" – and what Peter Coviello designates "the untimely" – the ways desire circulates in nineteenth-century American fiction that does not anticipate the medico-juridical taxonomies of sex at the beginning of the twentieth century but, rather, consists of a series of unpredictable forms of sexual intimacy, same-sex attachment, and erotic possibility.[10] And so Jordan Stein, in his reading of Nathaniel Hawthorne's *The Blithedale Romance*, does not dwell on the more obviously gay bits of the story such as Coverdale and Hollingsworth's homoerotic exchanges or the tense polyamorous love quadrangle among Coverdale, Hollingsworth, Zenobia, and Priscilla but on a moment of narrative suspension when Coverdale's scopophilic penchant for peeping into Zenobia and Priscilla's back window is interrupted by a waiter serving him a sherry-cobbler. For Stein, this interruption is a mark of the narrative's queer style that, in the absence of a fixed discourse on homosexuality, "provides the basis for a characterization of *Blithedale* as a queer novel before 'homosexuality.'"[11]

Hawthorne's novel, of course, is only one of any number of texts one could turn to when tracing a genealogy of queer theory's literary objects and the styles they engage. In American literature, certain authors have for some time now given shape to queer literary studies: Walt Whitman, Emily Dickinson, Gertrude Stein, Henry James, Claude McCay, Willa Cather, Jean Toomer, James Baldwin, and Nella Larsen have all been taken up in the work of Mae G. Henderson, Michael Moon, Charles I.

Nero, Betsy Erkkila, Michael Warner, Eve Sedgwick, Jonathan Goldberg, Peter Coviello, Heather Love, Michael Snediker, Siobhan Somerville, Dwight McBride, Dana Luciano, and other major contributors to the field. As a result, we have become privy to the homoerotic intimacies of Sarah Orne Jewett's spinsters and Walt Whitman's cruising poetics. We have taken succor from the styles of queer refusal and resistance in Emily Dickinson – "I'm Nobody! Who Are You? Are you – Nobody – too? Then there's a pair of us!" – and Herman Melville – in which Bartelby's famous response, "I prefer not to," has become a hallmark of queer negativity. We have noted Willa Cather's queer allusions ("the tan velvet on the collar" of Paul's Wildean overcoat, where he placed "an opal pin in his neatly knotted black four-in-hand, and a red carnation in his buttonhole") and Hawthorne's explorations of how the erotic is not what funds an easy queer sociality but, ultimately, what gives the lie to the nation form, caught up as that form is in the mutual entanglements of projective identification, the absent presence of desire, and the prohibition on sex.[12] We could also dwell with no small amount of erotic glee on the ending of Djuna Barnes's *Ladies Almanack* in which, when the lesbian lothario and main protagonist Dame Evangeline Musset dies and her body is cremated, "all had burned but the Tongue, and this flamed, and would not suffer Ash, and it played about on the handful that had been she indeed."[13] The tongue as both a sexual organ and an organ for speech that refuses to burn at the end of Barnes's work appears as a queer leitmotif in the frame narrative of Zora Neale Hurston's *Their Eyes Are Watching God* as well when Janie sits on the porch recounting her travels to her "kissin' friend" Phoebe, thus forging the narrative's final couple as one between women, and Janie avows, "Mah tongue is in mah friend's mouth."[14]

## Aesthetics and Politics

One of the things we learn from this body of work is that if desire can be seen as existing at the root of the organization of the social, then the aesthetic mediations of sex and sexuality can't be dismissed so easily as the "merely cultural."[15] Queer theory's interest in literary style is an interest in working through what kinds of relations between people can be figured. There is thus an ethical urgency about queer theory that is directed at the damage that sexual prohibitions do to people, but also at how literary form is crucial in confronting the various ways the social fabric does not unravel evenly. With particular emphasis on the dissonant effects of race on sexual experience, the work of Sandra Soto, Sharon Patricia Holland, David Eng, Aliyyah I. Abdur-Rahman, Jose Muñoz, and many others has argued for a queer analysis of the discursive relationship between racialization and sexuality in poetry, fiction, and cultural performance.[16] "Can work on 'desire' be antiracist work? Can antiracist work think 'desire'?" Holland asks.[17] Maybe, but only if we continue to grapple with the social and historical contingencies of "desire" and "pleasure" and their locations in nonuniversal, nonautonomous domains (as Holland also suggests). Toward this end, in *Against the Closet: Black Political Longing and the Erotics of Race*, Abdur-Rahman analyzes African-American literary depictions of black sexuality in order to illuminate how the erotic operates at the center of understandings of race in US culture. Tracing how African-American writers work to disavow the constraints of white heteronormativity, Abdur-Rahman moves from literature portraying white acts of aggression on black bodies to literature that explores forms of black desire (as well as the simultaneity of both). Abdur-Rahman thus reveals how narrative form aids us in confronting the racialized sexual tensions at the heart of the American national imaginary.

Along these lines, in key texts such as the slave narratives written by Harriet Jacobs and Fredrick Douglass we can trace the emergence of a black Bildungsroman. This is a specific narrative form that does not simply retread late eighteenth-century authorized conventions in which an individual's maturation requires their eventual acceptance of the values of their social world. Rather, it is a narrative form that must contend with the specific ways the sexual is fundamental to constructions of blackness in the acquisition and maintenance of white power in the US, necessitating a depiction of how the protagonist of the black Bildungsroman must engage in a narrative-long struggle with both sexual violence and sexual autonomy. In Jacobs's *Incidents in the Life of a Slave Girl*, for example, Linda Brendt must survive and escape from an unremitting context of sexual endangerment (the sexual violence of Mrs. Flint's nightly intrusions as much as Mr. Flint's relentless coercions) toward a possible sexual freedom. The harrowing narration of "the trials of girlhood" that unfolds, as Hortense Spillers and others have discussed, structurally maps how the black women's body under slavery, far from being marked in terms of gender or sexuality, is forced into availability for the projections of white male and female violence alike.[18] Jacobs's account of this endangerment and the possibility of escaping it thus requires different modes and styles of narration capable of recording the different sensory and sexual orientations to the world experienced by slaves as a result of the brutalities of dispossession.[19]

Understanding the aesthetic and social unfolding of this structure of what Roderick Ferguson terms "racialized sexuality" calls for an exchange between critical race theory and queer studies at the level of form as well as other styles of resistance – which means grappling with the myriad ways class, race, gender, and sexuality are shaped and reshaped in and through a number of overlapping, mutually informing histories, including racial capitalism, settler colonialism, the sexual politics of empire, and the dynamics of social reproduction and epistemic familialism.[20] As Cathy Cohen suggests, the political analysis of queer theory is damaged at its core if it cannot account for the interactions and mutual determinations of class, race, gender, and sexuality, not as a set of issues one "supports," or topics and populations one includes in a conference session, political rally, or anthology, but as intertwined historical, aesthetic, and political formations.[21] In this vein, queer styles of narrative pleasure and resistance are not reducible to aesthetic forms and poetic structures but need to be understood in relation to the various national, racial, gendered, classed logics they also inhabit. In this sense, too, in Gertrude Stein's poem "Susie Asado" sexuality is also a race. Read through the interventions of queer of color critique, Stein's poem, while working to move beyond the mandates of body and identity, nonetheless turns to a Spanish flamenco dancer as the impetus for its queer desires. This points us toward both Stein's specific appropriation of racial culture and, more largely, the often invisible racial structures of modernism.[22] It also underscores the point I have been making about how something like queer style is never not politically imbricated.

## Limits of Radical Worldmaking

What does this mean about the uneven democratizations of queer possibility? For Whitman, as scholars from Moon to Coviello suggest, sexual union figures the utopian possibilities of civic union. Expressing his polyamorous democratic vision through writerly experiment (parataxis, incantatory repetition, enjambment, assonance, consonance, and an almost drunken use of alliteration), Whitman endows male–male desire with the power to "make the continent indissoluble" by virtue of "the love of comrades, / With the life-long love of comrades."[23] Both in the "Calamus" poems and throughout *Leaves of Grass*, Whitman places ebullient and vigorous faith in writing as the means to fashion a queerer and thus more just world. For Whitman, queer love, and even more an ethics of queer care, just might have the power to end slavery.

The runaway slave came to my house and stopped outside,
I heard his motions crackling the twigs of the woodpile,
Through the swung half-door of the kitchen I saw him limpsey and weak,
And went where he sat on a log, and led him in and assured him,
And brought water and filled a tub for his sweated body and bruised feet,
And gave him a room that entered from my own, and gave him some coarse
    clean clothes,
And remember perfectly well his revolving eyes and his awkwardness, And
    remember putting plasters on the galls of his neck and ankles;
He staid with me a week before he was recuperated and passed north, I had
    him sit next me at table ... my firelock leaned in the corner.[24]

In the context of the Fugitive Slave Act of 1850, which authorized local governments to seize anyone thought to be an escaped slave and imposed penalties on those who aided their flight, Whitman imagines a scene of affectionate care between himself and a male runaway slave in defiance of the law. Both here and throughout the poem, Whitman refuses traditional syntactic arrangements of time, space, and people, opting instead to make nonhierarchical connections between and amongst them through his much-noted use of parataxis – the infinite addition, the thousand-comma sentence – in which no subordination between clauses and phrases can be said to exist. By doing so, he delineates the possibilities of cross-racial affinity infused with the vibrancy of desire akin to the love of comrades articulated in "Calamus." And yet. The act of queer love depicted here is such an intensely embodied consecration, an act stylized as much by an imagined and celebratory male capacity to nurture as by the relentlessness of the white male gaze, so tender but also so reifying as he makes visually manifest the slave's "sweated body and bruised feet," "his revolving eyes and his awkwardness," all the while, oh so fearlessly keeping his rifle in the corner. Is this, we might sincerely ask, an act of queer love or a white savior narrative? Does it sketch out the contours of a decidedly antiracist practice of intimacy or reinforce the sexual objectification of the black male body? All of this? Whitman's vision is at once a queer world-making practice and a will to visualization working to frame the other's legibility.[25] The point, I think, would not be to use the latter critique to indict and dismiss the former practice as much as to grapple with the co-occurrence of each and, correspondingly, to think about how the former practice doesn't exist without the latter in Whitman's articulation. Following Soto's understanding of "reading like a queer," it means directly engaging with, rather than trying to bracket or disentangle, a narrative's fundamental contradictions.[26]

We also read like a queer when we attend to the difference style makes. What happens when we consider sexuality in aesthetic rather than identitarian terms? If style in literature is the element that describes the ways that the author uses words – from word choice to syntactical arrangement to tonal variation to sentence structure – to produce moods, meanings, and sensations, then attending to what is queer about style (to what is provisional, experimental, strange, intervening, difficult, performative) makes queerness less constrained by historical discourse and sociological fact, more open to practice, change, and transformation – more possible.

## Queer Style and the Genres of Heterosexuality

Focusing on style means more expansive possibilities for criticism. Looking at texts not usually considered "queer" (either by authorship or content) provides particular affordances for how queer methods of reading for style help pry open a text to its own internal sexual imaginings. For example, in his short story "The Bride Comes to Yellow Sky," Stephen Crane, perhaps unwittingly, takes up the gauntlet thrown down by Whitman to forward the argument that the imposition of the modern regime of heterosexuality, indeed, ruins everything. "The Bride" can be read as much as a comic send-up of the logic of heteronormativity as a political commentary on how the same logic founds the violence of settler colonialism. As Mark Rifkin argues, one of the ways the process of settler colonialism simultaneously asserts and disavows itself is through the establishment of the conjugal couple form and its naturalized claim to property.[27] In "The Bride Comes to Yellow Sky," this plays itself out comically via the marriage plot. The first chapter begins in the space of a train – flagrant symbol of encroaching modernity – with Jack Potter and his new bride travelling west from San Antonio, Texas, where they have just been married, to the unsettled region of Yellow Sky. "Whirling onward with such dignity of motion," the train that carries "the newly married pair" thus equates marriage with the threshold of modernity as both plow their way headlong into the unconstructed West, figured in the story (not to mention the American imagination) as an extralegal space.[28] In the second chapter, the focalization shifts and we are now with the men of the town as they gather for a drink at "The Weary Gentleman's Saloon" and wait for Jack Potter to return. Soon after, they find that they must lock themselves in the bar because they hear that Scratchy Wilson is on a drunken tear, pistols flaring and looking for a fight. In chapter 3, the narrative focalization shifts once again as Scratchy Wilson, "the last one of the old gang that used to hang out along the river here," enters the scene (320). We now follow the narrative action from his point of view and thus come to inhabit the rough and rugged character of masculinity that he represents. He lusts so heavily for a fight that "the cords of his neck straightened and sank, straightened and sank, as passion moved him" (321). And not just any fight, but one with his beloved adversary, Jack Potter: "he moved in the direction of his desire, chanting Apache scalp-music" as if "on the war trail" (322). Placing Scratchy within native discourse, coupled with the story's scattered references to the presence of Mexicans (such as the two "Mexican sheep-herders who did not talk as a general practice in the Weary Gentleman's Saloon"), binds him to a settler narrative of coercive disappearance, in which his desire presents itself as in excess of or located somewhere beyond the dynamics of the law and the state that Jack Potter, as the Town Marshall, represents (318). Scratchy's presence testifies to prior contexts of Native and Mexican inhabitance of Texan land and simultaneously, or in fact as a result, functions as the story's site of queerness. This queerness comes to the fore in chapter 4 when Scratchy finds the object of his desire in the figure of Jack Potter: "The two men faced each other at a distance of three paces. He of the revolver smiled with a new and quiet ferocity" (323).

Scratchy soon discovers that their romance has been displaced by Jack Potter's new bride. "Married!" Scratchy Wilson shouts uncomprehendingly, "Married?" "No!" Noticing the bride standing by Potter's side for the first time, he was "like a creature allowed a glimpse of another world." "I guess it's all off now," Wilson shrugs, and then sadly, slowly walks away, making "funnel-shaped tracks in the heavy sand" (324). Like the perennial sands of time dropping through the funnel of an hourglass, Scratchy Wilson's retreat signals that the temporality of the modern is the time of heterosexuality. Melancholy sets in as Scratchy discovers he is not the story's vital pulse but a figure of the racial and sexual past, a sign of what has been lost, affectively, historically, spatially, sexually. The story of his defeat is a sustained meditation on heterosexuality and the marriage form that consolidates it as "The Bride" so precisely comes to allegorize the marital couple's elevation to the status of a racial and sexual norm.

The modern regime of sexuality is thus identified not only by "the feminization of American culture" indicated by the bride's presence, but also by the heterosexual contract with the feminine. In many ways, then, the narrative's sexism (its horror at the presence of the female body) is also its queerness. The bride's entry into Yellow Sky redefines, even repudiates, male–male relations, and this is what makes Scratchy so sad: "I guess it's all over then." The West is a space of male homosocial *and* homoerotic unconstraint – and the discourse on heterosexuality has disciplinary effects.

It marks a shift from the logic of masculine violence to one of decorum in the presence of ladies. This is simultaneously a shift away from the queer gunplay that Scratchy Wilson has a history of enjoying with Jack Potter and toward dyadic monogamy.

Ultimately, this is a profoundly Foucauldian tale about the modern implantation of the legitimate heterosexual couple. The melancholic ending laments the passing of male–male desire as heterosexuality establishes itself as the new order. The strange use of chapter breaks in the short story form (four such breaks in a nine-page tale) allows Crane to refocalize the narrative from multiple angles of vision. These chapter breaks interrupt the teleology of the narrative as an otherwise straightforward marriage plot and thereby act as a formal manifestation of the temporal and structural disorientations of modernity that the married couple also ushers in. At the same time, the use of chapters unsettles – cuts into, breaks up – both the narrative of settler colonialism and the implantation of white heterosexuality that supports it. On this reading, Crane's story can be understood as queer less because it features two men in desiring attachment to one another (though it does this too) but by way of its manner of narration, its queer style. Instead of the narrative unfolding from what Gérard Genette calls "zero focalization" (through the narrator's voice alone), it unfolds through the perspective of particular characters in a pattern of shifting focalization until it comes to reside with Scratchy Wilson.[29] It is ultimately through Scratchy Wilson's vision that the reader sees, which has the significant effect of cuing us to the potential of the narrative's nonnormative alliances. The result is a less sympathetic and totalizing narrative of the inevitability of modern sexuality and the episteme of the family that enables geopolitical usurpation and racial violence than one that, instead, opens up a discussion of how these forms get constructed in and by narrative. Rather than captivating the reader with the marriage plot, it makes visible that plot's structural perversity.

The obstinacy of heterosexuality as a genre of being that binds selfhood to society takes center stage in the work of Henry James as well. This is because James's queer style involves the formal conjuring of heterosexuality as a narrative impasse. He does so by unsettling the narrative emplotment of heterosexual romance with what we might think of as a form of queer narrative nonclosure. For Kevin Ohi, James's queer style is figured by his disorienting narrative temporalities in which a character's consciousness is continually out of sync with the experience it records.[30] We can see a similar temporal play in James's refusal of narrative closure, specifically in the deliberate ongoingness that his endings imply (more often than not of suffering, stuckness, ambivalence, and other affective microclimates of desire) – whether it is Isabel Archer's refusal to share whatever "straight path" she imagines for herself at the end of *Portrait of a Lady*; Kate Croy's inscrutable final line in *Wings of the Dove* ("We shall never be again as we were!"); Strether Lambert's mystifying (and for the most part unstated) decision to return home in *The Ambassadors* instead of remaining in the space of art and queer love with which Parisian life provides him; the closing lament of *The Bostonians* that, as a result of Verena Tarrant's decision to run off with Basil Ransom, "it is to be feared that with the union, so far from brilliant, into which she was about to enter, these were not the last [tears] she was destined to shed"; or – well, I could go on.[31] James eschews the kinds of coherence narrative closure affords, instead demonstrating how the imperative for closure has the tendency to wrap itself up in a coercive and false sense of heterosexualized stability. If the consolidating forms of the heterosexual romance and the marriage plot all promise to resolve the narrative crises of sexual confusion, wayward pleasure, bad object choice, and adolescent play, in James we are treated to the more agonizing ambivalences of, and thus more expansive possibilities for, love and desire. To ask of his narratives *how* they end – whether or not we should consider them tragic or triumphant – is to ask precisely the wrong question because it assumes that experiences of love and desire do end. Love objects and other sites of sexual desire may fade into the past, but do they disappear without a psychic or material trace? "We shall never be again as we were!": not because we were once comfortable and assured in our desires but because desire, love, and other modes of being-in-relation are as constitutively uncomfortable and uncertain as they are interminable. We shall never again inhabit that fantasy of ourselves that never was, for now we know it to have been a fantasy. This makes the supposition that there can be an "after" queer studies somewhat incomprehensible. From a Jamesian perspective, we could ask: Can queer desire be contained within a teleological narrative of beginnings and ends? Can ways of reading it? If, as readers, we crave a stable, simplified version of James's, or any, novelistic world as one way to simplify and stabilize the relations we have in our own, this wish for a resolution is precisely what James mirrors back to us and then refuses by confronting us with a narrative that insists – through its presentation of provisional and impoverished forms of perception, its exhaustive use of the prepositional clause as a way to mime the slow rhythms of thinking, its temporal discontinuities – upon the impossibility of an ending. In these writerly practices, these resolute attachments to irresolution, James shows himself at his most queer. To refuse the closure of the marriage plot is to refuse the time of hetero-sexuality. To embrace the structural and temporal vicissitudes of the narration of desire is to open up the categories of sexuality to greater, more multiple possibilities for attachment, intimacy, and sex.

## Dancing Queens

If narrative irresolution and nonclosure gives us James at his most queer, we also find in his work an instance of queerness at its nadir when, in the novella *Daisy Miller*, Winterbourne discloses that he hates to dance. "It's a pity these rooms are so small; we can't dance," Daisy Miller effuses to her moralizing counterpart. "I am not sorry we can't dance," Winterbourne returns; "I don't dance."[32] Bright, vivacious, and defiantly in violation of the norms of feminine sexual propriety, Daisy Miller disagrees, and it is this moment of unbridled attachment to dancing and other pleasures like it that garner her all sorts of social judgment, not least of which comes from the character that finds his desire for her so unbearable: Winter-bourne himself, shown up by James most scathingly at the moment he discloses his disapproval of the dance floor. "Of course you don't dance; you're too stiff," replies Daisy as she flounces off. For José Muñoz, we might recall, "dance is an especially valuable site for ruminations on queerness and gesture." Muñoz continues, "Queer dance is hard to catch, and it is meant to be hard to catch – it is supposed to slip through the fingers and comprehension of those who would use knowledge against us. Rather than dematerialize, dance rematerializes. Dance, like energy, never disappears; it is simply transformed."[33] Like James's narrative nonclosures, dance is another queer style, one that points us away from a critical timeline of befores and afters and toward the "ephemeral trace," which is to say the style, of the queer.

Might we revisit, for a third time, Stein's poem "Susie Asado" through this lens? By concentrating on the rhythms, gestures, and movements of flamenco, is it possible to steal back the dance form from modernism's appropriations? "Susie Asado which is a told tray sure. A lean on the shoe this means slips slips hers."[34] Functioning within both visual and aural registers as an image of a dancer and the sound of dance, Susie Asado is, to be sure, an object of lesbian desire, a treasure ("tray sure"), but also a series of movements ("A lean on the shoe this means slips slips hers"). By con-juring the visuality and aurality of flamenco, a dance that makes use of palmas (handclapping), pintas (finger snapping), and rhythmic stamping to express intense emotion and sexual intimacy, the dance can be said to exceed the words on the page that attempt to capture it.[35] Virgil Thomson's famous musical composition for "Susie Asado" not only confirms how the poem lends itself to music, but also how we cannot fully engage the poem's words referentially, only elusively through the sensory forms they evoke. Such an interpretation might allow the traces of flamenco in the poem to hold greater sway, to foreground the ways pleasure is summoned in and through the relationship between the utterance and that which surpasses it. We can, in this way, glimpse the poem's materialization of sensory relations that link the reader to the dance as an aesthetic event that bears with it the traces of queer desire and racial expression at the intersections. Of course, this is a strategic misreading along the lines of what Muñoz names "disidentification" – a mode of reading that does not identify with a text's ideology or only reject it but, rather, rereads the text according to one's own willful projections and pleasures and, as an effect, transforms it.[36]

How does this help us to imagine the significance of queer style within the discipline of queer studies? To be sure, the literary works adumbrated throughout this chapter offer an array of queer intimacies and attachments between women and between men, but they also invite readers to explore literary styles that reveal themselves as queer in myriad other ways: through narrative structure, poetic technique, genre transformation and reinvention, temporal distortion and resistance, and, as such, continuously renovate the very question of the potential of literary style for articulations of queerness. Just as significantly, these works and the ways of reading them I have gestured toward outline the multiple and capacious styles of queer literary criticism, styles that enable a reader to turn, again and again, to the same short poem and read its queernesses differently each time, queer styles that advocate improvisation, openness, renegotiation, and, above all, a willingness to be wrong. While there are many modalities of queer studies deserving of criticism, at its best it stands to be corrected, open to polyamorous dialogue and sensuous provocation, it aspires to participate in criticism as Daisy Miller might but Winterbourne never would; that is, it aspires to dance. In alliance with the inversions of queer style, then, permit me to end with where I could have begun, with an epigraph from Prince, who has taught us this all along: "Somebody say dance (dance), music (music), sex (sex), romance (romance). Everybody say dance (dance), music (music), sex (sex), romance (romance)."[37]

## Notes

1 Gertrude Stein, "Susie Asado," in *Selected Writings of Gertrude Stein*, ed. Carl Van Vechten (New York: Vintage, 1990), 549.

2 Dana Luciano and Mel Y. Chen, "Has the Queer Ever Been Human?," in *GLQ: A Journal of Lesbian and Gay Studies*, special issue *Queer Inhumanisms*, ed. Dana Luciano and Mel Y. Chen, vol. 21, nos. 2–3 (2015): 183–207.

3 Gertrude Stein, "Composition as Explanation," in *Selected Writings of Gertrude Stein*, ed. Carl Van Vechten (New York: Vintage, 1990), 511.

4 Gertrude Stein, "Preciosilla," in *Selected Writings of Gertrude Stein*, ed. Carl Van Vechten (New York: Vintage, 1990), 550.

5 Virginia Woolf, "A Sketch of the Past," in *Moments of Being* (New York: Harcourt, Brace, Jovanovich, 1985), 70.

6 Virginia Woolf, "Kew Gardens," in *Monday or Tuesday* (New York: Harcourt, Brace and Company, 1921), 55.

7 Lauren Berlant and Lee Edelman, *Sex, or The Unbearable* (Durham: Duke University Press, 2013), 6.

8 See Kristin Ross, *The Emergence of Social Space: Rimbaud and the Paris Commune* (Minneapolis: University of Minnesota Press, 1988).

9 Ariella Azoulay, "Potential History: Thinking through Violence," *Critical Inquiry* vol. 39, no. 3 (Spring 2013): 548–74.

10 Elizabeth Freeman, *Time Binds: Queer Temporalities, Queer Histories* (Durham: Duke University Press, 2010), xxiii; Peter Coviello, *Tomorrow's Parties: Sex and the Untimely in Nineteenth-Century America* (New York: New York University Press, 2013).

11 Jordan Alexander Stein, "*The Blithedale Romance*'s Queer Style," *ESQ: A Journal of the American Renaissance* vol. 55, nos. 3–4 (Winter–Spring 2009): 211–36.

12 Willa Cather, "Paul's Case," *Norton Anthology of Short Fiction*, 7th ed. (New York: W. W. Norton, 2006), 234. On Cather see Eve Kosofsky Sedgwick, "Across Gender, Across Sexuality: Willa Cather and Others," *South Atlantic Quarterly* vol. 88, no. 1 (Winter 1989): 53–72; Jonathan Goldberg, *Willa Cather and Others* (Durham: Duke University Press, 2001); and Michael Trask, *Cruising Modernism: Class and Sexuality in American Literature and Social Thought* (New York: Cornell University Press, 2003). In addition to Jordan Stein and Coviello cited above, on Nathaniel Hawthorne, see Lauren Berlant, *The Anatomy of National Fantasy: Hawthorne, Utopia, And Everyday Life* (Chicago: University of Chicago Press, 1991) and Elizabeth Freeman, *The Wedding Complex: Forms of Belonging in Modern American Culture* (Durham: Duke University Press, 2002).

13 Djuna Barnes, *Ladies Almanack* (Windsor Locks, CT: Martino Publishing, 2016), 84.

14 Zora Neale Hurston, *Their Eyes Were Watching God* (New York: Harper & Row, 1990), 6. Also see Carla Kaplan, "The Erotics of Talk: 'That Oldest Human Longing' in *Their Eyes Were Watching God*," *American Literature* vol. 67, no. 1 (March 1995): 115–42.

15 See Judith Butler, "Marxism and the Merely Cultural," *New Left Review* vol. 227, no. 1 (January–February 1998): 33–44.
16 See Sharon Patricia Holland, *The Erotic Life of Racism* (Durham: Duke University Press, 2012); Aliyyah I. Abdur-Rahman, *Against the Closet: Black Political Longing and the Erotics of Race* (Durham: Duke University Press, 2012); David L. Eng, *Racial Castration: Managing Masculinity in Asian America* (Durham: Duke University Press, 2001); and Sandra Soto, *Reading Chican@ Like a Queer: The De-Mastery of Desire* (Austin: University of Texas Press, 2010). For the two field-changing collections on blackness and queer studies see E. Patrick Johnson and Mae G. Henderson, eds., *Black Queer Studies: A Critical Anthology* (Durham: Duke University Press, 2005) and E. Patrick Johnson, ed., *No Tea, No Shade: New Writings in Black Queer Studies* (Durham: Duke University Press, 2016).
17 Holland, *The Erotic Life of Racism*, 3.
18 Harriet Jacobs, *Incidents in the Life of a Slave Girl*, 44.
19 See Hortense Spillers, *Black, White, and in Color: Essays on American Literature and Culture* (Chicago: University of Chicago Press, 2003), 156.
20 Roderick Ferguson, "Of Our Normative Strivings: African American Studies and the Histories of Sexuality," *Social Text* vol. 23, no. 3–4 (Fall–Winter 2005): 84–100.
21 Cathy Cohen, "Punks, Bulldaggers, and Welfare Queens: The Radical Potential of Queer Politics?," *GLQ: A Journal of Lesbian and Gay Studies* vol. 3, no. 4 (1997): 437–65.
22 See David Eng, "The End(s) of Race," *PMLA* vol. 123, no. 5, Special Topic: Comparative Racialization (October 2008): 1479–93.
23 Walt Whitman, *Complete Poetry and Prose*, ed. Malcolm Cowley (New York: Pelligrini, 1996), 134.
24 Walt Whitman, *Leaves of Grass: The Original 1855 Edition* (New York: Dover, 2007), 27.
25 This is akin to what Christina Sharpe describes as "the intimacy of violence" in *In the Wake: On Blackness and Being* (Durham: Duke University Press, 2016).
26 Soto, *Reading Chican@ Like a Queer*, 17.
27 Mark Rifkin, *Settler Common Sense: Queerness and Everyday Colonialism in the American Renaissance* (Minneapolis: University of Minnesota Press, 2012).
28 Stephen Crane, "The Bride Comes to Yellow Sky," in *The Great Works of Stephen Crane*, ed. James B. Covert (New York: Harper & Row, 1968), 313. All subsequent references cited parenthetically in text.
29 Gérard Genette, *Narrative Discourse: An Essay in Method*, trans. Jane E. Lewin (Ithaca: Cornell University Press, [1972] 1980), 186.
30 Kevin Ohi, *Henry James and the Queerness of Style* (Minneapolis: University of Minnesota Press, 2008).
31 Henry James, *The Portrait of a Lady* (New York: Penguin, 2003), 636; *The Wings of the Dove* (New York: Penguin, 2008), 533; *The Bostonians* (Oxford: Oxford University Press, 1998), 435.

32 Henry James, *Daisy Miller* (New York: Penguin, 1998), 88.
33 José Muñoz, *Cruising Utopia: The Then and There of Queer Futurity* (New York: New York University Press, 2009), 65, 81.
34 Stein, "Susie Asado," 549.
35 See Michelle Heffner Hayes, *Flamenco: Conflicting Histories of the Dance* (New York: McFarland, 2009), 53.
36 José Esteban Muñoz, *Disidentifications: Queers of Color and the Performance of Politics* (Minneapolis: University of Minnesota Press, 1999).
37 Prince, "D.S.M.R." *1999* (Warner Bros. Records, 1982).

# CHAPTER 3

# Queer Latinx Studies and Queer Latinx Literature "After" Queer Theory, or Thought and Art and Sex after Pulse

*Ricardo Ortiz*

> People talk about liberation as if it's some kind of permanent state, as if you get liberated and that's it, you get some rights and that's it, you get some acknowledgment and that's it, happy now? But you're going back down into the muck of it every day; this world constricts. You know what the opposite of Latin Night at the Queer Club is? Another Day in Straight White America. So when you walk into the club, if you're lucky, it feels expansive. "Safe space" is a cliche, overused and exhausted in our discourse, but the fact remains that a sense of safety transforms the body, transforms the spirit. So many of us walk through the world without it. So when you walk through the door and it's a salsa beat, and brown bodies, queer bodies, all writhing in some fake smoke and strobing lights, no matter how cool, how detached, how over-it you think you are, Latin Night at the Queer Club breaks your cool. You can't help but smile, this is for you, for us.
>
> (Justin Torres, "In Praise of Latin Night at the Queer Club," 2016)

Immediately following the mass atrocity committed at the Orlando, FL, nightclub Pulse on June 12, 2016, the writer Justin Torres published a lyrical, outraged meditation on the productive cultural and political work that intersectional spaces like Pulse had been managing to do over recent decades, particularly in bringing into intimately public contact folks living out their lives in terms of at least the dual identifiers, "latinx" and "queer," but often in a more densely intersectional dynamic including "trans-gender," "gender-queer," "female," "brown," "poor," and "(dis-)abled."[1] Torres' heartbreakingly gorgeous rumination invites as many interpretive approaches as there are readers in the world who might be drawn to it from a variety of perspectives and for a variety of desires. It serves as an evocative touchstone for where a recognizable "discourse" of the intersection of queerness with a particularly "latinx" brownness finds itself in the second decade of the twenty-first century, especially in the year that saw the Obama era of US cultural politics recede and the Trump era emerge. In

Torres' piece and the Pulse attack, this invocation of "Latin Night at the Queer Club" simultaneously measures both progress and regress in the opportunities afforded to queer, brown existence to express, assert, and celebrate itself in its full, deep, rich intersectional complexity: "Latin Night" might be a weekly event at the "Queer Club," but it's never the nightly rule; Torres knows better than to invoke the mirror prospect of "Queer Night" at the "Latin Club" (*just imagine*: a weekly "noche de jotería" at YOUR neighborhood straight salsa club!); and, finally, while dedicated queer latinx clubs do exist in and certainly beyond the US, they are far outnumbered by spaces that embrace one identity category in favor of the other, making opportunities for intersectional cultural practice feel marginal at best, sometimes available, perhaps, but also always vulnerable to displacement, and to danger, and to disappearance.

Torres' piece provides its own occasion, however, for thinking certain forms of intersectionality together through its particular strategy for rhetorical intervention: for all of its expository, conceptual power as a cultural analysis of brown latinx queer life in twenty-first-century America's clublands, it also works powerfully as a literary act, the use of the second-person "you," for example, driving an expressive performance of address that implicates the reader in a different kind of discursive exchange. It is, after all, "you" whom Torres imagines "walk[ing] through the door," hearing "a salsa beat," seeing "brown bodies, queer bodies, all writhing in some fake smoke and strobing lights," and having it all "break" your vaunted "cool," finding that "[y]ou can't help but smile, [because] this is for you, for us." As literary act in the service of political and cultural analysis, "In Praise of Latin Night" thus opens itself up to a broader conversation with a longer genealogy of historically situated discursive work that has imagined and theorized queer latinx life for more than the half century leading up to 2016, beginning at least as far back in literary terms with work by Chicanx male writers like José Antonio Villarreal (in *Pocho*, 1959) and John Rechy (see *City of Night*, 1963, *Numbers*, 1967), and in theoretical terms with foundational work by queer Chicanx women writers like Cherríe Moraga and Gloria Anzaldúa in their groundbreaking 1981 collection *This Bridge Called My Back: Writings by Radical Women of Color* (reprinted 1983, revised and updated, 2001 and 2015).[2] This discussion focuses on the theoretical work, only tracing possible lines in the literary genealogy of queer *latinidad* in a footnote. I thus use the terms of theoretical conceptualization and critique to lend an unruly mass of literary work some possible shape and to demonstrate along the way how literature and theory quite often manifest in the same discursive act. Here

we attend to the eventual encounter and ongoing interaction and integra-
tion of queer and latinx studies as intellectual, ideological and (eventually)
institutional discursive formations. This process of contact, conflict, and
collaboration has been unfolding at least since the appearance of Moraga
and Anzaldúa's collection nearly thirty-five years before the Pulse massacre
and Torres' response.

## Queer Latinx Feminism 1: Gloria Anzaldúa and Cherríe Moraga

AnaLouise Keating confronts this complex process in her "Introduction"
to the *Gloria Anzladúa Reader* (2009) when she asks:

> Why have theorists so often ignored Anzaldúa's groundbreaking contribu-
> tions to queer theory? ... Do many heterosexually identified scholars fear
> being censured or labeled as gay? Do they simply not see the provocative,
> transgressive elements in her work? Are most queer theorists so Eurocentric
> or masculinist in their text selections that they have entirely ignored *This
> Bridge Called My Back*, where Anzaldúa's queer theorizing began?[3]

Keating's questions foreground the challenges that queer *latinidad* faces
in its attempts to come to discursive and conceptual life in that dense
intersectional space where queer studies meets latinx studies: here, "theorists" and "scholars" still spin as primarily white, male, and straight, and
queer theorists (and therefore queer *theory*) still spin as primarily white and
male. Keating thus underscores how fully the challenge of critically racia-
lizing white-presumptive queer and gender theory hinges on a further
burrowing into the still buried interstitial nodes of the theory of intersectionality, burrowing perhaps so deeply as to break through and even
past the conventions of intersectionality theory itself. The question of
latinx studies' decades of encounter with queer theory of course exceeds
the contours of its embodiment in Anzaldúa, but it is not easily resolved,
let alone simplified, if we include figures as diverse, and as important to
the conversation, as Emma Pérez, José Esteban Muñoz, Juana María
Rodríguez, Frederick Luis Aldama, Alicia Arrizón, Lawrence LaFountain-
Stokes, Michael Hames-García, Ernesto Martínez, Sandra K. Soto, or
Hiram Perez.

Before turning to this crowded genealogy of queer latinx scholars and
theorists, it bears pausing to observe that Keating's more pressing questions
were anticipated and in some manner addressed, from the beginning, in
Cherríe Moraga's oft-anthologized 1979 essay "La Güera," which appears
in both *This Bridge* and in Moraga's 1983 collection *Loving in the War
Years*.[4] Moraga, Anzaldúa's early collaborator, observes in that piece that

"[i]n this country, lesbianism is a poverty – as is being brown, as is being a woman, as is being just plain poor," before famously concluding:

> The danger lies in failing to acknowledge the specificity of the oppression. The danger lies in attempting to deal with oppression purely from a theoretical base. Without an emotional, heartfelt grappling with the source of the oppression, without naming the enemy within ourselves and outside of us, no authentic, nonhierarchical connection among oppressed groups can take place.[5]

Moraga elaborates further, asking "To whose camp, then, should the lesbian of color retreat?" given that "[h]er very presence violates the ranking and abstraction of oppression." More than a decade before law scholar Kimberlé Crenshaw would definitively introduce the concept of intersectionality into critical race theory, Moraga articulates the impoverishing violence of the multimodal minoritization of a "lesbianism" compounded by "being brown, ... being a woman, ... being just plain poor," arguing against the corresponding inadequacy of a purely "theoretical" grasp of this kind of intersectional dynamic of "oppression," an approach too reliant on the protocols of (social) science and even reason. Against this abstract, theoretical path Moraga posits an "emotional, heartfelt grappling with the source of our own oppression," which includes the expressive, imaginative approach evinced by both Moraga and Anzaldúa in their respective embracing of intense, one might say fierce, discursive hybridity as performative manifestation of a more general writerly strategy to an at once creative and critical capture of queer mestizx experience and existence.

One could if one wanted devote the entirety of the present discussion to a description of how that queer mestizx practice unfolds across the artistic and intellectual careers of both Moraga and Anzaldúa, focusing as much on their distinct strategies for synthesizing prose and verse, argument and narrative, analysis and figurative, symbolic play, theory and literature, as on the impact that practice has had on the larger body of queer mestizx latinx literature and theory that has followed, accompanied, responded to, or emerged in proximity to theirs.[6] The current discussion, however, turns instead to two related theoretical debates that have shaped and driven queer latinx studies for the past two decades. The two debates can be summarized thus: (1) latinx studies scholars disagree about the deployment of post-structural critical theory to guide literary and cultural analysis, with some scholars critiquing post-structuralism's anti-ontological bent as abdicating the responsibility to account for the lived oppression of marginalized groups; (2) overlapping with the first debate, queer scholars of color confront the "antisocial, anti-relational" strain of queer theory, which they critique as presumptively male, white, and unconscious or repressive of how these markers of privilege ground the nihilism of a political vision that therefore offers no recourse for empowerment or liberation to queer groups marked as (for starters) nonwhite and non-gender conforming. My intention here is not to resolve these debates, or to decide how they might be concluded, but rather to describe them, to assess their impact on critical and scholarly responses to literary work, and to account for whatever might remain of their influence in the contemporary moment.

### Debate 1: (Queer) Latinx Studies' Post-Structural Anxiety

Ten years separate the publication of José Esteban Muñoz's two books on queer of color performance and cultural world making (*Disidentifications*, 1999; *Cruising Utopia*, 2009), but across and beyond that decade of work Muñoz's commitment to a specific theory of cultural subjectivity and politics remained steady.[7] While Muñoz's work ranges far beyond his specific interest in queer latinx performance and cultural practice, his focus on queer *latinidad* offers decidedly evocative articulations of "disidentification," his touchstone concept. "The disjunctures between queer and Latino communities are many," Muñoz tells us in *Disidentifications*, "The mainstream gay community ignores or exoticizes Latino bodies, while many Latino communities promote homophobia" (146). In this chapter, dedicated to Cuban-American AIDS activist Pedro Zamora's 1994 televisual work on MTV's *The Real World*, Muñoz argued that "the linkages between queerness and *latinidad* [had] never been more poignant," or more available to public witnessing and consumption. Through his activism against and his struggles with homophobia and AIDS, Zamora occasions Muñoz to elaborate subaltern counterpublicity as an enabling resource for queer of color subjectivity and both cultural and political assertion. "Counterpublicity," Muñoz explains, "is disseminated through acts that are representational and political interventions in the service of subaltern counterpublics" (147). Later, Muñoz elaborates that queer latinx cultural practices like Zamora's "publicize and theatricalize an ethics of the self ... [which] present strategies that resist, often through performances that insist on local specificities and historicity, the pull of reductive multicultural pluralism." Muñoz's tense conjunctions – citing "acts" that are "representational *and* political," that "publicize *and* theatricalize" – underscores his simultaneously symbolic and material understanding of culture's and consciousness's conditioning of social life.

This tense conjoining carries across the decade separating *Disidentifica-tions* and *Cruising Utopia*. In the first book, Muñoz concludes the Zamora chapter with an explicit insistence of the work of the symbolically cultural in the service of the material. In the second, he doubles down on the necessary participation of the aesthetic and symbolic in the futural forma-tion of consciousness, and certainly (queer, latinx) political consciousness: "Queerness," he famously argues in *Cruising Utopia*, "is that thing that lets us feel that this world is not enough, that indeed something is missing. Often," he insists, "we can glimpse the world proposed and promised by queerness in the realm of the aesthetic, . . . [which] frequently contains blueprints and schemata of a forward-dawning futurity" (1). For Muñoz, "the aesthetic" thus operates as an empowering and democratizing resource, utilizing both "ornamental" and "quotidian" elements to draw "a map of utopia that is queerness," and thereby offering "nothing like an escape from the social realm, insofar as queer aesthetics map future social relations." After *Cruising Utopia*, Muñoz's influence over and beyond queer latinx studies cannot be overstated, especially since his untimely death in 2013 at an obscenely early age, but that doesn't mean that his work hasn't received criticism, even from within the fields he helped to found and shape.

In 2005, for example, the prolific latinx studies scholar Frederick Luis Aldama included Muñoz within a larger category of post-structuralist and social constructionist cultural studies work whose "variously abstract and obscurantist formulations" Aldama critiques for "propos[ing] all aspects of our reality to be equal."[8] Against this theoretical school, Aldama "propose[s] that verifiable information and scientific hypotheses can pro-vide the raw material needed for us to pour a solid foundation for the building of a theory of what constitutes the self (ethnosexual or otherwise)" (5). For Aldama "the self" of "verifiable information and scientific hypoth-eses" is a more concrete, consistent, and knowable formation than post-structural theory, which levels unequal, hierarchical social relations in an impossibly symbolically undifferentiated "subject." "Whether we talk of Muñoz's 'disidentifications,' Butler's 'performative,' Derrida's 'operators of generality' or 'différance,' Lacan's 'Real,' 'Imaginary,' or 'Symbolic,'" Aldama argues, "we must ask, do such ideas and categories actually help further our understanding of queer (borderland, postcolonial, or other-wise) subjectivity and how oppressive social conditions might be trans-formed?" (40). Despite his critique, it is worth considering the resilient currency of the concepts he invokes as politically bankrupt (Muñoz's

"disidentifications" not least among them), as well as the supposed political
and intellectual damage such concepts have done since Aldama called them
out for the threat they posed to "the self (ethnosexual or otherwise)."

Still, aspects of Aldama's positivistic critique might resonate for some in
the current era of extreme political crisis in which intersectionally minor-
itized subjects find themselves under threat. Addressing abstract theory's
practical use in a world riven by violent material forces, Aldama's questions
ring with tangible urgency in 2018:

> Can there be slippage between signifier and signified? Is meaning really
> deferrable? Is the subject and the world experienced by the subject unstable
> and fragmented? If the subject and the world are linguistic constructs,
> then how can we account for the real stigmatization and real suffering
> and real pain that the ethnoqueer subject experiences in the real world
> "out there"? (40)

Aldama's polemical rejection of post-structuralism may set an extreme
limit on the debate that this essay stages, but it did not foreclose, as
it might have, the dynamic of intellectual exchange that has actually
informed queer latinx studies since *Brown on Brown* and Muñoz's partial
rejoinder in *Cruising Utopia*. Indeed, in the years leading up to and
following the publication of the latter text, Michael Hames-García and
Ernesto Martínez, both aligned with Aldama's positivist-realism, produced
*Gay Latino Studies: A Critical Reader* (2011), which included an important
early piece by Muñoz as well as essays by Antonio Viego and Lawrence
LaFountain-Stokes with a post-structuralist bent.[9]

Hames-García and Martínez's volume opens by articulating and embracing the terms of the debate, "highlight[ing] relationships among ongoing
intellectual projects that take the lives of gay, bisexual and queer latino
men as a starting point" (4). Across an array of intellectual approaches and
scholarly methodologies, their collection offered "a new attentiveness to
the politics and theorization of intersectionality, multiplicity, coalition,
and identity, including an overdue interrogation of racialized masculinities" (8). To their credit, Hames-García and Martínez include these
distinct accounts of racial, cultural, and sexual difference while foregrounding the differences of intellectual approach for further elaboration, such
as the debates still roiling between queer of color critique and white-
male-presumptive queer theory. "[E]ven among those contributors who
are most ambivalent toward identity as a stable or coherent category,"
Hames-García and Martínez write, "there is also a resistance to jettisoning
the experience of class, gender, race and sexuality as lived realities shaping

people's lives," tempering the extreme abstraction to which Moraga, Anzaldúa, and Aldama so strongly objected. That degree of skepticism about the solidity of social identity taints the work of the "mainstream" (mostly) white, (mostly) male "queer" theorists, which in part explains Hames-García and Martínez's strategic choice of "gay" over "queer" for their title. They argue,

> [T]he term queer, particularly in its development within the body of thought known as queer theory, has formed part of a much broader skepticism about identity categories per se[;] ... we believe that skepticism about identities, while sometimes justified, can often mistake political identities for attempts at transparent ethnographic description[;] ... such deep-seated, a priori, skepticism toward identity can also sometimes function as a cover for undertheorized racial politics. (10)

Hames-García and Martínez extend this critique in their own projects, starting with Hames-García's contribution to the *Gay Latino Studies*, "Queer Theory Revisited," and Martínez's *On Making Sense: Queer Race Narratives of Intelligibility* (2013).[10]

## Debate 2: Queer of Color Critique and the "Anti-Relational Thesis"

Alongside the "positivist-realist" and "post-structural skepticist" debate, another debate pits the latter group against what some queer latinx studies scholars see as an even more nihilistically pessimistic branch of white-presumptive queer theory. This debate is organized around what Muñoz in *Cruising Utopia* termed the "anti-relational thesis" that runs through work by Leo Bersani and Lee Edelman.[11] The "anti-relational" (or "antisocial") thesis "imagine[s] an escape or denouncement of relationality as first and foremost a distancing of queerness from what theorists seem to think of as the contamination of race, gender or other particularities that taint the purity of sexuality as a singular trope of difference" (11). Muñoz concludes that such "anti-relational approaches to queer theory are romances of the negative ... investments in deferring various dreams of difference," and he instead "insist[s] on the essential need for an understanding of [queerness as collectivity ... ] queerness [as] primarily about futurity and hope ... [as] always on the horizon." *Cruising Utopia* certainly didn't settle matters definitively, given that as recently as 2015 the debate appeared in even more elaborate form in Hiram Pérez's important study, *A Taste for Brown Bodies: Gay Modernity and Cosmopolitan Desire*.[12] Pérez traces a thread of the debate that goes back as far as the 2003 "Gay Shame" conference, which he attended. References to that conference appear in the book's introduction, and it is the central object of analysis in "You Can Have My Brown Body and Eat It, Too!," which critiques the racial unconscious that not only haunted a number of the projects presented there but the very conceptualization of the conference itself. For Pérez, as for Muñoz, the problem arises from the refusal of anti-relational queer theory to cop to its own normalizing white-presumptiveness when it insists on the irreducible specificity of queerness as *not* one marker of difference among others, but as the marker of social difference *qua non.*

The violence of this repressive (in both senses of the word) intellectual refusal manifested as deeply felt experience thanks to the fetishistic deployment of an eroticized latinx queer brown body in one presentation by a prominent white queer theorist and the reception of that work by a mostly white audience. The critical afterlife of Pérez's experience unfolds through the almost polemical characterization of queer of color critique's (and within it queer latinx theory's) relationship to what he calls "establishment-arian" queer theory. For example, Pérez reflects on identity constructs like "latino" and "brown" in terms that would likely peeve the positivist-realists before turning to "queer" theory itself: "The category 'Latino,'" he argues, "used as a racial descriptor rather than a political affiliation, is nearly as vague as 'brown,'" and in that vagueness provides (white) queer theory with a convenient alibi for its own indifference to whatever actual, relevant complexities might underlie that vagueness (117). Pérez argues:

> Remarkably, queer theory understands the politics of difference as funda-
> mental to its practice, yet it can participate in the circulation of categories
> like "Latin" without appreciating in the least its function within a complex
> web of identifications and desires. While the variations of the category
> "Latina/o" collapse innumerable differences, queer theorizing seems for the
> most part quite content to let that sameness alone ... [having thus]
> exchanged too hastily the politics of identity for the politics of difference.
> This is especially crucial where sameness makes itself transparent, as it does
> with whiteness ... Queer theory, when it privileges difference over same-
> ness absolutely, colludes with institutionalized racism in vanishing, hence
> retrenching, white privilege. It serves as the magician's assistant to white-
> ness's disappearing act. (118)

At this point, the reader may have noticed that these important debates within and across latinx/queer theory have also devolved into a male-only dynamic that may be as guilty of a failure to recognize its own political unconscious at the level of gender as we've characterized queer theory's failure to recognize its political unconscious at the level of race.[13]

## Queer Latinx Feminism 2: Beyond Intersectionality

Indeed, tracing the work of queer latinx studies and queer latinx theory through an alternatively explicit feminist genealogy enables us to revisit some spaces where the debates described above have taken us while also opening new paths and possibilities for the productive theorization, articulation, and manifestation of queer *latindad.* "Theory," Anzaldúa observed in 1991, "serves those that create it. White middle-class lesbians are certainly not speaking for me. Inevitably we colored dykes fall into a reactive mode, counter their terms and theories – as I am doing, as I have to do before I can even begin to write this essay" (qtd. in Keating 165); this disarmingly candid, blunt appraisal could serve as a clarifying gloss to the much more granular critique offered up nearly twenty-five years later by Pérez. However, in the same way that Pérez demonstrates how the queer of color critic can liberate themselves from that reactive mode, Anzaldúa herself offers perhaps the best "theory" to help align Pérez's practice: Anzaldúa too embraces what she calls the greater "flexibility" of the signifier "queer," its greater capacity to give her mind, and her activism "more room to maneuver" (qtd. in Keating 166). She observes,

> A mestiza colored queer person is bodily shoved by both the heterosexual world and by white gays into the "lesbian" or "homosexual" mold whether she fits or not. *La persona está situada dentro de la idea en vez del al revez . . .* The core question is: what is the power and what is the danger of writing and reading like a "lesbian" or a queer? Can the power and the danger be named and can queer writing be named?

Twenty years following Anzaldúa's posing of her "core" question, we find a direct response to it in the title of Sandra K. Soto's *Reading Chican@ Like a Queer.*[14]

In its commitment to a complex construction of subjectivity as always already discursive, and ambivalent, and protean, Soto's work might also provoke the positivist realist school.[15] Yet Soto exemplifies the possibility of being logoconscious without being logocentric, understanding as she does that stipulating the imbrication of subjectivity in the signifier (in and as writing) merely enables the situating of identity, consciousness, or agency; it is a *locating* that refuses, by demonstrating the very impossibility of, any *centering* of that subject. Soto offers an erstwhile, loyal, loving, and literary deconstruction of Crenshaw's conception of "intersectionality," which has authorized so much of critical race studies since the early 1990s. Soto writes:

> "[I]ntersectionality" is perhaps too spatially rigid and exacting a metaphor
> to employ when considering the ever-dynamic and unending process
> of subject formation [since ... ] race, sexuality and gender are much
> too complex, unsettled, porous ... mutually constitutive, unpredictable,
> incommensurable, and dynamic ever ... to travel independently of one
> another. But they would have to do so to be conceived of as intersecting, as
> eventually meeting one another here and there, crossing, colliding, passing,
> yielding or merging. (6)

Strategically literalizing what critical race studies offered and deployed as a
metaphorical concept allows Soto to make explicit theory's ongoing
dependence on, not to say addiction to, some rather nonrational, creative,
and decidedly figural rhetorical ploys in furthering its mostly rational,
analytical, critical work. Soto's argument recalls Moraga's warning, quoted
above, about conceptualizing "oppression purely from a theoretical
base."[16] Taking Moraga's cue, Soto refuses to replace the concept she's
just unpacked with an alternative that might better travel the routes
mapped by theory; instead, she opts (as Moraga encourages) for the
"emotional, heartfelt grappling" that feels as much as (or more than) it
thinks about power and oppression, and all the ways we might write, and
enact, ways around and out of them. "I do not want to offer a better
metaphor as an answer to this problem," Soto declares, "[but] to suggest
[instead] that we be wordy and contingent, that we not look for a
shorthand for naming or understanding or footnoting the confounding
manifold ways that our bodies, our work, our desires are relentlessly
interpellated by unequivalent social processes" (6).

## Queer Latinx Futures

One critic who takes up Soto's important call to refuse the conventional
distinction between the literal and the figurative, and to embrace forms of
critical practice that dare to favor being messily "wordy and contingent," is
Juana María Rodríguez.[17] Rodríguez situates her work explicitly in the
genealogy of debates elaborated here, but also models a critical practice
that brings theory into intimate contact with the affective, the expressive,
even the literary, using these intense points of contact to reconstrue "the
body" as simultaneously thinking and feeling, collective and individual,
public and private, political and erotic. In doing so, Rodríguez's project
opens queer latinx theory to a series of possible contacts with primarily
literary work, such as Torres'. In Rodríguez's hands, Torres' brown, queer
dancers and their "writhing" can occasion a theorization of *Latinidad*

through her detailed reflection on the excess of our "seemingly over-the-top gestures, our bodies betraying – or gleefully luxuriating in – our intentions to exceed the norms of proper corporal containment. Our bodies," she argues, "dispatch sweeping flourishes or hold back wilted wrists. We swish too much or speak too loudly" (*Sexual Futures* 2). Rodríguez is careful, however, not to allow this kind of potentially mystifying invocation of bodily tendencies to devolve into ethnosexual stereotype; in fact, her critical elaborations of queer latinx gesture and excess occasion instead a strategic re-theorization of any tendency toward essentialism and its concomitant political byproducts: complicity, conformity, and certainty.

"To the trained eye," Rodríguez observes:

"Latinidad," that ambiguous ethnic category that eludes binary racial registers, can be visually captured not in skin tone or phenotype, but in the reading of gesture ... In this text, gesture serves metaphorically to register the actions of the body politic, those activist interventions that push, jam, open, block, and twist social forces in the material world. But it is also used to name specific corporeal articulations of fingers, thighs, and tongues, the movement of the living body and her parts, the ephemera of affect that leaves no trace. Gestures are where the literal and the figurative copulate. (*Sexual Futures* 4)

One might argue with Rodríguez here that gestures aren't really places but moments (not "wheres," but "whens"), and that, strictly speaking, everything that we can speak of leaves a trace, but it may be more difficult to "argue" with the imaginative, and literary, proposition (in the figure of personification) that the "literal" and the "figurative" may be made to "copulate," or at least revealed as being able to do so. Rodríguez's *Sexual Futures* directly addresses the debates between "anti-relational" (white, male) queer theory and its refusals from various camps of queer and feminist of color critique, as well as the debate within queer latinx studies between the positive-realists and the post-structuralists. Engaging both debates at once, Rodríguez arguably settles many of their dialectical tensions enough to see a future past them, a future still violently unfolding. Against the "anti-relational" school, she too invokes Muñoz's call for a "[q]ueer theory" that "ask[s] us to consider the role of queer social bonds, community futures and the relevance of sex at this precise moment when the demands of neoliberalism emphasize individual exchange absent an analysis of differential social relationships to power" (*Sexual Futures* 9–10).

In the contemporary moment, it bears noting how resilient and potent Muñoz's concept of futurity has been both as a catalyst for the additional, additive unfolding of queer latinx thought and expression, and as a cautionary warning against our forgetting what has come before – from such violent traumas as the Pulse butchery, the deaths of thinkers as vital to our survival and our liberation as Muñoz and Anzaldúa, and all the other historical, bodily, and spiritual erasures that anti-brown, anti-queer oppression have wrought. But we also must remember the intellectual and creative work that critiques that oppression and imagines its dismantling. Readers can browse across the entire expanse of *Cruising Utopia* to find those gestures that remind them that they're in the presence of a writer who intimately understood his writing's relationship to time as much as its relationship to queerness and brownness: "It seems," Muñoz observes, "like the other's time is always off. Often," he concludes, "we are the first ones there and the last to leave. The essential point here is that our temporalities are different and outside" (*Cruising* 183). In the complexly overlaid temporalities of before, during, and after, of what's inside and outside time, one can do worse than imagine the temporal shifts and imaginative leaps that connect the dance club to the bedroom to the classroom to the streets to the written page to the performance space to the microphoned table at the conference panel, where all of these spaces might be invoked in the course of one smart, sexy session leading ideally to one smart, sexy collected edition of queer, brown scholarly work. For many of us who both worked and lived and played and read and thought through the three decades of history traced above, and who now find ourselves still here, alive if not exactly intact, it might be tempting to imagine ourselves in the suspended time of the post-club after-party, in the twilight of a dawn more defined by the night just dying than the day being born.

## After Pulse, the Comedown

Joshua Javier Guzmán has already theorized this moment out of queer brown life in "Notes on the Comedown."[18] Caught between "the event-ness of the high and the crash," the comedown "acts as the material dissolve between the high and the low, performing a sort of fading in and fading out from one another yet without any sort of directionality[, hence] ontologically ... recalibrating how the everyday is changed, altered, made altogether different" (60). While we may all have access to the kinds of ecstasy (chemical, erotic, emotional, spiritual) that always precede and often entail the comedown, and then the crash, Guzmán is clear that such access is almost always a function of one's positioning in spaces structured by power, making his specific account of the comedown "highly browned . . . [hence] a depressive posture or style, an inclination to both register and negotiate the historical particularities of dispossession and systems of disenfranchisement that cut across minoritarian populations in various ways" (61). However, despite disenfranchisement, there often is access, and whatever form our dosage takes, our ecstasy is always "a stepping out of straight time," making the inevitable comedown a "space between normative time and queer time, a spacing out, or [an] act of displacement . . . [that] is really about loss," a loss that Guzmán finally aligns with Muñoz's own characterization of queerness' elusive but necessary futurity, given its constant failure at the hands of the constant violence against it, in the present. "[F]or José," Guzmán confesses, "this loss was the loss of the future in the present" (65).

Certainly we risk trivializing the loss of life and hope at Pulse if all we do is compare it to or contextualize it with the melancholy of losing a certain relationship to time that Guzmán's narrative of ecstasy-comedown-crash dramatizes. Let's conclude, therefore, with this modest proposition: what would their futures have been had those murdered and injured at Pulse never been attacked, had instead just moved from one moment to the following, from the party to the after-party, from the high to the comedown to whatever might have come next? That even this humble likelihood could be rendered unthinkable by the systemic violence that targeted the innocents who were murdered and maimed that night tells us all we need to be told regarding that everyday "loss of the future in the present" that so much queer latinx thought, and so much queer latinx expression, has been marshalled to oppose, to deconstruct, to dismantle, and to survive.

## Notes

1 Justin Torres, "In Praise of Latin Night at the Queer Club," *The Washington Post*, June 13, 2016, www.washingtonpost.com/opinions/in-praise-of-latin-night-at-the-queer-club/2016/06/13/e841867e-317b-11e6-95c0-2a68730313 02_story.html.

2 José Antonio Villarreal, *Pocho* (New York: Doubleday and Company, 1959); John Rechy, *City of Night* (New York: Grove Press, 1963); and *Numbers* (New York: Grove Press, 1967); Cherríe Moraga and Gloria Anzaldúa, *This Bridge Called My Back: Writings by Radical Women of Color*, 4th ed. (Albany: SUNY Press, 2015); and Gloria Anzaldúa, *Borderlands/La Frontera: The New Mestiza*, 4th ed. (San Francisco: Aunt Lute Books, 2012).

66     RICARDO ORTIZ

3 AnaLouise Keating, *The Gloria Anzaldúa Reader* (Durham: Duke University Press, 2009), 5.
4 Cherríe Moraga, *Loving in the War Years: lo que nunca pasó por sus labios* (Cambridge, MA: South End Press, 2000).
5 Ibid., 44.
6 That literary genealogy could begin in the mid-twentieth century with José Antonio Villarreal and John Rechy, and would include names, representing deeply varied and multiple work, like María Irene Fornes, Arturo Islas, Richard Rodríguez, Alicia Gaspar de Alba, Rafael Campo, Rigoberto González, Richard Blanco, Ana Castillo, Michael Nava, Achy Obejas, Manuel Muñoz, Luis Alfaro, Francisco X. Alarcón, Francisco Aragón, Raquel Gutiérrez, Gil Cuadros, Justin Torres, Eduardo C. Corral, and Carmen Maria Machado. This partial and therefore unsatisfactory list includes mostly US-based writers who write in English and who have mostly enjoyed success with mainstream publishing, who have therefore received serious critical and scholarly attention, and who mostly embrace rather conventional, canonical forms of literary and artistic expression. They also mostly hail from the larger national groups (Mexican-Chicanx, mainland Puerto Rican, Cuban, Salvadoran) comprising the much more diverse Latinx population of the twenty-first-century United States. It also excludes writers who are not queer (or at least not out) themselves but who have explored queerness in their work in nuanced and impactful ways (e.g., Piri Thomas, Miguel Piñero, Julia Alvarez, Cristina García, Yxta Maya Murray, and Junot Díaz).
7 José Esteban Muñoz, *Disidentifications: Queers of Color and the Performance of the Political* (Minneapolis: University of Minnesota Press, 1999); *Cruising Utopia: The Then and There of Queer Futurity* (New York: New York University Press, 2009). Subsequent references cited in the text.
8 Frederick Luis Aldama, *Brown on Brown: Chicano/a Representations of Gender, Sexuality and Ethnicity* (Austin: University of Texas Press, 2005), 5. Subsequent references cited in the text.
9 Michael Hames-García and Ernesto Javier Martínez, eds., *Gay Latino Studies: A Critical Reader* (Durham: Duke University Press, 2011). Subsequent references cited in the text.
10 Michael Hames-García, "Queer Theory Revisited," in *Gay Latino Studies: A Critical Reader*, ed. Michael Hames-García and Ernesto Javier Martínez (Durham: Duke University Press, 2011), 19–45; Ernesto Javier Martínez, *On Making Sense: Queer Race Narratives of Intelligibility* (Stanford: Stanford University Press, 2013). In the introduction to *On Making Sense*, entitled "On the Practices and Politics of Intelligibility," Martínez offers a cogent encapsulation from the "realist" side of the debate just summarized above: "Realist arguments," he tells us, "manifest themselves frequently in the assertions queers of color make about how they acquire better and more accurate knowledge, and about how they make sense of their experiences. The full impact of these arguments, however, remains potentially unrecognized by contemporary critics because of the excessive skepticism that has dominated

academic discourse regarding the relationship between identities, experiences and objectivity" (5).

11 Lee Edelman, *No Future: Queer Theory and the Death Drive* (Durham: Duke University Press, 2004); and Leo Bersani, *Is the Rectum a Grave? And Other Essays* (Chicago: Chicago University Press, 2010).

12 Hiram Pérez, *A Taste for Brown Bodies: Gay Modernity and Cosmopolitan Desire* (New York: New York University Press, 2015). Subsequent references cited in the text.

13 While in recent decades much of this scholarly work has been produced by cis-gendered writers who only very unevenly interrogate the received binary logic of gender, the ground has been slowly shifting lately thanks to trans studies' contributions to gender theory and the critique of "cis." Important titles not discussed in detail in the body of this piece include: Alicia Arrizón, *Queering Mestizaje: Transculturation and Performance* (Ann Arbor: University of Michigan Press, 2006); Lawrence LaFountain-Stokes, *Queer Ricans: Cultures and Sexualities in the Diaspora* (Minneapolis: University of Minnesota Press, 2009); Lázaro Lima, *The Latino Body: Crisis Identities in American Literary and Cultural Memory* (New York: New York University Press, 2007); Emma Pérez, *The Decolonial Imaginary: Writing Chicanas into History* (Bloomington: Indiana University Press, 1999); Chela Sandoval, *Methodology of the Oppressed* (Minneapolis: University of Minnesota Press, 2000); and Antonio Viego, *Dead Subjects: Toward a Politics of Loss in Latino Studies* (Durham: Duke University Press, 2007). While trans-latinx studies remains an emerging scholarly field, readers can find promising examples of this work in collections like Yolanda Martínez-San Miguel and Sarah Tobias, *Trans Studies: The Challenge to Hetero/Homo Normativities* (New Brunswick: Rutgers University Press, 2016); and Reina Gossett, Eric A. Stanley, and Johanna Burton, *Trap Door: Trans Cultural Production and the Politics of Visibility* (Cambridge, MA: The MIT Press, 2017).

14 Sandra K. Soto, *Reading Chican@ Like a Queer: The De-Mastery of Desire* (Austin: University of Texas Press, 2010). Subsequent references cited in the text.

15 For a complementary account of the model of subjectivity that Soto offers in social-scientific terms, see Cristina Beltrán, *The Trouble with Unity: Latino Politics and the Creation of Identity* (Oxford: Oxford University Press, 2010).

16 Moraga, *Loving*, 44.

17 Juana María Rodríguez, *Queer Latinidad: Identity Practices, Discursive Spaces* (New York: New York University Press, 2003); and *Sexual Futures, Queer Gestures, Latina Longings* (New York: New York University Press, 2014).

18 Joshua Javier Guzmán, "Notes on the Comedown," *Social Text* 121, vol. 32, no. 4 (2014): 59–67. Subsequent references cited in the text.

# *Reading Queer Writers*

# Reading Queer Writers

CHAPTER 4

# Oscar Wilde and George Bernard Shaw in Queer Time
## Law, Lawlessness, and the Mid-Twentieth-Century Afterlife of a Decadent Persona

### Richard A. Kaye

> I read for the first time the (almost) complete account of Oscar's trials...It's very interesting and depressing. One of the surprising features is that he very nearly got off. If he had, what would have happened, I wonder? I fancy the history of English culture might have been quite different, if a juryman's stupidity had chanced to take another turn.
>
> (Lytton Strachey, Letter to Dora Carrington, September 25, 1921)

Lytton Strachey's counter-historical daydream speaks not only to the importance of Oscar Wilde well beyond his literary achievements but to the way the writer's fate – and those of others – were entangled with the unpredictable, seemingly arbitrary exigencies of the law. Strachey's fantasy, moreover, would appear to be taking place in what recent queer theorists call "queer time," a temporality outside of actual (often cruel) history or the ineluctable drive of linear, progressive time. Queer time often entertains a counter-historical, backwards-looking, or futuristic temporal directionality.[1] As José Esteban Muñoz notes, the very notion of the "queer" is indissociably interconnected to unrealized visions of utopia, an "ideality" that represents a "warm illumination of a horizon imbued with potentiality."[2]

A key figure in the history of attitudes about same-sex eros, Wilde holds literary significance in just such a future-tense queer temporality. Wilde's transtemporal import is captured in the opening chapter of Jonathan Dollimore's influential 1991 study *Sexual Dissidence: Augustine to Wilde, Freud to Foucault*, which sees Wilde as both ending a period of sexual history and inaugurating a modern understanding of same-sex erotics. Dollimore focuses on a series of pivotal encounters between Wilde and the French writer André Gide, in which the Irish-born writer repeatedly challenged and undermined Gide's sense of self – most specifically, his sense of sexual identity – through Wilde's insistence that Gide avail himself of the pleasures of Algerian youths. "Wilde is religiously trying to kill whatever remains of my soul," Gide wrote to Paul Valéry in 1891.[3] Another letter of the same month begins, "Please forgive my silence; since Wilde, I hardly exist anymore."

Those fraught face-offs culminated in what Dollimore considers a decisive 1895 nonencounter in Algiers when Gide, seeing the names of Wilde and Wilde's lover Alfred Lord Douglas on a hotel register, crossed out his own name and immediately left the hotel, an act of social retreat and, figuratively, of self-erasure. For Dollimore, the bruising conflict between Wilde and Gide speaks to opposite poles in the modern conception of dissident sexualities. From Dollimore's perspective, Wildean erotic individualism is radically self-subverting, creatively perverse, legally dangerous – "feasting with panthers," as Wilde memorably puts it – beholden to the "truth" of masks, and contemptuous of depth. Gidean individualism, on the other hand, is related to moral integrity, an essentialist faith in a "true" sexual self, as well as the affirmation of the "naturalness" of sexual inversion and therefore its legal legitimacy and moral integrity. In Dollimore's account, these two conceptions structure all future understandings of same-sex erotics.

Abundantly suggestive as the Wilde-Gide dyad is, I want to posit a different disjunction and attendant genealogy that I argue is equally illustrative of twentieth and twenty-first-century thinking regarding dissident erotics. I posit George Bernard Shaw and Wilde in terms of their competing conceptions of sexual modernism – one coordinated by a faith in law, the pragmatics of technological advancement, and welfare state progress, and the other in queer lawlessness, Symbolist mystery, and nostalgia for undestroyed lost civilizations. With the legal advances today governing same-sex behavior in Western countries, from the decriminalization of sodomy laws to the recent legitimization of marriage equality by the United States Supreme Court, it might seem that much of Shaw's conception of a utopian state has been increasingly achieved, although the triumph of nationalist politics in Europe and the 2016 presidential election in the United States pose substantial threats to those advances. Ironically, given his central role in a set of era-defining legal cases, Wilde was skeptical of – or perhaps simply uninterested in – issues related to the law. It is telling that not a single paragraph of De Profundis, a work written some two years into Wilde's imprisonment in bitter denunciation of his lover, Alfred Lord Douglas, explores the legal issues determining his trials, possibly because prison officials would find such reflections mutinous. Today, many queer thinkers and activists have similarly skeptical views of the law as an ultimate arena of redress and freedom. They question, for example, marital equality – not only because of marriage's history as a conservative institution but for its linking in the United States of basic human rights such as health to a spousal bond – and hate-crime laws for their strengthening of traditionally anti-queer agents (the police) and institutions (prisons).[4] While uninterested in the law, *De Profundis* did ponder a kind of queer time, ending its many rancorous regretful pages with a somewhat mystical observation that affirmed the subjective nature of time: "The past, the present, and the future are but one moment in the sight of God, in whose sight we should try to live. Time and space, succession and extension, are merely accidental conditions of Thought."[5] In Wilde's schema, the law was similarly subjective and arbitrary, having its foundation in conventional ethics, for Wilde a mostly bogus and bourgeois invention, encapsulated in his quip, "I love an ethical dilemma. It is so much more interesting than a real one."

To the degree that Wilde was interested in the law, he was concerned with infractions against unjust legal restrictions or flamboyant criminals such as Thomas Griffiths Waineright, whom Wilde described as "one of the most subtle and secret poisoners of this or any age," thus elevating criminality to an art.[6] The value of the law lay chiefly in the possibilities it created for principled dissent and for exploring the creative dimension in criminality. My discussion of Shavian and Wildean conceptions of utopia construes these writers as working in dialectical relation to each other within a late-Victorian context in which same-sex desire was being articulated in fundamentally new ways. Their utopianism was part of a turn-of-the-century zeitgeist in which writers such as H. G. Wells and William Morris expressed a keen interest in utopian schemes, but they entertained such fantasies at a historical moment when the law was becoming increasingly interested in punishing aberrant forms of sexual conduct.

Although the differences between Shaw and Wilde would seem to pivot on a sharp contrast between reason and unruly imagination – Shaw's hard-nosed utopia based on laws versus Wilde's dreamy utopia smitten with lawlessness – this distinction is misleading. To take one example: the law depends on an imaginatively manipulative use of language and may be as rhetorically creative as any literary text. Here, for example, is Henry Vincent, Director of Criminal Investigations at Scotland Yard, on the need for the Labouchère amendment:

> The increase of these monsters in the shape of men, commonly designated
> margeries, poofs etc., of late years, in the great Metropolis, renders it neces-
> sary for the safety of the public that they should be made known ... Will
> the reader credit it, but such is nevertheless the fact, that these monsters
> actually walk the street the same as the whores, looking out for a chance?[7]

This colorful condemnation, with its unending, knowing catalogue of
urban deviants, indistinguishable from the era's Fleet Street journalistic
rhetoric, is the agitated flipside of the amendment itself, whose dry, single-
sentence stipulation outlawing acts "of gross indecency" was vague enough
to implicate (notionally) large numbers of men. That today's laws often
function through literary effects seems inarguable. Thus, as Dale Carpenter
notes, the 2003 US Supreme Court *Lawrence* v. *Texas* decision striking
down sodomy laws did not simply validate a right to privacy but did so
through language that emphasized, as a corollary, the ability of gay men
and women to sustain *long-term* same-sex relationships. In his majority
decision, Justice Kennedy repeatedly used the word "relationship" in
invoking the potentiality of LGBT people to enter into an extended bond,
although, as Carpenter wryly observes, the incident that originally generated the court case – a random sexual encounter between two men (who
did not live together and were not in a long-term relationship) that led to
an arrest by the police (who either did or did not interrupt the men having
sex) – was hardly the exalted intimate affiliation evoked in Kennedy's
affirmative opinion.[8] For the Supreme Court, then, queer time only gains
legitimacy when it occurs within the context of a hallowed *protraction* of
same-sex relations.

Complicating my examination of Shavian and Wildean utopianism is
Wilde's posthumous mid-twentieth-century afterlife. Wilde's carnal utopianism troubled an Anglo-American liberal consensus on normative
sexuality. Before he emerged as a progenitor of 1970s Gay Liberation, a
Warholian avatar of style, and a twenty-first-century queer icon, Wilde was
seen by prominent mid-twentieth-century literary intellectuals as an
anarchistic, "decadent" figure overly captive to a covertly sexualized Hel-
lenism. That the most prominent exponent of that position, the poet and
critic W. H. Auden, was widely known as a gay man, represents not only a
salient biographical irony but speaks to how the fissures dividing Shaw and
Wilde – one heterosexually identified, the other scandalously not – ultimately emerged as divisions within twentieth-century queer culture itself.
Law and lawlessness continues to structure discussions of same-sex erotics –
and not without echoes of Victorian-era anxieties that defined Wilde's life
and work. For the present-day "normalization" of same-sex erotics stands

in tensile relation to a freewheeling, semiclandestine internet culture, with reverberations of the Victorian sexual "underground" that we know Wilde – and his fictional protagonist Dorian Gray – frequented.

## Utopias of Law and Realism/Utopias of Lawlessness and Artifice

A dialectic of law and lawlessness as well as one of forward-moving time and recessive time structures the divide between today's social egalitarians and queer critics, one whose genealogy may be traced to Shaw and Wilde's discordant relationships. This dialectic also pivots on the law's "realism" versus a visionary – and therefore unreal or unrealistic – conception of freedom. To Shaw's materialist stance insisting on social and economic justice, Wilde offers an antimaterialist credo of beauty that insisted on hierarchies in the aesthetic realm. Their disagreements comprise a creative dialectic and not simply a set of contradictions. For just as Shaw's faith in welfare state legal resolutions shorn of obfuscating mysticisms notionally allows for competing conceptions of eros, Wilde's defense of lawlessness in the political, social, and erotic domain depends on the existence of laws against which he took an oppositional stance. It is, however, in the aesthetic sphere that Shavian and Wildean political divergences are most evident. The realm of art, for Shaw, represented an opportunity for dramatizing the social obstacles to utopia, a utopia defined as a sphere in which nonnormative sexuality would be legal but also inconsequential or unnecessary. For Wilde, on the other hand, the aesthetic realm was the location for imagining the freedoms of a political utopia, one that would leave untroubled unruly desires defined by society as nonnormative.

Building on their contrasting notions of dissident erotics, I want to explore how Wilde's enduring decadent persona reproduces the divide between a legalistic conception of same-sex erotics and nonlegal conception that abjures simple classifications and a concomitant language of legal "rights." Tellingly, Shaw sensed that Wilde represented a challenge to his worldview; he doggedly followed Wilde's rise and fall and, in a sense, tracked Wilde's evolving persona. Initially Shaw became aware of Wilde as a dandified troublemaker, then saw him as a rival in the London theatre world, and later denigrated the playwright's increasing celebrity. Yet Shaw defended Wilde during the latter's legal travails and soon after Wilde's release from prison nominated him to be one of the "Immortals" for the Academy of Letters. After Wilde's death, Shaw became an obsessive epistolary tormentor of Alfred Lord Douglas for some twelve years. Shaw's

intellectual and emotional investment in Wilde – ambivalent, contradictory, excessive – at times resembles a vexed, one-sided romantic fixation.
The biographical asymmetry between these writers' interest in each other
aside, their relationship stands as an overwrought, overlooked, and defining
affiliation in critical accounts of Wilde's life and in the history of modern
conceptions of dissident sexuality.

Irish-born provocateurs as well as successful London playwrights, Wilde
and Shaw, who had some twelve personal encounters, shared much in their
public deportment and political sympathies. As Michael Holroyd observes,
"Both Wilde, the complete dandy, and Shaw, the rationale dress reformer,
were showmen ... Whenever these two noticeable figures met, they
treated each other with elaborate courtesy."[9] Shaw's first novel, *Immaturity*
(written in 1879 but unpublished until 1930) includes a character, Patrick
Hawkshaw, a dandy and poet, obviously modeled on Wilde, whose name
suggests Shaw's intense self-recognition in Wilde the aesthete even as he
depicts Hawkshaw in sexually ambiguous terms. It is likely, however, that
Shaw did not perceive Wildean aestheticism as a mask or code for same-sex
preferences. In fact, Shaw maintained that until the last of Wilde's trials he
had never conceived of his friend as having had sexual relations with other
men.[10] Alone among Shaw's literary acquaintances, Wilde signed a peti-
tion initiated by Shaw on behalf of Chicago anarchists involved in the
1886 Haymarket riots. Shaw rallied for his fellow Irishman several times –
notably a defense of Wilde in an article on Max Nordeau's best-selling
*Degeneration* (1892), a book that skewered Wildean aesthetics, and later
when Wilde was convicted for "gross indecency."

Their shared anarchist leanings and defense of artistic freedom are
complicated, however, by Shaw and Wilde's deep differences in political
belief and aesthetic outlook. Of his fellow Irishman, Wilde told Frank
Harris, "He is a man of real ability but a bleak mind. Humorous gleams of
wintry sunlight on a bare, harsh landscape. He has no passion, no feeling
and without passionate feeling how can one be an artist. He believes in
nothing, loves nothing, not even Bernard Shaw, and really on the whole,
I don't wonder at the indifference."[11] Wilde displays his elegant cynicism
here as well as the (less familiar) idealism at the core of his philosophical
outlook, which stressed the pleasures of fantasy and artifice in contradistinction to the bracing exposures of realism that were so basic to Shaw's
theatre. For his part, Shaw despised what he took to be Wilde's fraudulent
unconventionality ("never was there a man less an outlaw than he,"
claimed Shaw), casting aspersion on Wilde's writing for the theatre as
well.[12] *The Importance of Being Earnest*, Shaw declared, was Wilde's "first

truly heartless play." In a review of *The Ideal Husband*, Shaw dismissed Wilde as "absolutely the most sentimental dramatist of the day" (the play, he complained, "has no thesis").[13] The idea that a theatrical work would have an argument is obviously opposed to Wilde's aestheticist doctrine, which militated against edifying depth in works of art.[14]

The two writers' differing ideological positions on dissident sexuality echo in a present moment in which the neoliberal accommodation of same-sex erotics within the discourses of equality, marriage, and family opposes queer conceptions of dissident sexuality that resist normative systems and embrace an unstable, artificial component in sexual identity. Furthermore, as LGBTQ liberties are threatened by authoritarian regimes relying on punitive laws in Russia and parts of the Middle East, the asymmetries between Shavian and Wildean utopias still matter. For Shaw's politics were not just allied with egalitarian democratic ideals but held totalitarian inclinations that were utterly alien to Wilde's idiosyncratic anarchism, with its skepticism about limitations on individual freedom. As Ruth Lively notes, the "religion of socialism" characteristic of the 1880s Fabian movement emerged as a belief in a welfare state overseen by an enlightened intellectual leadership.[15] Further, as Matthew Yde demonstrates, Shaw's utopian politics frequently darkened into the idealization of "Superman" figures and tyrannous regimes.[16] Despite his support of anarchists, Shaw became beholden to visions of a smooth-functioning rationally cohesive social order that required a charismatic leader.

To be sure, Shaw was a maverick in his understanding of – and principled activism on behalf of – homosexual rights, particularly in the 1880s and 1890s during an intense social purity campaign in Britain. That assertive stance first was signaled in the playwright's 1889 letter to *Truth* magazine, the organ of the social purity campaigner Henry Labouchère, the architect of the so-called Labouchère Amendment under which Wilde would be prosecuted for "gross indecency" four years later. In his letter – either unsent or rejected for publication – Shaw denounced the arrest of men ensnared in a homosexual brothel scandal that erupted in London's West End, the notorious 1889 Cleveland Street case. Empowered by the recently passed "gross indecency" clause of the Labouchère law (and not, as Shaw's letter did not seem to recognize, by existing sodomy laws), police arrested several socially prominent men.

Shaw undermined the legitimacy of the legal charges by insisting on the temporal and geographical pervasiveness of same-sex erotic activity. "There are hundreds of others who might have been expelled on the same grounds," he wrote, "Greek philosophers, soldiers, sailors, convicts and

in fact members of all communities deprived of intercourse with women."
He further clarified that same-sex desire was not the prerogative of men
alone: "Women, from Sappho downward, have shewn that this abnormal
appetite is not confined to one sex."[17] Most importantly, Shaw protested
that the Labouchère law violated individual rights through misguided
religious injunctions that trespassed on the secular state:

> I appeal now to the champions of individual rights ... to join me in a
> protest against a law by which two adult men can be sentenced to twenty
> years and servitude for a private act, freely consented to and desired by both
> which concerns they themselves alone. There is absolutely no justification
> for the law except the old theological one of making the secular arm the
> instrument of God's vengeance (230).

As Morris Kaplan notes of this letter, Shaw was alone among observers of the
West End scandal to raise the issue of human rights.[18] Prophetically anticipating the logic of *Lawrence* v. *Texas*, his letter designated privacy as a basic
right, a central fundament of the recent liberal defense of same-sex eros.

Like Richard Burton, whose Orientalist "Terminal Note" to his 1885
translation of *One Thousand Nights and a Night* neutrally taxonomized
sodomy as geographically widespread, especially in Eastern locales, Shaw
maintained that the behavior exposed in the Cleveland Street case was
widely observable in different societies and historical epochs, implicitly
insisting on the tolerance of difference as a fundament of an enlightened
society. As Aleardro Zanghellini notes, Shaw's letter "normalizes homosexuality by historicizing it, by appealing to moral pluralism."[19] Of course,
Wilde – with the *fin de siècle* artist's characteristic backward-looking
idealization of mythic, artistic, or historical players – similarly appeals to
history in his famous speech at trial, in which he referenced the "great
affection of an elder for a younger man as there was between David and
Jonathan, such as Plato made the very basis of his philosophy, and such as
you find in the sonnets of Michelangelo and Shakespeare."[20] Rejecting
Wilde's nostalgic temporalizing, Shaw democratized illicit acts and actors –
hence the reference to those sailors, soldiers, and convicts, all of them
existing in the present and many of them, it is implied, *circumstantially*
drawn to their own sex. Hence, in his *Truth* letter, Shaw notes the
existence of a Norfolk penal colony as an instance of situational homosexuality wherein imprisoned men resorted to same-sex erotic activity
in the absence of women. With its forward-looking sexual modernism,
Shaw's emphasis on the *contingent* nature of queer carnal acts opposed the
prevailing late Victorian sexology's notion of *congenital* sexual "types."

Tellingly, although Shaw later made the case for prostitution as a victimless crime in *Mrs. Warren's Profession*, his *Truth* letter ignored the issue of sex work in the Cleveland Street case, focusing entirely on the question of sodomy. Shaw's elision signaled a shrewd awareness that the vendible economics disclosed by the Cleveland Street case could feed into a sordid narrative of cross-class exploitation – a specter that had inspired Labouchère when he sought support for his social purity legal activism in W. T. Stead's recently published 1885 "The Maiden Tribute of Modern Babylon," an expose in the *Pall Mall Gazette* dealing with allegedly widespread child prostitution in Britain. Rather, Shaw – at least publicly – preferred to see the case as wrongly turning a common vice into a new crime. Yet ignoring the issue of class exploitation effectively put Shaw – now an official advocate for working-class aspirations in his new role as a leader of the Fabian Society, established a year before – at some odds with Shaw the campaigner for the decriminalization of prostitution.

With his polemical defense of male same-sex amours – his speech at trial evoking Hellenic and Renaissance love – Wilde exalted dissident erotics by evoking classical and Renaissance models, affirming a utopia defined by *cross-generational*, as opposed to cross-class, affection. Yet it was precisely this heightened rhetoric of Hellenic and Renaissance love that doomed Wilde when the prosecution paraded before the court a group of lower-class young men with whom he had traded money for erotic favors. "Hellenic Wilde" was thus exposed as "Predatory Wilde," a member of an illicit brethren of relatively prosperous men that extended from the Lotharios depicted in Stead's 1895 "Maiden Tribute" article to the upper-class homosexual cenacles of Eton, Harrow, Oxford, and Cambridge. In this way, prosecutors demythologized nineteenth-century utopian discourse surrounding same-sex eros, extrapolating the economist logic that, for wholly different purposes, Shaw had invoked in considering the question of prostitution in *Mrs. Warren's Profession* (1893). Yet Wilde's theatrical persona may have predisposed the jury and the press to deem him anathema to a decent-minded public even before the trial's revelations of same-sex liaisons. Tellingly, *The Evening News'* early coverage of the proceedings foregrounded Wilde's quicksilver linguistic skills – not the specifics of his sexuality – as "the source of evidence" for his "strange personality."[21]

In his *Truth* letter, Shaw questioned the notion of sodomy as unnatural, deftly rebuking the Cleveland Street prosecutors for claiming that sodomitical acts were so "expressively disagreeable as to appear unnatural."[22] Notwithstanding this disruption of the "natural" as subjective and arbitrary, Shaw's utopian vision was almost entirely legalistic, economic, and moral, a socialist and humanist dream of rational discourse, secular laws, and freedom of expression. Broadly speaking, Shaw's "sexual utopia" depends on a structure of private individual "rights" secured by the state even as it conceives of dissident sexual acts as largely emerging from unequal social and economic conditions, exemplified by the imprisoned Norfolk men or Mrs. Warren's reliance on prostitution for financial independence.

More abstractly, Wilde's endorsement of utopian schemes is apparent in his much-quoted comment in "The Soul of Man under Socialism" (1891), "A map of the world that does not include Utopia is not worth even glancing at, for it leaves out the one country at which Humanity is always landing. And when Humanity lands there, it looks out, and, seeing a better country, sets sail. Progress is the realization of Utopias."[23] Unlike Shaw, Wilde distinguishes "individual" socialism from "authoritarian" (what he termed "bureaucratic") socialist societies that cause the "complete suppression" of original creative power," advocating what today we might recognize as a libertarian refinement of anarchist beliefs. Wilde's caution girds his fundamental point that "What is needed is Individualism. If the Socialism is Authoritarian; if there are Governments armed with economic power as they are now with political power; if, in a word, we are to have Industrial Tyrannies, then the last state of man will be worse than the first" (229). Yet Wilde's dominant concern is the aesthetic realm. As George Woodcock notes: "Wilde's aim in *The Soul of Man under Socialism* is to seek the society most favorable to the artist. ... for Wilde art is the supreme end, containing within itself enlightenment and regeneration, to which all else in society must be subordinated. ... Wilde represents the anarchist as an aesthete."[24] Moreover, to the extent that it evokes the law, his polemic explores occasions when the dissenting individual must choose to violate legal injunctions.

One may glean Wilde and Shaw's divergent conceptions of sexual utopia by considering *Salome* and *Mrs. Warren's Profession* in tandem. Both plays center on unruly women in fissured familial relationships. Both were originally banned from the London stage – *Salome* because of its use of biblical figures, deemed unallowable by the Lord Chamberlain's office, *Mrs. Warren's Profession* because of its sympathetic treatment of female prostitution. There the similarities end. The dilemma of Shaw's play is related to a dramatization of desire's wily management, and even then its subject is the cost of sexual dissidence to normative familial relations. Thus

Mrs. Warren struggles – after years of successfully working as a prostitute and then as a brothel-owner – with her daughter Vivie's bourgeois moralism, a disgust only partly camouflaged by Vivie's New-Womanish qualities. The play never wrestles with the more problematic aspects of prostitution – for example, whether prostitution, if legalized, might remain degrading to indigent women. Sidestepping such thorny issues by focusing on a prostitute of financial means – a bourgeois madam – the play steadily shifts to questions of motherhood, culminating in Mrs. Warren's confession to Vivie that she wishes she had been a better mother and her daughter's rejection of any relationship with her.

As Robert Brustein notes, "like Arthur Miller, Shaw envisions a reconciled society in which there will be no more tragedy – or mystery, since all human problems will be already solved."[25] Paradoxically, Shaw is contemptuous of Victorian pieties regarding social reform yet resorts to wellmade plays of dogged nineteenth-century realism indebted to Ibsen. In *Salome*, contrastingly, Wilde is absorbed in the ineluctable enchantments, symbolist inscrutabilities, and tragic potential of disorderly eros. There is no rectifiable Shavian "social problem." Also, Wilde not only inverted Victorian-era hypocrisies in plays such as *The Importance of Being Earnest*, in *Salome*, he absorbed the poetics of nineteenth-century Symbolism, repeatedly sequestering dissident erotics into a realm of mystery, opacity, and doubleness valued by the antirealist, largely French Symbolist movement exemplified by Stéphane Mallarmé and Odilon Redon. *Salome* depicts dissidence as almost entirely outside a circuit of repressed desires – except when Herod ultimately orders his stepdaughter Salome's execution, the climactic but sole law-substantiating act in Wilde's play. At the same time, we are left with a sense throughout *Salome* of sexual fantasies run wild, independent of any stable sexual "identity" in large part because Symbolism rejects the codes of realism.

A refusal of erotic identification is characteristic of Wilde's work and persona more generally. Today, we might understand this stance as presciently "posthumanist," a queer deflection of a univocal sexual identity. At the same time, Shaw and Wilde's contrasting outlooks on erotic futurity were entangled with radically opposed aesthetic values. Shaw – for Yeats, a "notorious hater of romance" – was skeptical of artifice and subterfuge, whereas Wilde was deeply committed to an aesthetics of the beguilingly artificial, what he called the "truth of masks," and the possibilities for sexual freedom that concealed or deferred identity allowed.[26] Wilde's aesthetic values were entangled with his overt utopian political ideas, as became clear with the critical dissent that Wildean ideas generated in the twentieth century when liberalism was being formed as an antidote to a supposedly misguided utopianism.

## Wilde's Aesthetic/Political Anarchism, W. H. Auden, and the Midcentury Backlash against Queer Temporality

Wilde's discomfort with strictly legal and scientific conceptions of dissident same-sex desire may be one reason he long has represented a problem for some prominent mid-twentieth-century humanist intellectuals, who saw in Wilde and his defenders at once an excess of Hellenic and Renaissance nostalgia and anarchist and socialist sympathies that threatened a liberal, law-based society as well as gender fixities.[27] That distrust may have stemmed from a number of extra-aesthetic positions, such as Wilde's disapproval of charity as demoralizing in "The Soul of Man under Socialism," his embrace of so-called paganism, his ostentatious openness to sensation, and his pioneering role in the creation of modern celebrity culture, all anathema to many midcentury American liberal intellectuals.

Nowhere is the mid-twentieth-century apprehension about Wilde's political imagination and Hellenic vision of same-sex *amours* more evident than in W. H. Auden's shifting responses to the playwright between 1941 and 1969. Although Auden's appreciation of Shaw was unbounded – he once called him "probably the best music critic who ever lived" – Auden's wariness about Wilde pivoted among caustic disavowal, overt hostility, and eventual admiration of Wilde's cultural impact if not his artistry.[28] In a 1941 essay on Byron, Auden noted that Wilde was one of only three writers with major reputations outside of Britain, the others being Shakespeare and Byron. However, in a striking about-face, in 1950, Auden – now a resident of the US and writing in a more politically conservative country and era – derisively dismissed Wilde as a mere performer. This claim appeared in a *Partisan Review* critique of George Woodcock's 1962 *The Paradox of Oscar Wilde*, one of the first scholarly works to comprehend Wilde in emphatically political terms – specifically, as a thinker with an idiosyncratic anarchist outlook. Negatively duplicating Woodcock's terms ("Playboy or Prophet" was one chapter title in Woodcock's account, which in measured terms judged him to be both), Auden derided Wilde as a consummate playboy as well as a failed prophet and artist. Auden claimed that Wilde authored only one significant work, *The Importance of Being Earnest*, which Auden read as indicative of Wilde's paltry vision. "At the end all secrets are out, there is no need for

Mr. Bunbury and Lady Bracknell surrenders," writes Auden. "In the Eden of Wilde's Hertfordshire all things are possible; in the late-Victorian Old Bailey, unfortunately, they were not."[29]

Auden's dilation on a Wildean carnal utopia syntactically forecloses that possibility through a semicolon that interrupts Wilde's progress, followed by a terse reference to Wilde's ghastly legal fate. The semicolon, in effect, denies Wilde the integrity of his utopian dreams. It is "gross indecency" law that, in Auden's telling, mockingly forecloses dreams of utopia, as if Wilde's erotic utopianism had been an entirely personal vision instead of one that may have been shared by millions of others. The history-determining law, given authority through its successful enactment, has the final word on Wilde. Auden's anti-utopianism then deduces in the play-wright's love of Hellenic ideals a common mistake of the *fin de siècle*, and exposes Wilde's true – but covert – merely personal interests:

> Of all men Wilde was least in the position to say "the real weakness of England lies . . . in the fact that her ideas are emotional and not intellectual" for in few cases is the emotional root of thinking so obvious as his.
>
> Thus, when, like all the nineteenth-century literary *école païenne*, he extols the Greeks, the Great God Pan, and the Beautiful Pagan Life, any resemblance to the historical reality is accidental and all he seems to mean is: I should like a world without Sunday closing, damp weather and overcooked vegetables but with plenty of sunshine and lots of yummy scantily-clad teenagers who can't say No. (186)

The Hellenic sympathies of the *fin de siècle* are reduced to the pitiful fantasies of a fussy ephebophile, whose biographical fate delegitimizes his utopian ideals. In Auden's rejection of a queer temporality of nostalgia, the law's "historical reality" is the restorative cudgel that recuperates pressingly real actualities. Put another way, for Auden, the (discretely gay-identified) humanist poet, the movement of history is indissociable from the workings of the law.

Writing in 1963 at the beginning of what would be a more sexually emancipatory period, Auden returned to Wilde in a review of a new collection of the playwright's correspondence, this time with far less bile. He observed, "From the beginning Wilde performed his life and con-tinued to do so even after fate had taken the plot out of his hands" – an acknowledgement that Wilde was not reducible to his imprisonment and that he existed in future-tense queer time.[30] Still, Wilde's utopianism continued to trouble *bien pensant* intellectuals worried about the social impact of a lawless imagination, particularly given the ascendant counter-culture. "The claim of the artist to express everything is subversive in one especially acute sense: the claim to express everything can only exacerbate feelings of being nothing," wrote Philip Rieff in 1970. "In such a mood, all limits begin to feel like humiliations. Wilde did not know that was prophesying a hideous new anger in modern men, one that will render unexcited peaceable existence even more Utopian than before."[31] Yet Wilde came to have a far more powerful set of cultural effects than as an actor in a Victorian – or present-day – morality tale or as a mere instrument in the liberalization of attitudes related to same-sex eros.

For Dollimore, Gide's essentialist and Wilde's destabilized notions of erotic identity represented an unresolvable disjuncture – and one that vexingly endured into the present. But the theoretical fissure that I have highlighted between utopias of law and lawlessness – the inheritance of Shavian and Wildean ideological skirmishes that has been revived in mid-twentieth-century critical debates about Wilde – is arguably less deeply ingrained. Moreover, the aesthetic realm for Wilde was not opposed to politics but was the very location for the potential for a political utopia. If, following Lytton Strachey, I may indulge in a queer counter-history – and thus a queer counter-futurity – I might wish that the juryman's stupidity at the last Wilde trial might have been undone through some lawless feat of the imagination.

## Notes

1  See, for example, Heather Love, *Feeling Backward: Loss and the Politics of Queer History* (Cambridge, MA: Harvard University Press, 2007).
2  José Esteban Muñoz, *Cruising Utopia: The Then and There of Queer Futurity* (New York University Press, 2009), 1.
3  André Gide, Letter to Paul Valéry (December 4, 1891), quoted in Jonathan Dollimore, *Sexual Dissidence* (New York: Oxford University Press, 1991), 4.
4  For a superb collection of essays from this perspective, see Ryan Coward, ed., *Against Equality: Queer Revolution, Not Mere Inclusion* (Oakland, CA: AK Press, 2014).
5  Oscar Wilde, *De Profundis*, in *The Soul of Man and Prison Writings* (Oxford: Oxford University Press, 1990), 158.
6  Oscar Wilde, "Pen, Pencil, and Poison," in *The Soul of Man under Socialism and Other Essays*, ed. Philip Rieff (New York: Harper Colophon, 1970), 90.
7  Quoted in Neil McKenna, *The Secret Life of Oscar Wilde* (London: Century, 2003), 81.
8  Dale Carpenter, *Flagrant Conduct: The Story of Lawrence v. Texas* (New York: W. W. Norton, 2012).
9  Michael Holroyd, *Bernard Shaw. Volume III. 1918–1950. The Lure of Fantasy* (New York: Random House, 1991), 190.

10 Shaw's apparent ignorance of Wilde's same-sex propensities confirms Alan Sinfield's argument that so-called effeminacy at the *fin de siècle* did not register as a homosexual identity until the Wilde trials. Alan Sinfield, *The Wilde Century* (New York: Columbia University Press, 1994).

11 Quoted in Frank Harris, *Oscar Wilde: His Life and Confessions* (Ware: Wordsworth Editions, [1916] 2007), 260. Wilde once commented acerbically: "Mr Bernard Shaw has no enemies, but is intensely disliked by his friends." Quoted in Holroyd, *Bernard Shaw*, 194.

12 Quoted in Holroyd, *Bernard Shaw*, 192.

13 George Bernard Shaw, "Review," *Saturday Review* (January 12, 1895).

14 Shaw's early plays often dealt with socially topical themes (restrictive marriage laws, prostitution, and slum-lordism), although after the 1880s Shaw claimed to have tired of what he called his "Blue Book" plays, a reference to British government reports, bound in blue covers, addressing pressing societal problems.

15 Ruth Livesey, *Socialism, Sex, and the Culture of Aestheticism in Britain, 1880–1914* (Oxford: Oxford University Press, 2007).

16 Matthew Yde, *George Bernard Shaw and Totalitarianism: Longing for Utopia* (New York: Palgrave, 2013).

17 George Bernard Shaw, *Collected Letters. 1874–1897*, ed. Dan Laurence (New York: Dodd Mead, 1965), 231, Subsequent references will appear parenthetically in the text.

18 Morris B. Kaplan, *Sodom on the Hudson: Sex, Love, and Scandal in Wilde Times*. (Ithaca: Cornell University Press, 2005), 191.

19 Aleardo Zanghellini, *The Sexual Constitution of Political Authority* (New York: Routledge, 2015), 154.

20 Quoted in H. Montgomery Hyde, *The Trials of Oscar Wilde* (New York: Dover, [1948] 1973), 236

21 Quoted in Ed Cohen, *Talk on the Wilde Side* (New York: Routledge, 1992), 152.

22 Shaw, *Collected Letters, 1874–1897*, 231.

23 Wilde, *The Soul of Man under Socialism and Other Essays*, 246. Subsequent references in text.

24 George Woodcock, *Anarchism: A History of Libertarian Ideas and Movements* (Cleveland: Meridian, 1962), 447.

25 Robert Brustein, "Bernard Shaw: The Face behind the Mask," in *G. B. Shaw: A Collection of Critical Essays*, ed Ralph James Kauffman (Upper Saddle River: Prentice Hall, 1965), 102.

26 William Butler Yeats, *Autobiographies* (London: Macmillan, 1955), 283.

27 The so-called New York intellectuals were especially caustic about Wilde. Alfred Kazin contrasted writers who followed "Wells, Shaw, and Kipling" with the "sickly exoticism that merely ran after Pater and Huysmans and Oscar Wilde." See *On Native Grounds* (New York: Doubleday, [1942] 1956), 53. In 1948, the anticommunist and anti-anarchist *Partisan Review* published Mary McCarthy's essay, "The Unimportance of Being Oscar," which states

"There is something *outré* in all of Wilde's work that makes one sympathize to a degree with the Marquess of Queensberry; this fellow is really insufferable." Mary McCarthy, "Theatre Chronicle," *Partisan Review* (Summer 1948): 302.

28 Quoted by Eric Bentley, Introduction to *Shaw on Music* (New York: Doubleday, 1955), 4.

29 W. H. Auden, *Prose: Volume III: 1949–1955*, ed. Edward Mendelsohn (Princeton: Princeton University Press, 2008), 186. Subsequent references in text.

30 W. H. Auden, "An Improbable Life," *Forewords and Afterwords* (New York: Vintage, 1973), 302–24. This was one of two appreciative responses to Wilde that Auden published in the 1960s, one in 1963 and the other in 1969.

31 Philip Rieff, Introduction to *The Soul of Man under Socialism and Other Essays*, xxxii–xxxiii.

# CHAPTER 5

# After Queer Baldwin

## Matt Brim

As his presence in the current volume suggests, James Baldwin has been figured and refigured by scholars of queer theory. His work continues to animate the field. But just how did James Baldwin become so important for and useful to queer theory? This essay examines the resurgence of interest in Baldwin by, first, considering the relationship between Baldwin as an object of analysis and queer theoretical approaches that attend to the pleasures and difficulties that Baldwin presents.[1] It then, necessarily, moves "after queer theory" to explore the disciplinary innovations by which black queer studies has emerged as a privileged site for reading Baldwin as a black queer writer. My most basic assertion in this regard will be that the work of critically queering Baldwin has become more interesting as *black queer studies* has proliferated and coalesced. In the ongoing queer of color moment "after queer theory," readers have more reason than ever to address Baldwin in all his queer complexity.[2]

### Baldwin as Black Queer Writer: Troubling Identity

The apparently good fit between Baldwin and queer theory stems from their shared project of troubling identity, often by undermining normative naming practices. To forge that connection, I want to make an important distinction between two seemingly similar descriptions of the author: Baldwin the "black gay writer" and Baldwin the "black queer writer." While the most obvious difference here is between "gay" and "queer," the racial designation "black" also had multiple, complicated meanings for Baldwin.[3] Both instances of complex naming practices point to one of Baldwin's most enduring literary and political commitments: to reveal and reject identity categories as constructed, confining, and impoverishing. For Baldwin, the writer's dilemma emerged from the necessity of *inventing* the terms of his own existence in the face of a world that ferociously demanded that he bow to its definitions of him. For example, Baldwin was born into

a time and place where he was frequently called "nigger" or, in its flatly
derogatory sense, "queer." Baldwin perceived, even in his youth, that he
was neither and that he must be at war with these terms if they were not to
consume him. He realized, for one thing, that such words were not only
distortions but also projections and that the racial and sexual "other" was
thus a feature of the speaker's unexamined self:

> I know, and I've always known – and really always, that's a part of
> the agony – I've always known that I am not a nigger. But if I am not
> the nigger, and if it's true that your invention reveals you, then who is the
> nigger? ... [Y]ou still think, I gather, that the nigger is necessary. Well he's
> unnecessary to me, so he must be necessary to you. I give you your problem
> *back*. You're the nigger, baby, it isn't me.[4]

The racist or homophobic epithet said more about the construction of
whiteness and the demands of sexual conservatism than they did about
Baldwin. Yet Baldwin also knew that he was inescapably implicated by the
words he refused to own. In one of his last essays, the ostensible topic of
which is androgyny and the actual topic of which is the refusal to confront
the terrifying otherness in the self, Baldwin writes,

> But we are all androgynous, not only because we are all born of a woman
> impregnated by the seed of a man but because each of us, helplessly and
> forever, contains the other – male in female, female in male, white in black
> and black in white. We are part of each other. Many of my countrymen
> appear to find this fact exceedingly inconvenient and even unfair, and so,
> very often, do I. But none of us can do anything about it.[5]

Try as we might to drive ourselves apart with word and deed, according to
Baldwin we are all "brothers." Categorical "labels" or "cells" undermine
the possibility of genuine human connection by blunting the capacity
to recognize our interdependence. Baldwin called that capacity "love."
The cost of facing that nearly unbearable connection was, in his words,
"the price of the ticket" for all Americans.

In Baldwin's lifetime, which saw the rise of both the Civil Rights
Movement and gay liberation, the language used by others to define him
would change. Yet the alternate and more positively inflected terms
"black" and "gay" did not so much erase the violence of the earlier epithets
as reshape the linguistic cage Baldwin sought to escape. "Some things had
happened to me because I was black," Baldwin wrote in 1977, "and some
things had happened to me because I was me and I had discover the
demarcation line, if there was one ... There was absolutely no way *not* to
be black without ceasing to exist. But it frequently seemed that there was

no way to be black, either, without ceasing to exist."[6] The writer from Harlem thus formulated his blackness as a crisis, lived close to the bone, a phenomenological and ontological paradox. Baldwin felt more directly at odds with the word "gay." Though he claimed a responsibility to his "brothers and sisters" who identified with "the phenomenon we call gay," he saw it as "a word that has very little to do with me, with where I did my growing up. I was never at home in it."[7] Though different from outright racist and homophobic epithets and indeed different from each other, "black" and "gay" identities also fit too tightly for the writer despite the value the latter categories could offer as politically galvanizing identity formations. The point is that *all* of these terms sent Baldwin in search of his own name.

Thanks in large part to his endless troubling of identity, Baldwin emerged as an object of analysis in the field of queer theory, for queer theory provides a language and theoretical architecture for productively exploiting such instances of category failure. It offers, for example, leverage against simplistic claims that Baldwin's rejection of the category "gay" reflected nothing more than his own internalized homophobia (a charge still frequently leveled at black communities). The word "queer" itself exposes all kinds of conceptual trouble within modernity's vast project of categorization. Queer is, definitionally, strange. But more importantly, queer is *strange-making* in its capacity to divest identity of its quiet power to seem natural and unremarkable. Ecumenical in its approach, queer theory critiques an increasingly wide swath of norms, but it initially privileged sexuality and heteronormativity as especially deserving of critical undoing.[8] Certainly queer theory's focus on upending heterosexuality as the unquestioned sociosexual norm aligned with Baldwin's explicit vision in his second novel, *Giovanni's Room*.[9] Donald Hall argues in this vein that *Giovanni's Room* represents an "exemplary queer text":

> But certainly the lingering possibility that individuals can resist by living and loving in excess of preexisting social categories does make [*Giovanni's Room*] a thoroughly queer [novel]. It suggests that desire can manifest itself in the most surprising ways and in nonexclusive terms. It suggests mutability in sexual relationships over time and also in ways that exceed a simple hetero/homo binary. It suggests strongly that individuals have the ability and responsibility to allow for human complexity outside the starkness of received social definitions and valuations, even as it does not deny the power of those contextual forces. It evokes the possibility of a different set of sexual relationships and definitions without prescribing exactly what the future might hold.[10]

An indictment of heteronormativity, *Giovanni's Room* frames the man/woman dyad as an overwhelming expectation, a paralyzing formal construct, a trap. The book pushes further: not only does compulsory heterosexuality offer up an emotional and erotic dead end for David, the white American protagonist; not only does the homophobic imperative that grounds white American masculinity and that forbids homosexual desire prove deadly for David's darker Italian lover, Giovanni; but, in very queer fashion, the category of homosexuality or gay identity, rather than being the thwarted ideal for David and Giovanni, itself becomes yet another prison cell. Baldwin refuses his characters and his readers the comfort of *any* sexual category (including, arguably, bisexuality). The solution for the doomed lovers, David and Giovanni, would not be an admission and acceptance of white homosexual identities but, rather, liberation from the raced sexual categories that artificially divide them. In their final lovers' quarrel before David leaves him, Giovanni (here a mouthpiece for Baldwin, surely) distinguishes his notably anti-American – and queer – perspective from David's highly taxonomic worldview: "You are the one who keeps talking about *what* I want. But I have only been talking about *who* I want."[11] "Who" versus "what" neatly encapsulates one queer critique of *Giovanni's Room*: we cannot love categories but individuals. Eventually, Giovanni's execution and David's crushing alienation literalize the stakes of failing to love queerly, beyond the bounds of hetero- or homonormativity.

I want to pause to note a queer tension that arises in Baldwin's turn to the "individual," "the person," and "human connection" as signifiers that transcend stifling sexual and racial labels. Anti-categorical – and thus queer – on the one hand, these terms also seem to appeal, on the other hand, to an essentialist understanding of personhood and humanity that runs counter to much of queer theory's post-structuralist, anti-foundationalist impulse. Queer theory, in other words, questions not only the "what?" of sexual categories but the status of the "who" – that expressive agent of love that grounds Giovanni's theory of his attachment to David. In this way, Baldwin, contra queer theory, seems not radically anti-categorical in his deconstructive vision. At the same time, Baldwin's "humanism" must be distinguished from the humanism of the Enlightenment and Western philosophy that Baldwin ceaselessly undermined and that, as Robert Reid-Pharr has recently argued, has proven itself to be resolutely, vulgarly antiblack and thus a partial, deeply impoverished knowledge-making system of thought.[12] We might better consider Baldwin's humanist compromise by turning to Ernesto Martínez's study of queer of color writers, including Baldwin, who work in a "realist" tradition that recognizes the constructedness of the social world (a queer perspective) while also recognizing the life-shaping *reality* of the social upon oppressed people:

> Throughout his career Baldwin was emphatic about the constructedness of black and white identities, showing us how profoundly and inelegantly these identities produce opacity in the lives of everyday Americans. But he was equally attuned to the tangible reality of living in a world organized so predictably and systematically on the subjugation and distortion of what black people feel and know.[13]

Martínez thus argues for queer of color reading strategies that allow for a supple, marked, negotiable objectivity to undergird the text. Baldwin's "individual," in resisting ready-made labels of straight or gay, does not operate outside of the objective world in some queer freespace but rather helps to discover how the struggles around identity "make possible better and worse knowledge about the world" (8).

The category troubles associated with racial and sexual identities were further complicated for Baldwin by the relationship these terms have to each other, and here it is instructive to consider a post-Baldwin moment in "black gay" literature. Published at the end of the first decade of the ongoing US black AIDS epidemic, the anthology *Brother to Brother: New Writings by Black Gay Men* (originally published in 1991) signaled a renaissance in literary representation by black same-gender-loving (SGL) men.[14] As new scholarship attests, there had been individual and even some collective efforts to assert "black gay male" identity before the 1980s.[15] Certainly the Harlem Renaissance had produced a cadre of ambiguously queer authors and texts, including Langston Hughes, Countee Cullen, Claude McKay, and Richard Bruce Nugent. However, these writers lived in a sociolinguistic space where "gay" had not yet settled into its current usage, largely solidified only after midcentury. The black gay writers of *Brother to Brother* could thus repeatedly and explicitly trace their literary inheritance back to one figure more than any other: midcentury writer James Baldwin. Baldwin became the black gay "forefather" upon whom many of his literary inheritors, such as Joseph Beam and Essex Hemphill, relied for a model – not only a model of literary excellence but also "evidence of being." Baldwin proved that black gay writers existed and that they could produce outstanding works of literature. In the face of renewed forces of racism and homophobia that fueled the AIDS epidemic and that actively engineered the extinction of racial and sexual minorities, black gay men saw in Baldwin irrefutable evidence that their own lives as artists were possible. This is one of the immeasurable benefits of the politics of representation: the possibility of forging a self-image thanks to the visibility of others. For powerful historical and political reasons, then, Baldwin was situated by black gay writers themselves at the personal and literary intersection where black authorial identity and gay authorial identity meet and thrive.

There is a problem, however, with using Baldwin to help construct a "black gay" intersection, and that problem has had important implications for renewed interest in Baldwin in the academy and in queer studies in particular. The politics of representation rely on a model of identity that Baldwin rejected in a number of ways. As a novelist, Baldwin intuitively understood there to be a link between the characters he created and the possibilities for imagining the complexity of "the human being" off the page. In an early exploration of that connection, he wrote that "the failure of the protest novel lies in its rejection of life, the human being, the denial of his beauty, dread, power, in its insistence that it is his categorization alone which is real and which cannot be transcended."[16] Unfortunately, this sentiment, repeated by Baldwin in innumerable ways over his long writing career, did little to prevent reviewers and critics from reading his first two novels in precisely the ways Baldwin strained against. His 1953 novel, *Go Tell It on the Mountain*, established the young author on the national stage, yet it did so on the strength of its supposedly authentic black voice. Largely read and reviewed as a "black experience novel," the book contributed to Baldwin's reputation as a "representative" black writer, just the kind of categorization against which Baldwin recoiled. That connection was secured by the seemingly autobiographical nature of *Go Tell It on the Mountain*, which tells the story of young John, a boy trying to negotiate his entry into manhood in the context of a black evangelical home and church in Harlem. This was, on its face, Baldwin's story, and this was his unmistakable powerful voice – two authenticating features of the "Negro spokesman."

*Giovanni's Room* garnered a similar kind of attention. This time, however, the explicit love between men that centers the book gave critics all the license they needed to categorize it as a "gay novel." This label *seemed* all the more logical because the book contains no black characters. Though written by the same author, Baldwin's early novels were read in ways that not only privileged fixed, single-axis identity categories as foundational to each book's message and meaning but also insisted upon the exclusivity of those terms. These readings largely ignored the homoerotic dynamics of John's maturation in *Go Tell It on the Mountain*, and they completely ignored the white racial dynamics of *Giovanni's Room*. In the popular press and, for many years, in the academy alike, *Go Tell It on the Mountain* and *Giovanni's Room* were used to implicitly stage "black gay" as an unthinkable intersection. Baldwin became, impossibly, simultaneously representative of *either* black *or* gay literature. In the face of that kind of bad thinking, reading Baldwin as black *and* gay seems like an improvement, as indeed it is. But recall that Baldwin eschewed the underlying logic of this admittedly more complex identity construction. Valuable on the one hand for its precision, "black gay" nevertheless makes the same mistake twice by assuming the stability and referentiality of its two constituent terms.

## Baldwin, Black Queer Studies, and Embodied Intersectionality

Baldwin has not only helped queer theorists pursue their critique of fixed identity categories; he has also helped the field of queer theory to be more self-critical. With Baldwin as one of its luminaries, *black queer studies* coalesced as a new academic formation in relationship to – though not circumscribed by – the institutional forces by which queer studies too often became (white) queer studies.[17] That is, black queer studies names the broad effort to confront queer theory's unexamined whiteness and to theorize nonheteronormative blackness, while also giving other disciplines with more identitarian approaches to knowledge production a way of reviewing the sex and gender norms that inform their work. These can be difficult academic bridges to cross. The increased attention within queer theory to an analysis of race and sex was not simply an "evolution" in the field. Rather, this change required disciplinary struggle and stressful innovation that, ultimately, realigned the field of (no longer? white) queer theory. "Black queer studies," sometimes called "quare" studies,[18] names the academic formation that has, arguably, best realized the potential for reading Baldwin through a queer theoretical lens. It also offers key interdisciplinary methodologies – chief among them intersectional queer of color critique – for taking up Baldwin's legacy of thinking race and sex together and deconstructing whiteness as a register of eroticized power. It is no surprise that of the seventeen essays that comprise the groundbreaking 2005 anthology *Black Queer Studies: A Critical Anthology*, three focus primarily (and others secondarily) on the work and influence of James Baldwin.[19]

I want to note that, implicitly, my disciplinary narrative frames the story of black queer studies as one that takes shape "after queer theory." And while "black queer studies" nominally emerges after "queer theory," that is only half the story. Certainly black queer studies vigorously responds to the whitewashing dynamics of queer theory and the straightwashing dynamics of black studies. However, it is also true that black queer thought enjoys multiple critical genealogies, perhaps most significantly its connections to black women's studies and the extracurricular black lesbian feminist theory upon which that field was conceptualized and created.[20] Further, because queer theory at least in part owes its own emergence to 1970s and 1980s black lesbian feminist analysis, millennial black queer studies – in that it thinks back through its black lesbian feminist "mothers" – operates as *both* call and response to queer theory.[21] (White) queer theory, in short, was never really white, and black queer studies was never brand new. I will use a double narrative, then: black queer studies responds to (white) queer theory even as black lesbian feminist thought grounds queer theoretical inquiry. As black queer studies casts its light backward to illuminate the whitening tendencies of queer theory, it also illuminates the black lesbian feminist roots of intersectionality as an analytic tool in the service of social change.

Because Baldwin's fiction does not settle for a black + gay model of representation, it offers a set of rich target texts for queer of color intersectional analysis of the ways normative social systems interact with and interanimate each other to create complex experiences of oppression and privilege. Baldwin refuses to understand himself as fixed as a "black gay writer," and neither does intersectionality merely name a critical method of pinpointing the location where one's multiple identities overlap, as the metaphor of the intersection can seem to imply. Intersectionality describes not a location but a methodology for conceptualizing "the problem [of compound discrimination] that attempts to capture both the structural and dynamic consequences of the interaction between two or more axes of subordination. It specifically addresses the manner in which racism, patriarchy, class oppression and other discriminatory systems create background inequalities that structure the relative positions of women, races, ethnicities, classes – and the like."[22] It offers a "way of thinking about the problem of sameness and difference and its relation to power. This framing – conceiving of categories not as distinct but as always permeated by other categories, fluid and changing, always in the process of creating and being created by dynamics of power – emphasizes what intersectionality does rather than what intersectionality is."[23] Black queer studies has become such a powerful optic not because the composite term "black queer" somehow succeeds in stabilizing an intersection but precisely because its terms are held in productive intersectional tension, allowed to operate in shifting relation to each other. Black queer studies and queer of color critique recognize these multidimensional relationships, just as they anticipate the terms of class, gender, and nation that they at least nominally hold in abeyance. Far from a totalizing impulse, black queer studies has energized Baldwin studies by marking a racial and sexual connection, the specifics of which enrich (and often explode) the very terms used to frame the debate.

Baldwin's bestselling third novel, *Another Country*, was published in 1962, well before intersectional analysis was named as such, yet the novel calls the reader to do just the kind of difficult conceptual work that an intersectional approach facilitates.[24] Set once again in New York, the novel redoubles Baldwin's efforts to expose the uselessness and, indeed, the danger of racial and sexual categories. But with its more racially and sexually diverse cast of characters, and written after Baldwin's temporary return to the US in 1957 and his subsequent involvement with the burgeoning Civil Rights Movement, *Another Country* became the crucible in which Baldwin's universalizing poetic of brotherhood would be most severely tested. Again acting as a witness to our flawed but common humanity, Baldwin confronted in *Another Country* the fundamental, but not reciprocal or symmetrical, interdependence that exists *across* lines of race and sexual difference. The novel stages any number of intimate crossings over – interracial, intersexual, interclass – as it asks how white and black, gay and straight, rich and poor can love across these lines of power.

On the one hand, the theme of crossing over in *Another Country* invites an intersectional analysis of interlocking systems of social power. The mobility of black bodies, women's bodies, gay bodies, and poor bodies is never unfettered in the novel, particularly in relation to the straight white male body that has access to each of them. And crucially, black, female, gay, and poor bodies are entwined in their own power relations, with racism, sexism, homophobia, and class conflict operative among them, not just upon them. On the other hand, however, Baldwin insists more adamantly than ever on the ultimate importance of "the person," whose incarnation can never be explained by a calculus of oppression. Baldwin's intersectionality is less a gauging of social power arrangements than a confrontation with history at the level of the interpersonal: how can individuals, brought face to face, grapple with themselves as "historical creations"[25] in order not to escape that history but rather to begin to change it in the only way possible, that is, together? In the alchemy of

Baldwin's social realism, intersectional vectors of power both crystalize and potentially dissolve at the level of human engagement. The opposite of categorization for Baldwin is not some sort of utopian queer category-lessness; it is the agony of relationality, interdependence, even intersubjectivity.

One relationship in *Another Country* exemplifies Baldwin's intersectional vision. Foreshadowed by my reference to bodies above, this example locates social power dynamics at the level of embodied experience, thus materializing the forces of history and blurring, upon the flesh, facile distinctions between the social and the self. Ida Scott, an aspiring blues singer, prides herself on "knowing the score" as a black woman who must negotiate the tricky and, indeed, deadly race and gender dynamics that threaten her, including in the context of her relationship with her white boyfriend, Vivaldo Moore. Ida cannot afford *not* to reject the liberalism of this white man's claim that he loves her: "[H]ow can you talk about love when you don't want to know what's happening ... How can I believe you love me?" (324–5). In Ida's experience, people, both black and white, make the cheap trade. They pay with their money or with their bodies rather than entering into the more difficult and perhaps impossible exchange by which blacks and whites might actually attempt to know each other. She tells Vivaldo, who as a writer is in the business of imagining others' lives and who insists that he wants to spend the rest of his life finding out about Ida, that he is not truly willing to do so. "And, listen," Ida concedes, "I don't blame you for not being willing. I'm not willing, nobody's willing. Nobody's willing to pay their dues" (325). The price, she knows, would be too high. Ida therefore sees Vivaldo's attempt to love across the color line as a white liberal fantasy that blacks, who know the score, cannot afford to share.

Yet in their last scene, Ida and Vivaldo do share a breakthrough, perhaps beginning to pay off the race debts that are their unequal American inheritance. Confessing her opportunistic affair with an influential white music producer, Ida begins to tell Vivaldo something of her connection to her dead brother, Rufus, of their mutual lost innocence, of their experience as African Americans living in a white world. Vivaldo, shedding his liberal skin, feels, in turn, that Ida "was not locking him out now; he felt, rather, that he was being locked in. He listened, seeing, or trying to see, what she saw, and feeling something of what she felt" (415). When Ida breaks down sobbing on the floor, Vivaldo's "heart [begins] to beat with a newer, stonier anguish, which destroyed the distance called pity and placed him, very nearly, in her body, beside that table, on the dirty floor ..., her sobs seeming to make his belly sore" (426). The scene ends with Ida "stroking his innocence out of him" (431). At the novel's close, then, Vivaldo seems willing to trade his white innocence as he attempts to imagine, both more personally and more historically, Ida's life. Ida, in turn, appears willing to accept the legitimacy of that crossracial exploration, as their black and white body barriers seem almost literally to dissolve.[26]

Drawing on women of color feminism's insight that social power plays out on the body, black queer studies offers a ready framework for reading corporeal boundary dissolutions such as this one in *Another Country*. It enables us to ask, "What does it feel like to be enmeshed in regimes of power?"[27] "Enmeshed" conveys the physicality that accompanies the discursive and historical production of subjectivity at the level of the lived body. As Baldwin implies with Ida and Vivaldo, to be enmeshed in webs of power is not only to be stuck but also pulled apart, shot through, and it is on the "sensational flesh"[28] where racialized and sexualized power threatens most intimately and paradoxically. The queer pleasure/danger of raced and sexed embodiment emerges most consistently in Baldwin's depictions of the homoerotic dependence of white straight male power on black men's bodies.[29] However, if body boundaries can blur and dissolve in pleasure and pain, they can also stubbornly refuse to yield. The pain of corporeal/psychic dissolution surely aches differently for Ida than it does for Vivaldo, who seems to be coaxed and coached by the black woman. In this respect we can also wonder about the total absence of lesbian erotics in Baldwin's writing. To the extent that the physical enactment of desire in Baldwin's fiction seems to require the presence of a man, his work contributes to the erasure of the lesbian body. His frequent references in interviews and essays to "his woman" and "his children" – references that along with the language of "brotherhood" rhetorically position him as the straight black male – further suggests that Baldwin was invested in what might be called a black (queer) masculinism at the price of female (homo) eroticism. Intersectional analysis must take account of such gender differentials that arise within Baldwin's "queer" oeuvre.

## After Queer Baldwin

Despite these gender troubles, queer theory's fascination with Baldwin's anti-identitarian project threatens to make him something of a posterboy, a bit too perfectly queer. That version of Baldwin may be a useful object with which to demonstrate queer critique, but it would no longer be the Baldwin who refused to be a spokesman for any group. Creating him as a fixture within queer reading practices is the risk, not the payoff, of queering Baldwin. Black queer studies and queer of color critique have thus far kept Baldwin an unfixed object, a queerly moving target. Yet as academic fields mature, even their most dynamic texts can become too familiar, even foundational. Fortunately, at least one piece of evidence suggests that a productively loose textual/critical "fit" between Baldwin and black queer studies is being sustained.

Methodologically speaking, the critical tools and conceptual approaches deployed in reading Baldwin have changed as black queer studies has become the most dynamic site of engagement with his work. True, literary studies continues to ground much of black queer studies and much of Baldwin studies. Yet Baldwin's non-fiction essays – and Baldwin is perhaps the greatest American essayist of the twentieth century – constantly entice scholars from outside literature departments to work on Baldwin. Further, the long-awaited acquisition of Baldwin's personal papers by the Schomburg Center for Research in Black Culture is sure to propel Baldwin scholarship into even more unpredictable disciplinary orbits. Anticipating that exciting work, I want to end with a comparison of two dazzling anthologies in black queer studies that reflect a dynamic relationship between Baldwin and queer of color critique. The previously mentioned volume that helped to define the field, *Black Queer Studies: A Critical Anthology* (published in 2005 and developed from the "Black Queer Studies at the Millennium" conference of 2000), draws most heavily on scholars located in English departments, many of whom also have cross-disciplinary homes in African-American studies, American studies, performance studies, and cultural studies. Their repeated object of analysis is Baldwin. By comparison, the 2016 follow-up volume, *No Tea, No Shade: New Writings in Black Queer Studies* (edited by E. Patrick Johnson, who was one of the *Black Queer Studies* coeditors), while it includes several literary analyses, reflects a much more explicitly interdisciplinary orientation.[30] Only one of the twenty-two contributors is housed in an English department. Interestingly, most come from women's, gender, and sexuality studies departments – long a site of interdisciplinary teaching and research – as well as African and African-American studies and ethnic studies. Rather than a statement about the passé nature of literary inquiry and close textual analysis, *No Tea, No Shade* powerfully demonstrates how far and fast black queer studies has run in the last decade.[31] And just as there is a paucity of English professors in the volume, there is also a striking absence of Baldwin criticism. These shifts, to my mind, reflect welcome field-mobilizing editorial decisions, for they decenter Baldwin and therefore make good on a queer commitment – easier said than done – to anti-hierarchical methods of knowledge production, including decisions around how to expand the archive of black queer studies after queer Baldwin.

### Notes

1  The resurgence of interest in Baldwin has been widespread. Emblematic in this regard was the extensive series of events that comprised the 2014–15 "Year of James Baldwin," conceived and organized by Rich Blint. Recent national and international James Baldwin conferences speak in particular to the increased critical attention to diasporic blackness and the global south in Baldwin studies. See the 2011 NYU conference, "James Baldwin's Global Imagination," www.cs gsnyu.org/wp-content/uploads/2011/02/James-Baldwins-Global-Imagination-schedule.pdf. See also the 2016 American University of Paris conference, "'A Language to Dwell In': James Baldwin, Paris, and International Visions," www.aup.edu/news-events/lectures-conferences/james-baldwin-conference, especially Robert Reid-Pharr's and Bill Mullen's plenary talks on Baldwin in Paris and Palestine respectively. Magdalena Zaborowska's *James Baldwin's Turkish Decade: Erotics of Exile* (Durham: Duke University Press, 2009) still sets the standard for work on Baldwin as a transatlantic queer commuter. Karen Thorsen's important documentary, *James Baldwin: The Price of the Ticket* (California Newsreel, 1989), was redigitized in 2015, and Raoul Peck's *I Am Not Your Negro* (Magnolia Pictures, 2016) was nominated for a 2016 Academy Award in documentary film.

2  Queer communities of color, the Movement for Black Lives, and people whom Baldwin once described as "the relatively conscious whites and the relatively conscious blacks" come to Baldwin in the current moment of US racism and imperialism for intellectual, strategic, political, affective, and spiritual reasons. See "The Fire Next Time," in *The Price of the Ticket: Collected Nonfiction, 1948–1985* (New York: St. Martin's, 1985), 379. Baldwin's timeliness, I want to emphasize, is not only an academic matter.

3  Even the descriptor "writer" was complicated for Baldwin. His beginnings were in oratory as a child preacher, and later he would position himself as working in the tradition of blues musicians.

4  *Take This Hammer*, directed by Richard O. Moore (1964; San Francisco, CA: National Education Television).

5  "Here Be Dragons," *The Price of the Ticket*, 690.

6  "Every Good-Bye Ain't Gone," *The Price of the Ticket*, 642–3.

7  "'Go the Way Your Blood Beats': An Interview with James Baldwin," in *James Baldwin: The Legacy*, ed. Quincy Troupe (New York: Simon and Schuster, 1989), 174.

8 The centrality of sexuality to queer theory has become an active and ongoing question for the ever-developing field.

9 James Baldwin, *Giovanni's Room* (New York: Delta, 2000).

10 Donald Hall, *Queer Theories* (New York: Palgrave Macmillan, 2003), 160.

11 *Giovanni's Room*, 142.

12 Robert Reid-Pharr, *Archives of Flesh: African America, Spain, and Post-Humanist Critique* (New York: New York University Press, 2016).

13 Ernesto Martínez, *On Making Sense: Queer Race Narratives of Intelligibility* (Stanford: Stanford University Press, 2012), 7.

14 Essex Hemphill, ed., *Brother to Brother: New Writings by Black Gay Men* (Washington, DC: RedBone Press, 2007).

15 See, for example, Kevin Mumford's *Not Straight, Not White: Black Gay Men from the March on Washington to the AIDS Crisis* (Chapel Hill: University of North Carolina Press, 2016).

16 "Everybody's Protest Novel," *The Price of the Ticket*, 33.

17 Alison Reed's essay "The Whiter the Bread, the Quicker You're Dead: Spectacular Absence and Post-Racialized Blackness in (White) Queer Theory," in *No Tea, No Shade: New Writings in Black Queer Studies*, ed. E. Patrick Johnson (Durham: Duke University Press, 2016) explores the ongoing, troubling pattern of the critical reinscription of whiteness into queer theory.

18 See E. Patrick Johnson's "'Quare' Studies, or (Almost) Everything I Know about Queer Studies I Learned from My Grandmother," in *Black Queer Studies: A Critical Anthology*, ed. E. Patrick Johnson and Mae G. Henderson (Durham: Duke University Press, 2005), 124–57.

19 Patrick E. Johnson and Mae G. Henderson, eds., *Black Queer Studies: A Critical Anthology* (Durham: Duke University Press, 2005).

20 See Gloria T. Hull, Patricia Bell-Scott, and Barbara Smith, eds., *All the Women Are White, All the Men Are Black, but Some of Us Are Brave: Black Women's Studies*, 2nd ed. (New York: Feminist Press, 2015).

21 See Amber Musser's chapter (Chapter 7) in this volume.

22 Though this passage is excerpted from Kimberlé Williams Crenshaw's "Background Paper for the Expert Meeting on the Gender-Related Aspects of Race Discrimination" (United Nations, 2000), I quote from and want to draw attention to the noteworthy anthology, Patrick R. Grzanka, ed., *Intersectionality: A Foundations and Frontiers Reader* (Boulder: Westview Press, 2014), 17.

23 See Sumi Cho, Kimberlé Crenshaw, and Leslie McCall, "Toward a Field of Intersectionality Studies: Theory, Applications, and Praxis," *Signs: Journal of Women in Culture and Society* vol. 8, no. 4 (2013): 795.

24 James Baldwin, *Another Country* (New York: Vintage, 1993).

25 Baldwin, "White Man's Guilt," *The Price of the Ticket*, 410.

26 I have argued elsewhere that the Ida/Vivaldo sexual relationship stands in sharp – and problematic – relief against two other erotic couplings in the novel, the flashpoints for which are the "almost sex" scene between Vivaldo and Rufus, which is plagued by racial and gendered paralysis, and the fully

realized sex scene between Vivaldo and (white gay) Eric, which is characterized by sexual and emotional access. See chapter two of Matt Brim, *James Baldwin and the Queer Imagination* (Ann Arbor: University of Michigan Press, 2014).

27 See Uri McMillan, "(Black) Power Bottoms, Stickiness, and Receptivity," *GLQ: A Journal of Lesbian and Gay Studies* vol. 22, no. 3 (2016): 472.

28 See Amber Jamilla Musser, *Sensational Flesh: Race, Power, and Masochism* (New York: New York University Press, 2014).

29 See, for instance, Baldwin's 1965 short story, "Going to Meet the Man," in *Going to Meet the Man* (New York: Dell, 1966).

30 Patrick E. Johnson, ed., *No Tea, No Shade: New Writings in Black Queer Studies: New Writings in Black Queer Studies* (Durham: Duke University Press, 2016).

31 In her foreword to *No Tea, No Shade*, Cathy Cohen writes, "I remember attending the Black Queer Studies conference in 2000 planned by E. Patrick Johnson and Mae G. Henderson and never believing that the group assembled there would in a decade help to revolutionize our study and understanding of black intimacy, sex, and community. And yet, here we are, the many of us, having built the academic field of black queer studies that has come to be respected, critiqued, and institutionalized" (xi).

## CHAPTER 6

# Revision, Origin, and the Courage of Truth
### Henry James's New York Edition Prefaces

### Kevin Ohi

Among the questions that might remain "after" queer theory (so far) is that of origin; queer theorists have been reluctant to touch it, except to warn of its risks.[1] Eve Kosofsky Sedgwick, though much of her work turned on gay "incipience" and was energized, ethically and affectively, by invocations of proto-gay kids, spelled out reasons to steer clear of the etiological questions that preoccupied many early advocates of gay liberation: in "How to Bring Your Kids Up Gay," she suggested that, whether turning to nature or nurture, explorations of etiology are perhaps impossible to insulate from a fantasy of homosexual extirpation.[2] Current doxa agrees: to question why people become gay is taken to imply that they might become (or have become) something else; to assert that homosexuality is not a "choice" is now shorthand for sexual tolerance. Sedgwick's essay might give one pause in too quickly embracing the natural or given as shelter from homophobic fantasies (or it may be practices) of intervention, and it is still worth emphasizing how far short avowals of tolerance fall, and even how destructive they can be, and to admire, therefore, Sedgwick's polemical argument for a "strong, explicit, *erotically invested* affirmation of some people's felt desire or need that there be gay people in the immediate world" (164). Yet the eschewing of questions of origin is not merely pragmatic; the essay's peroration protects gay incipience by subjecting it to a horizon that resolves it in an identity – those gay people we want to people our immediate world. Sedgwick's "reparative" account seems to have two objects at least nominally at odds: the proto-gay child in a state of potentiality (what Kathryn Bond Stockton calls the "interval" of the queer child)[3] and the gayness that seeks to emerge from that potentiality, and, in emerging, to dissolve it. That tension is perhaps visible throughout her work – as, perhaps, in queer theory more generally, especially when it comes closest to the anti-homophobic commitments that animate it. To dwell on questions of origin might help to sustain that "proto-gay" thread of potentiality, even within the actualization that makes it retrospectively legible – and to link it with questions of literary creation.

Sedgwick notes the particular biases that reflexively cast gay emergence in terms of deficiency or mistake; her insistence on her "felt desire or need that there be gay people in the immediate world" is also a defense of gay incipience. Yet the powerful critique of ego psychological models targets their identitarian premises: assumptions that equate psychological health, reified egos, identities, and gendered identities (assumed in turn to be isomorphic with biological sex, however tendentiously conceived). Hence, Sedgwick notes, to be tolerated by these psychologists, gay men must be grown up, already gay, and recognizably masculine. In the very risk that the proto-gay might not, after all, become gay, the "etiology question" brings into view the threshold of becoming that divides any identity from itself – a queerness inherent to human consciousness to the degree that it cannot originate itself. Foucault's late writing on parrhēsia takes up the question of how thought might animate a life; I will suggest that Henry James's accounts of literary origins bring that latter question into contact with this originary queerness.

## Origin Stories

The question of origins is repeatedly confronted by James's late writing – after the major novels, from 1904 until his death in 1916. Personal origins to begin with: his return to America in *The American Scene* or to his younger years in the three volumes of the autobiography. And the New York Edition prefaces: written for the reissue of (some of) his works, the prefaces, which arguably initiate criticism of the novel in English, are often framed by origin stories.[4] Straightforward anecdotal accounts, however, are almost the exception, and, more often, the moment of origination is forgotten, suppressed, or lost in a retrospect that can find no moment when the idea wasn't already "there."

At a cursory glance, James's narratives of inception are deceptively simple, and present parallel accounts: of what occasioned an idea or story and, more often, of where James wrote them (locations that are rarely, if ever, the "settings" of the texts that result). These latter are usually cast as memories of composition that come back to James as he rereads his texts, and that originating scene, inaccessible, of course, to a reader because never "depicted" in the text, hovers there, to be seen by the author – much like, as we will see, the inevitable new term in the revised text. There is to my

mind no systematic account of the relation between the narratives of
compositional situations and those of the germs that form the minimal
ideas providing plot or character or situation. Thus, in the preface to
*The Portrait of a Lady*, for example, James moves from his memories of
writing in Venice to a discussion of the structuring role of character in the
origination of a novel – to characters' "germinal property and authority"
(1073). He writes:

> There are pages of the book which, in the reading over, have seemed to
> make me see again the bristling curve of the wide Riva, the large colour-
> spots of the balconied houses and the repeated undulations of the little
> hunchbacked bridges, marked by the rise and drop again, with the wave, of
> foreshortened clicking pedestrians. The Venetian footfall and the Venetian
> cry . . . come in once more at the window, renewing one's old impression of
> the delighted senses and the divided, frustrated mind. (1070–1)

The text, reread, calls back into view the scene of its creation – albeit with
a typically Jamesian complication (the pages "have *seemed* to make me see
again. . .") – and that recovered scene thwarts the composition that has, of
course, already occurred. At the time of composition, Venice embodies an
excess that frustrates writing – too rich, and too interesting, it figures, as
the limit case of the superabundant actual, the ways that the world exceeds
containment by a text. Too suggestive, it overwhelms and divides the
mind: such places "are too rich in their own life and too charged with their
own meanings merely to help him out with a lame phrase; they draw him
away from his small question to their own greater ones; so that, after a
little, he feels, while thus yearning toward them in his difficulty, as if he
were asking an army of glorious veterans to help him arrest a peddler who
had given him the wrong change" (1070). The multiple layers of incommensurate exchanges (the wrong change, the army of glorious veterans
assigned a task demeaning to their glory, the incommensurate relation of
this incommensurability to the exchange it purports to figure) thus stand
in for the relation between art and life explored by these prefatory narratives. In a perhaps characteristic structure, the "divided, frustrated" mind,
remembered, is harmonized by the remembering mind – divided, therefore, between its present reading and its memory of the past – which is
also to say that one's divided attention turns out, in retrospect, to have
been productive: "one's book, and one's literary effort were to be better
for them. Strangely fertilizing, in the long run, does a wasted effort of
attention often prove" (1071). The revising mind makes these discrepancies "fertilizing." In the unrationalized interplay between these different
forms of inception there is an implicit reckoning of the relation between

life and art; confounding the inside and the outside of the text, the parallel narratives of origination figure that relation, and link it to what James calls revision.

In the *Portrait of a Lady* preface, the incommensurability of inside and out appears, further, in the second term of what I have called an "unrationalized" relation: turning to the origin (in a different sense) of the text, the preface explores the "germinal property and authority" of character – a discussion that, personifying character, seems in various ways to *de*personify the author. His "dim first move toward 'The Portrait'" (1075), the grasp of a single character ("an acquisition I had made … after a fashion not here to be retraced"), raises the question of how the vivid character is "placed" – how the book is generated that contains the initiating presence of Isabel Archer:

> One could answer such a question beautifully, doubtless, if one could do so subtle, if not so monstrous, a thing as to write the history of the growth of one's imagination. One would describe then what, at a given time, had extraordinarily happened to it, and one would so, for instance, be in a position to tell, with an approach to clearness, how, under favour of occasion, it had been able to take over (take over straight from life) such and such a constituted, animated figure or form. The figure has to that extent, as you see, *been* placed – placed in the imagination that detains it, preserves, protects, enjoys it, conscious of its presence in the dusky, crowded, heterogeneous back-shop of the mind very much as a wary dealer in precious odds and ends, competent to make an "advance" on rare objects confided to him, is conscious of the rare little "piece" left in deposit by the reduced, mysterious lady of title or the speculative amateur, and which is already there to disclose its merit afresh as soon as a key shall have clicked in a cupboard-door. (1076)

The narrative progression of the preface points again to the intertwining of two forms of originating personification that are at the same time consequences of the forms they initiate or imagine: the character who instigates the novel's genesis and the authorial consciousness – or, rather, its retrospective narration, the "so subtle, if not so monstrous" project of writing "the history of the growth of one's imagination," an imagination that it seems cannot, under normal conditions, say "what, at a given time, had extraordinarily happened to it." To add to the quandaries of origin, the figure for the waiting idea derives from, or retells, a central episode in *The Golden Bowl*: Charlotte and the Prince's visit to the Bloomsbury shop containing the eponymous bowl, the visit that catalyzes the novel's plot and establishes its symbolic structure. To say only the least complicated thing about the relations thereby established, the novel would seem to be the "source" of the originating consciousness more than its result. As the preface continues, the "spacious house" still further confounds the novel's "organizing [of] an ado about Isabel Archer" (1077) with the authorial consciousness that conceived it.

When, therefore, the prefaces produce origin stories as (self-consciously) retrospective reconstructions, at issue is perhaps both the curiously provisional quality of authorial consciousness and its dependence on the texts that it ostensibly creates. These origin narratives, then, are "revisions" in the sense that rereading creates them, and the author is himself marked by the virtuality of events in the fiction. Authorial consciousness and germinating character alike are at once originating and self-consciously posited, lending a certain groundlessness to the figures of organic wholeness that describe the remembered emergence of the texts.

> These are the fascinations of the fabulist's art, these lurking forces of expansion, these necessities of upspringing in the seed, these beautiful determinations, on the part of the idea entertained, to grow as tall as possible, to push into the light and the air and thickly flower there; and quite as much, these fine possibilities of recovering, from some good standpoint on the ground gained, the intimate history of the business – of retracing and reconstructing its steps and stages. (1072)

"These necessities of upspringing in the seed": James's term for origination is "germ," and the difficulty of locating an origin is echoed by the term's multivalent figural resonances. Seed and sprout, a sprouting or the germination that presages it, the germ's connection to what germinates can be direct (a seed becoming a plant) or indirect (as a germ triggering an illness): thus the author's consciousness or sensibility is the "soil" in which a seed is planted (1074, 1140) and, at other moments, an organism infected by a "virus." The results, cultivated or nurtured, can also be involuntarily caught. "Germ," etymologically, is both the ovum (or ovary – in botany, the pistil) and the sperm; fertilized and fertilizing, it, like the author's consciousness, both acts and is acted upon – thereby naming the indeterminate agency in "having" an idea. The metaphor is also spatially multivalent: seed and sprout, it can name the seed that contains the sprout, what sprouts from the seed, and the embryonic plant contained within the seed. In the several prefaces where James emphasizes the "quite incalculable tendency of a mere grain of subject-matter to expand and develop and cover the ground when conditions happen to favour it," the "unforeseen principle of growth" (1120) that makes "projected ... small things" into "comparative monsters," he exploits the non-resemblance between the seed and what it becomes. A germ is also, simply, a small amount of something; the inspired writer, James asserts, wants only the merest hint of inoculation – too much information, and it will cease to be suggestive. And the term invokes the characteristically retrospective temporality of Jamesian thought – the essence, what an idea, under analysis, later boils down to – its central grain. In James's disorienting terms in the preface to *The Ambassadors*, "nothing can exceed the closeness with which the whole fits again into its germ" (1305).

This inside-out structure emblematizes the way these origin stories are also readings of the prefaced texts – and emblematizes the complex relation of authorial life to work. To forget the germ of "The Beast in the Jungle" (as James claims to do) is to locate the story's beginning in a repetition of Marcher's own initiating forgetfulness; likewise for the repeated note of "failure" in the preface to *The Wings of the Dove* – the novel's realized aesthetic form in some sense *is* Milly Theale's foreshortened life, Kate Croy's baffled scheme, and Merton Densher's thwarted love – a realized form of potentiality, the paradoxical mode whereby the authorial life enters the work – and disappears there. Even at a cursory glance, James's texts valorize tact in approaching the author's life; one thinks of "The Death of the Lion" or "The Aspern Papers" or "The Birthplace." Yet, at the same time, the search for the origin is not to be renounced. The failure to find the biographical source ("a torment," James writes of Shakespeare, "scarcely to be borne" [1215])[5] is, like the putative aesthetic "failures" confessed in the prefaces, a mode of sustaining (perpetuating, but also enduring) this mode of creation. The successful artist, James suggests many times, disappears, and, like Milly Theale or John Marcher, or like Shakespeare in *The Tempest*, turns his back on us, and escapes.

The prefaces' confessions of putative failures thus ask to be read as complex markers of authorial presence, even of his person. The discussion of bewilderment in the preface to *The Princess Cassimassima*, or the "failure" outlined by the preface to *The Wings of the Dove*, like other such moments, make such confessions interchangeable with another sort of authorial disappearance – into the potentiality of art. The "was to have been" that, in the *Wings of the Dove* preface, describes various plans that fail to come to fruition is a characteristic orientation of Jamesian verbs: suspending "happening" between two temporalities (one marking what was to happen and then did, and another marking what was to happen but then didn't), this complex verbal form is often how the late novels articulate, simply, what occurs in them. Thus, what from one angle looks like failure from another looks like the securing of potentiality, an ever-renewed possibility of beginning again. If, to judge from the explicit assertions of the prefaces, the Jamesian artist fails more often than he succeeds, failure is another name for the creative act.

## Revision

Hence the proximity of the prefaces to the autobiography under the aegis of what James calls revision: "The rate at which new readings, new conductors of sense interposed, to make any total sense at all right, became, to this wonderful tune, the very record and mirror of the general adventure of one's intelligence," he writes of *The Golden Bowl* (1335); in the preface to *The American*, it is the "joy of living over, as a chapter of experience, the particular intellectual adventure" (1060). James's central statement on revision is the preface to *The Golden Bowl*, which articulates a complex relation between revision and the authorial life. "To revise," he writes, "is to see, or to look over, again – which means in the case of a written thing neither more nor less than to re-read it" (1332). Rereading is not rewriting (a "task so difficult, and even so absurd, as to be impossible") because the new terms are already there: "the act of revision, the act of seeing it again, caused whatever I looked at on any page to flower before me as into the only terms that honorably expressed it," "the particular vision . . . that experience had at last made the only possible one." To revise is thus to perceive potentiality – what might have been, but wasn't; like James's visions of past compositional milieux, they impose themselves on his imagination as visions of the texts in potential. "The deviations and differences," he writes, "became . . . my very terms of cognition" (1330). The gap between old and new readings thus limns the history of the authorial life – becomes "the very record and mirror of the general adventure of one's intelligence" (1335):

> The interest of the question is attaching . . . because really half the artist's life seems involved in it – or doubtless, to speak more justly, the whole of his life intellectual. The "old" matter is there, re-accepted, re-tasted, exquis- itely re-assimilated and re-enjoyed – believed in, to be brief, with the same "old" grateful faith . . . ; yet for due testimony, for re-assertion of value, perforating as by some strange and fine, some latent and gathered force, a myriad more adequate channels.

The reread text is at least double: the old matter, reassimilated, reveals new terms that impose themselves as inevitable. Various figures render this doubleness: children or old people made presentable for company, garments repaired, properties renovated, new terms "looking over the heads" of older ones, "alert winged creatures, perched on those diminished summits and aspir[ing] to a clearer air" (1332–3). Thus to see the old and new is to retrace the growth of the artist's taste, "to hold the silver clue to the whole labyrinth of his consciousness" (1333).

Discrepancies, and the relation to the productions of one's past dictated by a shifting consciousness, make reading "a living affair" (1335), which will link revision to "responsibility." That note is struck early in figures amply commented on – by, for example, J. Hillis Miller[6] – where revision is the effort to follow footprints after one's gait has changed:

> Anything, in short, I now reflect, must always have seemed to me better . . . than the mere muffled majesty of irresponsible "authorship." Beset constantly with the sense that the painter of the picture or the chanter of the ballad . . . can never be responsible *enough*, and for every inch of his surface and note of his song, I track my uncontrollable footsteps, right and left, after the fact, while they take their quick turn, even on stealthiest tiptoe, toward the point of view that, within the compass, will give me most instead of least to answer for. (1322–3)

This figure recurs throughout the preface, where revision raises the question of whether "the march of my present attention coincides sufficiently with the march of my original expression," whether the "imaginative steps" of the reader he has become sink into the "very footprints" of the younger composer he was: "it was, all sensibly, as if the clear matter being still there, even as a shining expanse of snow spread over a plain, my exploring tread, for application of it, had quite unlearned the old pace and found itself naturally falling into another, which might sometimes indeed more or less agree with the original tracks, but might most often or very nearly, break the surface in other places." The "spontaneity" of these "deviations and differences," matters, he asserts, "not of choice but of immediate and perfect necessity," is what is "predominantly interesting."

The asynchronicity of consciousness might be said to enter the prefaces through figural discrepancies (of seed and germ, for example); the authorial life unifies, in its disappearing shadow, those discrepancies. And the *Golden Bowl* preface figures that very process – makes discrepancy harmonious by articulating figures of bodily movement (tracing his uncontrollable footsteps) with figures of vision (falling into a gait and seeing the tracks of one's footsteps over a plain of snow). The first difference, seen, turns discrepancy into the mark of perspective. Hence the first line of the preface: "Among many matters thrown into relief by a refreshed acquaintance with 'The Golden Bowl' what perhaps most stands out for me is the still marked inveteracy of a certain indirect and oblique view of my presented action" (1322). Later, those terms evoke a coincidence of original and retrospective vision more possible with recent works, the reader's footsteps sinking "comfortably" into the author's, so that "his vision, superimposed on my own as an image in cut paper is applied to a sharp shadow on a wall, matches, at every point, without excess or deficiency" (1329). With the passage of time coincidence gives way to discrepancy, and hence to "relief": "This truth throws into relief for me the very different dance that the taking in hand of my earlier productions was to lead me; the quite other kind of consciousness proceeding from *that* return." Throwing a discrepancy into relief, the retrospective gaze makes it a unified vision. The maneuver is all the more complex in that refracted vision is his method of narration – "the marked inveteracy of a certain indirect and oblique view of my presented action," the mediation through a "center of consciousness" that, as opposed to "an impersonal account of the affair in hand," presents "my account of somebody's impression of it," the impression of the author's "concrete deputy or delegate," the "convenient substitute or apologist for the creative power otherwise so veiled and disembodied" (1322). The authorial life could here be said to be the anthropomorphizing shadow of a disembodied form – an indirection of view.

   It is perhaps difficult to grasp how James moves from focalization to revision, but revision, too, is an indirect view – of new terms mediated by old ones. Moreover, I have simplified things; the preface's highly abstract opening suggests that in *The Golden Bowl*, the technique of an indirect view mediated by an unimplicated observer (typical of the shorter works) is paradoxically embodied by the central characters (whose vision is then described as refracted); the Prince and the Princess are at once characters and anthropomorphic mechanisms of narrative method. The "mere muffled majesty of 'irresponsible' authorship" describes an unmediated, or perhaps "omniscient," narration; implication, and responsibility, come, in the first place, with focalization. Maggie and the Prince personify focalization, and turn mediated vision into "direct" contact, pulling the author "down into the arena" with "the real, the deeply involved and immersed and more or less bleeding participants" (1323). (In short, the involvement here is perspectival; his angle of view places the author in the fray.) By the end of the preface, the language of responsibility shifts to a different register of implication. The final paragraph begins by asserting the salience of the literary "deed," established through the felt unity of our actions and our expressions. It is as if the freedom of our capacity for expression made it one with our actions, and therefore susceptible to, and worthy of, ethical consideration: "with any capability, we recognize betimes that to 'put' things is very exactly and responsibly and interminably to do them. Our expression of them, and the terms on which we understand that, belong as nearly to our conduct and our life as every other feature of our freedom" (1340). "Literary deeds" enjoy an advantage over "other acts": "their attachment and reference to us, however strained, needn't necessarily lapse." Thus:

> Our relation to them is essentially traceable, and in that fact abides ... the incomparable luxury of the artist ... Not to *be* disconnected ... he has but to feel that he is not; by his lightest touch the whole chain of relation and responsibility is reconstituted. Thus if he is always doing he can scarce, by his own measure, ever have done ... Our noted behaviour at large may show for ragged, because it perpetually escapes our control; we have again and again to consent to its appearing in undress – that is in no state to brook criticism. But on all the ground to which the pretension of performance by a series of exquisite laws may apply there reigns one sovereign truth – which decrees that, as art is nothing if not exemplary, care nothing if not active, finish nothing if not consistent, the proved error is the base apologetic deed, the helpless regret is the barren commentary, and "connexions" are employable for finer purposes than mere gaping contrition. (1340–1)

The claims at the end are built, in more than one way, on "connexion" – that, most immediately, linking us to our words – a joining together material or immaterial, physical or rhetorical. The word appears ten times in the preface (eleven if one includes "disconnexion"), most often as a synonym for context. The final paragraph makes the connections between words or ideas[7] into material, bodily, or tangible relations (evoking the group of meanings of the word centering on sex, intimacy, and family). That link is also enacted in the peroration's own connections – the rhetorical assimilations of parallel rhetorical forms, most immediately, but also the crossing of registers that assimilates words, actions, and emotional states, makes a deed "apologetic" and a "regret" a "commentary." "Traceable" explicitly evokes rereading, James's tracking of his footsteps – or the silhouette that later reading seeks to retrace. Tracing an outline or deciphering a trace, rereading asserts various forms of connection.

## Parrhēsia and Potentiality

James's claims evoke other moments in the late writing – for example, in "Is There a Life After Death?," which asserts that connections will not lapse, that death will not rupture the links among us because we are capable of thinking them in the first place.[8] The traceable relation is our relation to our words – our words as actions, and the ethical dimension, therefore, of what we say; at the end of the preface, that dimension turns on the claim that connection is, ultimately, our capacity to revise: not to be reduced to mere gaping contrition, not to reduce care to passivity, is to assert the claims of connection by seeing, perpetually, our words afresh. That question in late James calls to mind Foucault's exploration, in his final seminars, of parrhēsia – a mode of truth-telling to be distinguished from others in ancient Greece and Rome. Couched as historical investigation – a systematic outline of this particular mode of veridiction – it is also a theory of speech acts, and one that, separating truth from propositional content, shifts attention toward the context of utterance, and, most often, to a risk incurred by the speaker: a frequent example is telling someone you love them, and the risk is an isolation whose ultimate horizon is social ostracism. For parrhēsia entails a relation; it takes place "between two partners" (fundamentally, between friends) (240, 244).[9] The term evolves in complex ways; in political speech, it is, initially, the honesty that the benevolent ruler (forestalling flattery) will allow or invite. But it later becomes a mode of assuming a life: "I must be myself in what I say ... I do not content myself with telling you what I judge to be true. I tell this truth only inasmuch as it is in actual fact what I am myself; I am implicated in the truth of what I say," as Foucault puts it in a commentary on Seneca (247). I find moving and compelling in these late texts the way his interest in parrhēsia and the "care of self" tends to escape containment in the genealogy of confession's production of docile subjects that ostensibly motivates it.

This is not merely, in other words, the familiar story of subjects produced by a discourse of truth about sex; Foucault's courage of truth meets Jamesian revision in what Agamben calls potentiality. In *Il fuoco e il racconto*, Agamben suggests why the work cannot be finished – why, to echo the prefaces, no work fully realizes the author's intentions, fully actualizes what was to have been: does not every book contain "a residue of potentiality, without which its reading and reception would be impossible? A work in which creative potentiality [*la potenza creativa*] were totally exhausted [*spenta*] would not be a work but the ashes and sepulcher of the work" (94/98/109, translation modified).[10] This has nothing to do with perfectionism, with an anecdotal sense that nothing is ever finished, or with academics' laborious cultivation of writer's block. It has rather to do with potentiality, with a capacity that remains sheltered, as potential, within the creative act that actualizes it, with the words that peer out, in James's image, above or beyond the words that one has written. Potentiality is thus the central term for Agamben's reading of Deleuze's late lecture on the act of creation. Agamben reminds us that all creation, for Deleuze, is an act of resistance – "to death ... but also... to the paradigm of information media, through which power [*il potere*] is exercised in ... 'control societies'" (33/39). The elaboration of the concept of potentiality that comprises the bulk of Agamben's essay is a complementary explication of the act of creation as resistance. Deleuze's own (idiosyncratic) account of Foucault in the seminar on his friend and fellow philosopher affirms this connection. In the seminar, which preceded by a year the lecture on creation, Deleuze devotes considerable time to resistance, which, he says, emerges between *Discipline and Punish* and *The History of Sexuality*. In the lecture of February 25, 1986, for example, Deleuze links "resistance" to a "beyond."[11] Resistance is not a term or a vector of force within the "disciplinary diagram" but that which escapes capture in it. So, if discipline (on the one hand) takes any group whatever and forces it to perform any task whatever and (on the other hand) cultivates, manages, fosters a population, resistance is not a counterforce to either procedure. Likewise, it is not a resistance "to" either knowledge or power, which Deleuze conceptualizes according to formal, molar forces (on the one hand) and informal (de-forming) or molecular forces (on the other). It is rather what remains beyond, or unrealized within, that schematization. And, outlining Foucault's characterization of power in the first volume of the *History of Sexuality*, he suggests that resistance is not to be confused with either "spontaneity" or "receptivity," with either the "power to affect" or the "power to be affected." In Deleuze's rendering, resistance is primary; it precedes relations of force. Potentiality in Agamben's account of the 1987 lecture offers a way to gloss Deleuze's understanding of "resistance" as a "beyond" that is not a form of transcendence. Or to frame the centrality of origins to James's account of revision.

As in Agamben's other writings on potentiality, creation cannot consist purely in the passing into act of what was potential. Potentiality is sustained in the work by a trembling between creation and decreation, necessity and contingency – by "revision." Thus, every "authentic" creative process is "suspended between two contradictory impulses: upsurge [*slancio*] and resistance, inspiration and critique" (43/48/53). Artistic capacity is lined with a fundamental incapacity that one might call resistance – a potential-not-to that is a resistance internal to potentiality or power that prevents its being "exhausted" in its actualization; revision is the cipher of the authorial life because it bodies forth this contradiction, the suspension within creation that Agamben links to the nontrivial self-reflexivity of great poetry. Such poetry "says not only what it says but also the fact that it is saying it" – says "the potential/power and the impotential/impotence of saying it" (58). Such self-reflexivity does not mean that poetry is the "subject" of "poetry," or "thought," of "thought."[12] Rather, "the painting of painting" means "that painting (the potentiality of painting...) is exposed and suspended [è eposta e sospesa] in the act of painting, just as the poetry of poetry means that language is exposed and suspended in the poem" (50/55 [translation modified]). What remains potential within thought makes thought possible; the work, subject to revision, lays bare what Agamben calls "materiality," language as such prior to any meaning.

In "Opus alchymicum," Agamben asks why the ethical project of the self's transformation needs to pass through an opus – in spite of the great temptation to dispense with that seemingly unnecessary detour. A preliminary problem is logical or grammatical; the self is not a "subject" that can transform or work "on" itself: "The pronoun 'se,' the marker of reflexivity in Indo-European languages, therefore lacks the nominative case. It presupposes a grammatical subject that reflects upon itself but can never itself be in the position of subject. The self [sé], to the degree that it coincides with a reflexive relation, can never be a substance, or a substantive." "The idea of an ethical subject," therefore, "is a contradiction in terms."[13] This aporia, Agamben notes, menaces every effort to work on the self: "there is no subject prior to the relation to the self: the subject is this relation itself and not one of the terms of the relation" (151–52).

Hence the transformation of the self has to pass through an "opus," and hence I think James's characterization of revision might speak to the intimate question of why one writes – and, in the present context, to the future of queer theory. Queer theory, like many liberationist critical practices, asserts a connection to the world, even aspires to an alchemical power to counteract its injustices. In Sedgwick and others, this imperative often takes the form of a guilty conscience about writing, which, bringing the prose alive, nevertheless deforms the thought. This is the tension between the "proto-gay" child and the gay person whose necessity in our immediate world we are (I would say justly) enjoined to avow. It perhaps also marks Sedgwick's turn to shame and affect, which is formulated in her brilliant reading of James's prefaces – an account that might be better known to readers of queer theory than are the prefaces themselves.[14] On the one hand, shame allows Sedgwick to posit queer identity in the mode of its suspension: "Shame interests me politically, then, because it generates and legitimates the place of identity – the question of identity – at the origin of the impulse to the performative, but does so without giving that identity space the standing of an essence" (*Touching Feeling*, 64). On the other hand, the brilliant reading of the prefaces' "lexicon" is partly enabled by a reification of the authorial consciousness that the prefaces themselves put into question – or posit as a belated consequence of the writing itself. The positing of James's psychological reactions – to the failure of *Guy Domville* and the lackluster sales of the New York Edition, to the physiological experience of constipation – seem, like the generalizations about the "kinds" of persons who might vibrate to the key of shame, both true (because they resonate with experience and observation in profound ways) and false (because reductive of, most importantly, the relation between identity and writing explored by the prefaces' probing of origins). Insofar as shame, in her account, begins with a dynamic of (albeit thwarted) recognition, the account is grounded in a supposedly identifiable, psychological, and – harsh to say – therefore banalizing context. In other terms, for all its opening of disparate questions of affect, by beginning from shame (especially as formulated by Tomkins) it makes recognition (given or withheld) the primary mode of relation to the world.[15] (The lurid thematics of fisting also has a curiously sublimating effect, since shame is made queer while also being divided from its more obvious occasion in gay male sexuality: anal sex.)[16] Arguably, this reifying of identity has been the career of shame in queer theory; it has allowed critics, because they were saying something true, to avoid the truth of the texts they read – and to take as given queer identity precisely to the degree that, as a "subject" of constatation, it is presumed to be suspended. That criticism might thereby become a psychologistic, sociological, and largely descriptive enterprise is not seen as regrettable by some. That turn perhaps brackets questions of identity that – by refusing to resolve them – previous instantiations of queer theory found so productive. Partly, this is a (justifiable) shift away from the closet as a governing trope for understanding sexuality, and therefore a muting of the largely epistemological questions that shaped that earlier theory. And yet the turn to shame and affect might also short-circuit the passage through the work that might be named by James's "revision."

"It is not writing that is happy," says Foucault; "the happiness of existence is suspended in writing, which is slightly different."[17] In Agamben's gloss: "Happiness – the ethical task par excellence toward which all work on the self tends – is 'attached' to writing ['*sospesa' alla scrittura*], that is, becomes possible only through a creative practice. The care of the self necessarily passes through an *Opus*, implies an ineluctable alchemy" (134/138 [translation modified]). Thus, for Agamben, the transformation of the self through the creative act is made possible only if it constitutes a relation to a potentiality not exhausted by the work. The poet-become-seer contemplates language itself – "not the written work but the potentiality of writing" (156), like James, confronting the new terms as they impose themselves on his vision, or tracing his uncontrollable footsteps across a plain of snow. The transformation of the self returns the work to potentiality. "Truly poetic," Agamben writes, "is that form of life that, in the work, contemplates its own power to do and to not do and finds peace in it (137/141 [translation modified]). This is one way to read James's rendering of revision as autobiography, and of autobiography as revision: a life suspended in, maintained in perpetual relation to, the potentiality of the creative act by way of a work that, ever to be revised, is thus perpetually unwritten, a life, and work, that consume themselves in the origin where language speaks itself. The emphasis on the performative in queer theory has become, in shorthand, a critique of identity, and of identity politics. But it is also a querying of origin: "coming out," as a defiant political gesture is, in its performative dimension, an enactment of origin's recursive structure. I am gay because I say I am, and, by saying it, I bring my visible identity into line with the condition my utterance retrospectively constitutes. My implicit claim in this chapter is that, quite apart from whatever doctrinal distinctions one would want to make about whatever theoretical arguments seem pressing at any given historical moment, queer theory has provided, at least for me, a way to begin to confront such fundamental questions of a life suspended within the imponderable origin of literary creation.

## Second Chances

This structure of origin is allegorized by James's story "The Middle Years," whose title, in a well-known, but not the less cryptic for that, gesture, he borrowed for the final (unfinished) volume of his autobiography – and which derives, in the story, from the title of the main character's final book.[18] An ailing writer named Dencombe, receiving an advance copy of "The Middle Years," discovers that he has, at last, and belatedly, achieved clarity about his aesthetic project even as death threatens to make him unable to realize that vision. Just then, he meets a devoted young reader, Dr. Hugh. A fuller reading would dwell on, among other things, that erotic relation. In this context, at issue is the story's consideration of revision. It is not merely that Dencombe never stops revising, marking up (as James did) even published copies of his work. More crucially, the story explores what a life given over to revision might be. Notably, it begins with a caesura; Dencombe has completely forgotten his book. This caesura makes possible something like a literal experience of revision: he reads the text again and sees that it is good:

> Everything came back to him, but came back with a wonder, came back above all with a high and magnificent beauty. He read his own prose, he turned his own leaves, and had as he sat there with the spring sunshine on the page an emotion peculiar and intense. His career was over, no doubt, but it was over, when all was said, with *that*. (81)

The encounter with Dr. Hugh makes him dream that "ebbing time" and "shrinking opportunity," that his sense that "he hadn't done what he had wanted" (80) might be vanquished, makes him dream of a second chance whereby his discovery of his capacity could structure his life:

> It came over him in the long quiet hours that only with "The Middle Years" had he taken his flight; only on that day, visited by soundless processions, had he recognised his kingdom. He had had revelation of his range. What he dreaded was the idea that his reputation should stand on the unfinished. It wasn't with his past but with his future that it should properly be concerned. Illness and age rose before him like spectres with pitiless eyes: how was he to bribe such fates to give him the second chance? He had had the one chance that all men have – he had had the chance of life. (90–1)

"I want another go," he later explains; "I want an extension" (95, 6).

It would be easy enough to read in the story a renunciation of the aesthetic life in favor of what might crudely be understood as erotic fulfillment. For the story ends with Dr. Hugh and Dencombe together, Dr. Hugh pronouncing him a "great success," "putting into his young voice the ring of a marriage-bell" (105). Ironized or not, the offered erotic consummation as a substitute for the aesthetic life is turned down by the writer, who, "taking this in," demurs: there are no second chances, except to the very degree that no first chance is ever fully realized. Consummation would, of course, entail a contradiction; only their shared passion for Dencombe's work urges them toward the literal consummation in which they might dispense with it. The more crucial point is that the fantasy of second chances is also the fantasy that work could be something other than "unfinished," that the aesthetic life could be complete. Dencombe's demurral – one of the most frequently quoted passages in James – is a comment on the authorial life suspended in revision:

"A second chance – that's the delusion. There never was to be but one. We work in the dark – we do what we can – we give what we have. Our doubt is our passion and our passion is our task. The rest is the madness of art."

The tones of ethical exhortation are unmistakable; also unmistakable is a typical rhetorical structure in James: it has all the appearance – all the sound, and, to read, all of the satisfactions – of formal closure, but that form conceals, or rather discloses, terms that prove unexpectedly elusive. The satisfying closure comes from the series of repetitions – "We work in the dark – we do what we can – we give what we have" – followed by the (also ostensibly parallel) terms of a chiasmus, sealed by the certainty of the paired copula: "Our doubt is our passion and our passion is our task." Paraphrased, this might assert that doubt – not being certain of our aesthetic vocation, or of writing's purchase on the world – makes for the passion that is, in turn, our ethical imperative. I think, however, that we are meant to be struck by the unresolved heterogeneity of the terms – doubt, passion, passion, task, all linked by "is." This isn't – as it has often been understood – a claim for art's transcendence, and not only because art is put in a possibly ambiguous relation to "madness" (is the genitive objective or subjective; is all art mad, or just a part of it?), but because what is thus defined – doubt and passion, passion and task – forms a totality that excludes art, or produces it as a remainder: "the rest is the madness of art." The satisfying formal closure, whatever it might actually mean, thus bears on everything that *isn't* the statement's primary concern. The last claim, then, links "art" to the unwritten; in context, "the rest" has previously been defined: the "pearl," Dencombe asserts, isn't the public's admiration; "the pearl is the unwritten – the pearl is the unalloyed, the *rest*, the lost!" (104). No doubt, too, James was thinking of *Hamlet*: "the rest is silence." The madness of art is what remains unsaid or unexpressed, consists, perhaps, in the gap between the formal closure of this peroration and its content. That gap, one might say, is life as revision, or as potentiality.

The search for origins might be understood as a search for transcendence, a desire to escape history in a return to an uncorrupted state. In "The Middle Years," when Dencombe is confronted with what loyalty will cost his young friend, the blow – and the renunciation he resolves on, of nothing less than his "second chance" – evokes *Genesis* prior to creation: "Oh yes, after this Dencombe was certainly very ill . . . [I]t was the sharpest shock to him to discover what was at stake for a penniless young man of fine parts. He sat trembling on his bench, staring at the waste of waters, feeling sick with the directness of the blow" (100).[19] The echo of the story's opening – "He sat and stared at the sea, which appeared all surface and twinkle, far shallower than the spirit of man. It was the abyss of human illusion that was the real, the tideless deep. He held his packet, which had come by book-post, unopened on his knee" (77–78) – is perhaps less important for the tone of near despondency that marks the baffling of his hopes than for the formal return to the beginning, with (moreover) its evocation of the unread, the unopened, the forgotten book. In that echo, the story intimates that there dwells, in the baffled hope of second chances, a perpetual return to potentiality in writing's search for its origins. Thus to step outside history is not to secure transcendence for the work of art but, by consigning it to revision, to make it what James calls "a living affair" (1335), structured by the imperfections of created beings; suspended within this return to the origin, the writer strives to hear the exhortations of truthful speech, and to bear the risks of its equivocal importunings.

## Notes

1 Among the exceptions is Valerie Rohy, *Lost Causes Narrative, Etiology, and Queer Theory* (Oxford: Oxford University Press, 2014).

2 Eve Kosofsky Sedgwick, "How to Bring Your Kids Up Gay: The War on Effeminate Boys," in *Tendencies* (Durham: Duke University Press, 1993), 154–64.

3 Kathryn Bond Stockton, *The Queer Child, Or Growing Sideways in the Twentieth Century* (Durham: Duke University Press, 2009).

4 All quotations from the New York Edition prefaces are from the Library of America edition (Mark Wilson and Leon Edel, eds., *Henry James: Literary Criticism, Volume Two: French Writers, Other European Writers, Prefaces to the New York Edition* [New York: The Library of America, 1984]).

5 Henry James, "Introduction to *The Tempest*," in *Henry James: Literary Criticism*, Vol. 1, *Essays on Literature, American Writers, English Writers* (New York: Library of America, 1984), 1205. I discuss this torment in greater detail in Kevin Ohi, *Henry James and the Queerness of Style* (Minneapolis: University of Minnesota Press, 2011), 109–47.

6 J. Hillis Miller, *The Ethics of Reading: Kant, de Man, Eliot, Trollope, James and Benjamin* (New York: Columbia University Press, 1987).

7 "The linking together of words or ideas in speech or thought"; "Consecutiveness, continuity or coherence of ideas"; "a connecting passage, word, or particle"; "the condition of being related to something else by a bond of interdependence, causality, logical sequence, coherence, or the like; relation between things one of which is bound up with, or involved in, another" (OED).

8 Henry James, "Is There a Life After Death?," in *Henry James on Culture: Collected Essays on Politics and the American Social Scene*, ed. Pierre A. Walker (Lincoln: University of Nebraska Press, 1999), 115–27.

9 Foucault, "Parrēsia," trans. Graham Burchell, *Critical Inquiry* vol. 41, no. 2 (Winter 2015): 219–53. See also Michel Foucault, *The Courage of Truth: The Government of Self and Others II, Lectures at the Collège de France, 1983–1984*, ed. Frédéric Gros, trans. Graham Burchell (New York: Palgrave Macmillan, 2011); and *Fearless Speech*, ed. Joseph Pearson (Los Angeles: Semiotext(e), 2001).

10 G. Agamben, *The Fire and the Tale*, trans. Lorenzo Chiesa (Stanford: Stanford University Press, 2017). Translation of *Il fuoco e il racconto* (Rome: Nottetempo, 2014). Hereafter, when there are multiple page references, the first is to the English translation; the second, to the Italian text; and the third, to the French edition, which I also consulted: *Le feu et le récit*, trans. Martin Rueff (Paris: Éditions Payot & Rivages, 2015).

11 La Voix de Gilles Deleuze en Ligne: www2.univ-paris8.fr/deleuze/article.php3? id_article=453; www2.univ-paris8.fr/deleuze/article.php3?id_article=454; and www2.univ-paris8.fr/deleuze/article.php3?id_article=455. My translations.

12 See also Agamben's comments on the thought of thought in Aristotle – in "Bartleby, or, On Contingency," in *Potentialities: Collected Essays in Philosophy*, ed. and trans. Daniel Heller-Roazen (Palo Alto: Stanford University Press, 1999), 243–71.

13 See also "*Se*: Hegel's Absolute and Heidegger's *Ereignis*," in *Potentialities*, 116–37. And Michel Foucault, "Self Writing," in *Ethics: Subjectivity and Truth*, ed. Paul Rabinow, trans. Robert Hurley and others (New York: The New Press, 1997), 207–22.

14 Eve Kosofsky Sedgwick, "Shame, Theatricality, and Performativity: Henry James's *The Art of the Novel*," *Touching Feeling: Affect, Pedagogy, Performativity* (Durham: Duke University Press, 2003), 35–65.

15 A more detailed reading of Sedgwick's argument might begin with its very curious beginning: where Sedgwick looks down toward lower Manhattan at the missing World Trade Center towers and feels (of all things) *shame*. For another account critical of queer theoretical uses of shame, see John Limon, "The Shame of Abu Ghraib," *Critical Inquiry* vol. 33, no. 3 (Spring 2007): 543–72. Leo Bersani is also critical of the way that queer theory's use of shame produces a kind of innocence – which projects all unseemly forms of violence outward on to a persecuting social. Bersani, "Aggression, Shame, and Almodóvar's Art," in *Is the Rectum a Grave? And Other Essays* (Chicago: University of Chicago Press, 2010), 63–82, esp. 68.

16 See Leo Bersani, "Shame on You," in Leo Bersani and Adam Phillips, *Intimacies* (Chicago: University of Chicago Press, 2008), 31–56.

17 Agamben, 134; Agamben cites only the lines about happiness (not those about obligation or absolution). Source: Foucault, *Speech Begins After Death*, ed. Philippe Artières, trans. Robert Bononno (Minneapolis: University of Minnesota Press, 2013), 64. Translated from Foucault, *Le Beau Danger. Entretien de Michel Foucault avec Claude Bonnefoy* (1968), Paris, EHESS, 2011, 56. Agamben cites an Italian translation: Foucault, *Il bel rischio*, trad. It di A Moscati (Napoli: Cronopio, 2013), 49: "Non è la scrittura che è felice, è la

felicità di esistere che è sospesa alla scrittura, il che è un po' diverso." "Sospesa," here translating "*suspendu*," which Bononno renders as "attached," is the word Agamben also often uses to describe the way that potentiality and impotentiality are maintained within the actualization that ostensibly resolves them.

18 Henry James, "The Middle Years," *The Novels and Tales of Henry James: New York Edition*, Vol. XVI (New York: Houghton, Mifflin & Company, Harper & Brothers, and The Macmillan Company, 1909), 75–106.

19 I was thinking of Robert Alter's translation of *Genesis*, which James obviously could not have read (Alter, *Genesis: Translation and Commentary* [New York: W. W. Norton, 1997]): "When God began to create heaven and earth, and the earth then was welter and waste and darkness over the deep and God's breath hovering over the waters, God said, 'Let there be light.'" But the language does appear in a hymn by Bishop William Walsham How: "O'er the shoreless waste of waters / In the world's primeval night, / Moved the quickening Spirit, waking / All things into life and light." (www.histori chymns.com/HymnPage.aspx?HymnalNumber=31&Hymn_Number=268& TextID=2206).

# CHAPTER 7

# All About Our Mothers
## Race, Gender, and the Reparative
### Amber Jamilla Musser

More than twenty-five years after her death from cancer in 1992, Audre
Lorde remains a vibrant figure within queer studies. Her fusion of overlapping and diffuse identities – "Woman, a black lesbian feminist mother
lover poet" as she wrote in *The Cancer Journals* – draws attention to the
importance of working outside of identity politics toward a theorization of
community built on differences rather than an assumed sameness.[1] From
this perspective we see Lorde as a theorist whose work presaged queer
theory's investment in politics of marginality, intersectionality, and affect.[2]
Linda Garber describes Lorde as "stand[ing] historically and rhetorically at
the crux of the so-called generation gap between lesbian-feminist and
queer theoretical notions of identity."[3] While this universalization of
Lorde and her politics has appeal, I am interested in what is left out of
the mix – namely her investment in the fleshy, the feminine, and the
maternal. Elsewhere, I argue that Lorde's theory of the erotic might offer
an alternative formation to Foucault's notions of bodies and pleasures
where corporeal sensation and local community are privileged over subversion.[4] Why can we embrace Lorde as a prototype, a mother, shall we say,
of queer theory, but we have difficulty grappling with what she says about
the mother? That Lorde is admired is a given, but I am interested in the
moments of friction, the work that is not cited, and the types of mother
love that she does not inspire. This chapter delves into Lorde's theories of
the maternal to ask how we might reinvigorate formations of the mother
within women of color feminism in order to rethink racial mattering and
the politics of making reparations.

## Lorde and an Erotics of the Maternal

While Lorde's investment in mothering is marked by her use of the label
mother, her grappling with maternity is also a way to understand her
formulation of the erotic. In "Uses of the Erotic," Lorde describes the

erotic as "a measure between the beginnings of our sense of self and the chaos of our strongest feelings;" it is this feeling that builds community.[5] Further, she explicitly sees that the erotic "as assertion of the lifeforce of women; of that creative energy empowered" both belongs to individuals and cannot be contained by them (55). It is easy to focus on the affective community that Lorde summons with these words, but it is equally significant that she invokes the possibility of a different future by using the trope of children and implicitly connecting the erotic to mothering: "The aim of each thing which we do is to make our lives and the lives of our children richer and more possible." While this moment of optimism, figured through the child, is complicated – especially when we consider the work of Lee Edelman and the imperative of reproductive futurity – I argue that it signals Lorde's use of the maternal as both actual (experiential) and virtual (abstract) modes of being.[6]

In her discussion of the erotic, Lorde shows us the possibilities of maternity and femininity and allows us to reread women of color feminism and lesbian feminism's investment in communities of women as articulating modes of being and connecting that have to do with optimism, care, and eccentric kinship. This maternal is feminine, but not necessarily connected to the act of carrying a child. If conventionally the concept of mothering attaches maternity to absence, origins, and loss, Lorde's version of mothering is emphatically different from such a portrait of negation and loss of self. Lorde's maternity is about the crossings of time and space, in terms of being a daughter and thinking about history, ancestors, and migration. Thus, Lorde works to nuance a position that is frequently overdetermined with the language of essentialism.

We see this expanded version of maternity in her biomythography, *Zami: A New Spelling of My Name*, which begins with an explicit move away from the paternal toward the matrilineal. In the prologue, Lorde writes, "I have felt the age-old triangle of mother father child, with the 'I' at its eternal core, elongate and flatten out into the elegantly strong triad of grandmother mother daughter, with the 'I' moving back and forth flowing in either or both directions as needed."[7] She is also quick to describe the way this grandmother-mother-daughter relationship is felt in her body through the language of landscape, writing, "Woman forever. My body, a living representation of other life older longer wiser. The mountains and valleys, trees, rocks. Sand and flowers and water and stone. Made in earth" (7). While *Zami* tells the story of a black lesbian in New York in the 1950s, these moments of reflection about the mother and place are peppered throughout. The novella itself begins with Audre (Lorde's eponymous heroine) traveling to her mother's homeland: "When I visited Grenada I saw the root of my mother's powers walking through the streets. I thought, this is the country of my foremothers, my forebearing mothers, those Black island women who defined themselves by what they did" (9). This displacement does not last long, but it sets the stage for the recollection of Audre's early years as she comes to terms with the world that her mother has created for her. In her reflections, Audre's mother's omnipotence melds together with an eroticism that becomes Audre's lesbianism, creating a sensuous brew of tactile mother love, lesbian desire, and diasporic yearning. These blend together as Audre brings her mother into a lineage of lesbians: "But that is why to this day I believe that there have always been Black dykes around – in the sense of powerful and woman-oriented women – who would rather have died than use that name for themselves. And that includes my momma" (15). This mother love is born from acts of mothering, which are a form of sensuous pedagogy that also initiate Audre into a community of blackness:

> I remember the warm mother smell caught between her legs, and the intimacy of our physical touching nestled inside of the anxiety
>
> pain like a nutmeg nestled inside its covering of mace.
>
> The radio, the scratching comb, the smell of petroleum jelly, the grip of her knees and my stinging scalp all fall into – the rhythms of a litany, the rituals of Black women combing their daughters' hair. (33)

Lorde's lyricism evokes the sensuality that underlies mothering and infuses the maternal with a type of eroticism. This is rendered even more explicit when Audre narrates her mother's appearance in one of her sexual fantasies: "Years afterward when I was grown, whenever I thought about the way I smelled that day, I would have a fantasy of my mother, her hand wiped dry from the washing, and her apron untied and laid neatly away, looking down upon me lying on the couch, and then, slowly, thoroughly, our touching and caressing each other's most secret places" (78). The epilogue also bears the mark of this mother love. The book ends with these words, "Once *home* was a long way off, a place I had never been to but knew out of my mother's mouth. I only discovered its latitudes when Carriacou was no longer my home. / There it is said that the desire to lie with other women is a drive from the mother's blood" (256).

This fusion of sensuality, maternity, and geography is a powerful indicator of the ways that race *matters*. It matters as a connection to place and to lineages (both abstract and actual), and it comes to matter through the tactile acts of mothering that Lorde describes. Through Lorde, we can see that the materiality of the flesh matters in very particular ways. While she formulates this as a particular attachment to a black and lesbian identity, Lorde enables us to think in terms of solidarity rather than identity and to think difference relationally instead of through a rhetoric of inclusion that we might be tempted to utilize given her own claimed sexual and racial identities. In other words, I am not claiming that Lorde speaks for difference because she speaks as a black lesbian. This would repeat the silencing of the black queer female body that Sharon P. Holland critiques in *The Erotic Life of Racism*. Instead, I argue that Lorde opens the door toward thinking about difference in corporeal terms.[8] I also think that Lorde gives us another perspective on racial mattering, which Mel Chen uses to describe the way race works to produce matter in different modalities. In their analysis of the harms done to children with lead paint, Chen articulates a hierarchy of children's bodies that become apparent over concerns with safety and the various structures that value some children's lives over others. In the narrative Chen provides, fear over the white child's impaired cognition spurs recalls of lead toys without acknowledging the conditions of the Asian people who made them and the black children who also get caught in the crossfire as the rhetoric of lead exposure becomes a way to signify poor African-American parenting choices.[9] Chen's analysis shows the way that race matters in that it differently animates bodies and our responses to them. Lorde's version of the maternal also articulates an understanding of racial mattering, but it is through touch. She asks: How does race impact what we feel when bodies touch, what are the histories and places summoned? The structural components of race still undergird the matter of race, but in addition to an abstract hierarchy of marginalization, Lorde tells us how this difference feels and invites us to rescript prevailing narratives using these sensational differences.

## The Legacy of Our Lorde

My move to Lorde is part of a larger gesture to incorporate women of color feminism, especially its intersections with lesbian feminism, into contemporary queer theory. Scholars such as Roderick Ferguson, José Esteban Muñoz, Linda Garber, and Grace Hong have worked with these feminisms to produce new lineages of queer theory that are centered on race and structural inequalities.[10] Hong argues that the discourse of women of color feminism emerges from liberal capitalism – its exclusions and values produce the conditions of possibility for this mode of thinking – but that its product marks spaces of rupture within this system. Hong writes, "Women of color feminist practice marked the return of the repressed of possessive individualism, and thus emerged as the *crisis* of capital's national phase, at the very moment when capital was transitioning from its national to its global phase. It did so by suggesting modes of subjectivity and collectivity unimaginable under nationalism" (xiv). I am dwelling on Hong's description of women of color feminism because of the explicit connections that she draws between it and the state, capitalism, and liberal subjectivity. These formations have traditionally been aligned with the Oedipal subject, so these feminisms' protest against them also illuminates new models of kinship.

Through their attention to the way affective and sensual constructions of community illuminate the embeddedness of the familial within histories of capitalism, colonialism, and racism, Lorde and other women of color feminisms provide arresting foils for thinking about non-Oedipal possibilities. In particular, they hit on the politics of the matter of the mother. The mother here is more than psychic space or actual person; it is flesh, place, and touch in addition to political alternative. Often, however, the maternal is not addressed when others take up women of color feminism. In *Aberrations in Black*, Roderick Ferguson, for example, draws on women of color feminism to formulate queer of color critique, writing "Queer of color analysis extends women of color feminism by investigating how intersecting racial, gender, and sexual practices antagonize and/or conspire with the normative investments of nation states and capital."[11] For Ferguson, women of color feminism helps to identify the ways in which race, gender, and sexuality are produced through capitalism and the ways in which capitalism coopts these formations. The task of queer of color critique is to "ask the question of what possibilities they offer for agency. We must see the gendered and eroticized elements of racial formations as offering ruptural – i.e. critical – possibilities" (17). In particular, Ferguson gravitates toward women of color feminism's theorization of coalition and difference because they "attempted to devise notions of culture and agency that would alienate heteropatriarchy and liberal ideology" (116). Black lesbian feminism especially offers a way to negate heteropatriarchy: "Black lesbian feminists helped to render the imagination into a social practice that utilized cultural forms precisely because of the overlapping gender, sexual, class, and racial exclusions that constituted forms of nationalism" (118). In this way black lesbian feminism could be said to enable an imagination outside of what already was.

In later consolidations of queer of color critique, women of color feminisms become largely synonymous with Lorde, whose work on the erotic especially becomes a touchstone for those who wish to take up women of color feminism in the service of offering critique and the possibility of something that has not quite arrived.[12] In narrating Lorde's contribution to imagining an anticapitalist, antiracist, and antipatriarchal world as separate from her attachment to lesbian feminism, we see a tendency to view lesbian feminism as white and racist, severing both women of color from this strand of feminism and ignoring the antiracist work that white feminists performed.[13] We also see that black feminism becomes attached to its own type of pastness. By using Lorde, who died in 1992, as the voice of black feminism, the knowledge contributions of black feminism are framed as passé (even if prescient). Even in progressive projects, which aim to invigorate theory with the bodies of black women, black women occupy the space of historical stasis. As we can see through the persistent use of Lorde, black female theories come to symbolize a type of unchanging otherness from which more contemporary theory is drawn. Holland writes, "But the categories 'black,' 'colored,' female, queer point to a persistent problem in queer theorizing – how to have our queer theory and our feminism while still seeing the colored body or how to have our colored criticism while still seeing the female and the queer body and so on."[14] Further, Holland argues "her figuration at this point in our critical history looks profoundly like that of . . . a dead zone (think 'impasse')." By this Holland means that she is a reminder of historical wrongs, but not assimilated into a political future.

More richly, however, Holland argues that Lorde's critique should be read as a moment where black feminism illuminates the importance of thinking about different types of relationships to history. That is to say that objectification impacts women differently depending on their material conditions. Holland emphasizes the importance of black feminist thought for thinking through the erotic by using this antipornography moment as a mark of the specificity of the black female body's experience. In positioning difference at the center of the erotic, Holland wants to show how it has been erased by queer theory and ways that it need not be this way. She writes, "absenting *these* somewhat conservative black feminist opinions from the women of color intellectual project performs damaging work" (59). In citing this moment as a rupture between sexuality studies and black feminism (and lesbian feminism), it is easy to see where conflict between lesbian feminism and queer theory might occur. However, there are benefits to reading this moment into queer theory because it complicates our understanding of desire and helps to work against much of queer theory's tendency to privilege discourses of sexuality without acknowledging the work of race or gender.

When we work with Lorde, the theories that have had staying power are those that engage with theories of marginalization and community. That these theories are also attached to lesbian feminism and femininity is explained away historically. With her critique of structural inequality within the landscape of sexuality, Lorde is understood to be thwarting "our" progress toward sexual liberation. Lorde's unwillingness to embrace pornography and S&M becomes a symptom of lesbian feminism's antisex values despite the fact that Lorde herself had a deep investment in the sensual and the erotic. This characterization of Lorde casts aside her particular vision of sexuality and works to produce her in the image of the mammy – asexual, sage, nurturing, and beloved. While Lorde argued against sexual practices that she found objectifying, she advocated for a diffuse nongenital sexuality – something that might be discussed alongside Michel Foucault's bodies and pleasures. Lorde describes the erotic in physically diffuse terms. She finds it, "In the way my body stretches to music and opens into response, hearkening to its deepest rhythms, so every level upon which I sense also opens to the erotically satisfying experience, whether it is dancing, building a bookcase, writing a poem, examining an idea."[15] At the end of the essay, Lorde writes "For not only do we touch our most profoundly creative source, but we do that which is female and self-affirming in the face of a racist, patriarchal, and anti-erotic society" (59). The multiplicity of the feminine is part of Lorde's articulation of the maternal and the work of mothering. Rather than restrict the feminine to a site of reproduction and absence, Lorde's invocation of the maternal opens the feminine toward a space where touching across difference and relating to otherness are profoundly important. As I argued in my analysis of Lorde's theorization of the maternal, scripting mothering as pedagogical gives us a way to access the particular sets of knowledges that inhere in occupying marginalized positions. This knowledge is transmitted through sensual exchanges and works to shape worldviews and possibilities. Building on this understanding of mothering, Alexis P. Gumbs argues that the black mother is political and pedagogical. She writes, "the pedagogical work of mothering is exactly the site where a narrative will either be reproduced or interrupted. The work of Black mothering, the teaching of a set of social values that challenge a social logic which believes that we, the children of Black mothers, the queer, the deviant should not exist, is queer work."[16] For Gumbs, this politicization of mothering is queer because it speaks to people and experiences that have traditionally been denied recognition, but can be called into existence through the care and optimism that is part of mothering and its movement toward a more progressive future.

## Moraga, Touch, and the Politics of Making Maternal Reparations

In order to amplify our understanding of the mother, I turn now to Cherríe Moraga's writings in the 1980s. They echo Lorde's call for a return to the mother through touch, but Moraga is more attentive to the vulnerability that a turn toward touch entails and she explicitly formulates the return to the mother as a political gesture of making reparations. This alternate version of maternity gives us another way to think about the process of grappling with difference.

Like Lorde, Moraga understands racial and gendered difference through the figure of the mother, but this difference is overtly politicized. Instead of Lorde's sensual brew of grandmother-mother-daughter relations, Moraga's rediscovery of her mother occurs through the filter of white supremacy, capitalism, and racism. "La Güera" begins with the acknowledgement of the difference between her and her mother: "I am the very well-educated daughter of a woman who, by the standards in this country, would be considered largely illiterate."[17] For Moraga, this difference had been the source of internalized racism and classism: "I have had to confront the fact that much of what I value about being Chicana, about my family, has been subverted by anglo culture and my own cooperation with it" (46). However, as Moraga becomes more politically entrenched in feminism and as she awakens toward her lesbianism, she begins to understand these differences as a matter of structural inequality and she works to embrace her mother, Chicana identity, and the possibility of revolution. This means refusing many positions of privilege that she inhabited due to her white father: "I am a woman with a foot in both worlds. I refuse the split. . . . The real power, as you and I know well, is collective. I can't afford to be afraid of you, nor you of me. If it takes head-on collusions, let's do it" (50–1). The mother is central to this new vision in that she is a symbol of the space of difference, yet she is also incidental in that it is *through* this love for her that a new politics and ethics are born. Moraga's insistence on thinking about difference as the embodiment of structural inequality positions the mother as that which has been created as external through colonialism, capitalism, and patriarchy. Though this version of the mother is created through different sets of violence and exclusion, her position on the outside also offers an opportunity to think otherwise.

This explicit externalization of the mother means that the pedagogical work of mothering that Lorde describes is rescripted as a form of political work, a mode of making reparations, a process that we might see as allowing an understanding of otherness altogether. In her discussion of the mother-infant relationship, Melanie Klein describes making reparations as coming to terms with separation from the mother and the guilt and hatred that surround her absence and the infant's dependence. She writes, "in our unconscious phantasy we make good the injuries which we did in phantasy, and for which we still unconsciously feel very guilty. This *making reparation* is in my view, a fundamental element in love and in all human relationships."[18] Drawing on this relationship between making reparations and the social, David Eng writes,

> If the infant succeeds in mitigating this psychic violence, then it can "repair," "reinstate," and "restore" the mother as a separate object – indeed, a separate subject with agency and will – initiating an object relation not just with her but with the rest of the world beyond her and the many creatures in it. From this perspective, we might describe reparation as the psychic condition of possibility for the precipitation of both the (m)other and the social worlds themselves.[19]

Through making reparations, then, the possibility of otherness emerges. The ability to mark difference as a form of relationality allows us to imagine the space of the maternal – the space of the other – as a space where racial and gender difference might reside in the multiple.

It is this plurality of difference that Sandra Soto highlights in her discussion of Moraga's efforts to become brown through her lesbianism, which I read as her form of making reparations. Moraga, she writes:

> rearranges and reconfigures the epistemological and ontological tropes that we expect to find in accounts of difference, and – to put it rather schematically for the moment – identifies her sexuality as "brown"; explains that her ethnonationalist politics became available to her only through her public avowal of a lesbian identity; hinges her narratives of lesbian initiation and desire for butch competency on race; writes an urgent manifesto for a "queer Aztlan," and elaborates a butch identity that is as resolutely maternal as it is masculine.[20]

In Soto's analysis of Moraga's mode of becoming brown as a form of sexuality, we gain an alternate understanding of Moraga's use of touch. For example, the poem "For the Color of My Mother," which begins with these words: "*I am a white girl gone brown to the blood color of my mother / speaking to her through the unnamed part of the mouth / the wide-arched muzzle of brown women*" frames brownness as inhabitable through the parameters of sex.[21] Unsurprisingly, this racialized version of touch springs from the maternal, which Moraga alludes to in "La Dulce Culpa":

> What kind of lover have you made me, mother
> who drew me into bed with you at six/at sixteen
> oh, even at sixty-six you do still
> lifting up the blanket with one arm
> lining out the space for my body with the other...
>
> (8)

Love, here, is not abstract, but about touch and the ability to be touched. Throughout *Loving in the War Years,* Moraga's embrace of her brown mother is literal. In another essay, she writes, "if I were to build my womanhood on this self-evident truth, it is the love of the Chicana, the love of myself as a Chicana I had to embrace, no white man. Maybe this ultimately was the cutting difference between my brother and me. To be a woman fully necessitated my claiming the race of my mother. My brother's sex was white. Mine, brown" (86). Love, here, is doing a lot. Moraga's love understands racial difference and its accompanying emotions of guilt and shame. That Moraga is embracing her mother allows us to see ways gender is also aligned with brownness and difference. Further, that the embrace is between women allows us to figure this love in explicitly queer terms since Moraga describes her lesbianism as her mode of accessing this difference. Recall that in "La Güera," Moraga writes, "When I finally lifted the lid to my lesbianism, a profound connection with my mother reawakened in me. It wasn't until I acknowledged and confronted my lesbianism in the flesh that my heartfelt identification with and empathy for my mother's oppression – due to being poor, uneducated and Chicana – was realized. My lesbianism is the avenue through which I have learned the most about silence and oppression, and it continues to be the most tactile reminder to me that we are not free human beings" (44). Here, Moraga uses touch and sex to love (recover – a word that frequently turns up in her writing) her mother and to forge a bridge with difference.

Moraga's relationship with touch, however, is complicated. In her extended vision of matrilinearity, Moraga incorporates figures like La Malinche, the translator for Cortez who was accused of betrayal for working with him. La Malinche, whom she refers to as La Chingada (the fucked one), becomes a figure who stands for the vulnerability of Chicana/Mexicana women. Moraga writes, "If the simple act of sex then – the penetration itself – implies the female's filthiness, non-humanness, it is no wonder Chicanas often divorce ourselves from the conscious recognition of our own sexuality" (119). Even as touch and sexuality are part of her mode of accessing brownness, Moraga has difficulty with this form of vulnerability. She writes, "I have not wanted to admit that my deepest personal sense of myself has not quite 'caught up' with my 'woman-identified' politics ... I have sometimes taken society's fear and hatred of lesbians to bed with me. I have sometimes hated my lover for loving me. I have sometimes felt 'not woman enough' for her. I have sometimes felt 'not man enough'" (49). In Moraga's partial identification with butchness, we can read, following Jack Halberstam's analysis of stone butchness, an aversion to touch and the vulnerability that it produces.[22] This theme also comes through in her poem *Passage* when she writes "So that when you touch me / and I long to freeze, not feel / what hungry longing I used to know / nor taste in you a want / I fear will burn / my fingers to their roots" (38). Moraga does narrate coming to terms with touch by merging her desire for women with her desire to unite with other Chicanas. This reparative work doesn't foreclose vulnerability, but brings Moraga to a different understanding of it. Sex, desire, touch, and the communal come together in Moraga's description:

> Yo recuerdo a Carmela – su mano trazando los círculos de mis senos around and around bringing her square small hands down, shoving my legs apart, opening my lips hovering, holding me there, her light breath on my thighs. No me lame, pero espera, mirándome, diciendo, "¡Qué rica! ¡Ay mujer, qué rica tú eres!" And I can't quite believe my ears, she is talking about the taste of me *before* su boca lo sabe. She knows *before* hand and mouth make it possible. She tells me my name, my taste, in Spanish. She fucks me in Spanish. And I am changed. It is a different kind of passion ... something remembered. I think, *soy mujer en español*. No macha pero mujer. Soy Chicana – open to all kinds of assaults. (132)

Fusing making reparations with sex makes it clear that the stakes are powerful, political, and embodied. Additionally, Moraga's writing makes clear that touch opens toward other sensations – smell, taste, sound. The narrative Moraga provides in this instance is that learning to love her mother means learning to love herself and learning to love her femininity and her brownness and to accept being touched. In granting access to her body, Moraga joins touch with vulnerability – an idea that Ann Cvetkovich traces back to Freud's notion of trauma.[23] Yet Moraga's insistence on linking this with pleasure and the possibility of mutual touching suggests a sense of mutual vulnerability, mutual embrace, and mutual pleasure. This version of touch is about being in the world in the present, articulating multiple aspects of sexuality, and the possibility of making reparations. Working through the maternal and her desire for her mother reorganizes her relationship to touch. Her body comes to have a different meaning when she associates it with touch. That this new spatial awareness is simultaneous to Moraga's decision to learn Spanish, her mother tongue, is significant in its alignment of the maternal, desire, and lesbianism. If touch is our access point into the relational, Moraga illustrates the ways that race and gender exert their own pressures and histories.

## Toward Recuperating These Other Maternalisms

The question that comes to mind at this juncture, then, is why the focus on Lorde, what about the work of other women of color feminists? In thinking about the dominance of Lorde's legacy, we might dwell on her frequent use of the second person, which permits readers to position themselves within her words and identify with them. In relation to that, we might also think critically about the appeal of imagining Lorde as mammy, a formulation in which black female sexuality is diluted in favor of nurturing others. We might also argue that Lorde's death has augmented a fondness for her in a way that Moraga's continued discussion of current issues has made her controversial. In particular, Moraga's *Xicana Codex's* elegy for butches has been criticized for being transphobic and her 2009 essay "Still Loving in the War Years" offers a negative assessment of current LGBTQ movements. In addition to decrying the focus on marriage equality, she takes trans activism to task for reinforcing gender norms. In her understanding of trans, the identity forces people to choose a gender rather than residing in the space of ambivalence: "the transgender movement at large, and plain old peer pressure, will preempt young people from residing in that queer, gender-ambivalent site for as long and as deeply as is necessary."[24] Given the capaciousness of trans, critics argued that Moraga based her arguments on an imagined trans community of post-operative people who live in heterosexual communities while denying the breadth of ways to be trans.[25]

Despite Moraga's difficulty grappling with transness, we might think about how to work with her theorization of the maternal as a version of making reparations particularly because it requires an acknowledgment of one's embeddedness within racial, gender, and classed hierarchies and looks toward assuming responsibility for violence while finding ways to embrace difference. This is not about a politics of community formation, but a politics that is reliant on understanding one's identity as malleable. One might approach the mother, for example, by becoming brown, bridging difference through incorporation. This may not be literal, but it does speak to a particular ethics of reading. Muñoz and Hong both draw extensively on Moraga and this articulation of relational difference in identity. Hong writes, "Moraga's analysis secures an understanding that different racial and gender formations are not produced in isolation, but relationally ... she also refuses the project of valorizing such subjects through an identity politics" (ix). For Hong, "women of color feminism is not a reified subject position but a reading practice, a 'way of making sense of' that reveals the contradictions of the racialized and gendered state" (x). Similarly, Muñoz argues that Moraga (and Gloria Anzaldúa) produces an early articulation of disidentification, the critical hermeneutic that locates the performances of self at the juncture between essentialism and constructivism to produce identities in difference. Muñoz writes, "these identities-in-difference emerge from a failed interpellation within the dominant public sphere. Their emergence is predicated on their ability to disidentify with the mass public and instead, through this disidentification, contribute to the function of a counterpublic sphere."[26] Muñoz and Hong center Moraga's ability to articulate identity as always relational and potentially disruptive of the norm. This, however, is a difficult aspect of considering identity. As Muñoz warns, these performances of disidentification risk being illegible and collapsing into overdetermination. In Moraga's emphasis on the possibilities of becoming, especially in the way that she describes becoming-brown through embracing her mother and lesbianism, we see the slipperiness of relationality, we see the vulnerability, the insistence on the present, and the ambiguity of the future. Lorde's erotic with its optimistic future, mutable affective qualities, and more hidden maternal offers no such danger.[27]

The differential legacies of Moraga and Lorde bring us to another reason to rethink racialized maternity in feminist and queer theory. By differentiating between diffuse modes of apprehending the mother and the stakes of these different encounters, we gain rich non-Oedipal sensual universes and numerous possibilities for thinking about the politics of solidarity and coalition. Importantly, these new maternalisms offer the possibilities of producing new world orders without reifying the mother as essentially female or feminine. She is a set of practices, a mode of touching, or a figure through which one understands difference. In both scenarios, she offers tools to think against white supremacy, capitalism, and racism.

## Notes

1 Audre Lorde, *The Cancer Journals* (Argyle, NY: Spinsters Ink, 1980), 25.

2 See for example: Jennifer Nash, "Practicing Love: Black Feminism, Love-Politics, and Post-Untersectionality," *Meridians: Feminism, Race, Transnationalism* vol. 11, no. 2 (2013): 1–24; and Sara Ahmed, *Living a Feminist Life* (Durham: Duke University Press, 2017).

3 Linda Garber, *Identity Poetics: Race, Class, and the Lesbian-Feminist Roots of Queer Theory* (New York: Columbia University Press, 2001), 97.

4 Amber Jamilla Musser, *Sensational Flesh: Race, Power, and Masochism* (New York: New York University Press, 2014).

5 Audre Lorde, "Uses of the Erotic: The Erotic as Power," *Sister Outsider* (Berkeley: Crossing Press, [1984] 2007), 54.

6 Edelman gives us the most direct rejoinder against wholeheartedly embracing the figure of the child and reproductive futurity, but we might also think with Kathryn Bond Stockton's formulation of the sideways growth of children and Jack Halberstam's arguments about the queerness of childhood as complicating Lorde's assertions. Lee Edelman, *No Future: Queer Theory and the Death Drive* (Durham: Duke University Press, 2004); Kathryn Bond Stockton, *The Queer Child, or Growing Sideways in the Twentieth Century* (Durham: Duke University Press, 2009); and J. Jack Halberstam, *Gaga Feminism: Sex, Gender, and the End of Normal* (New York: Beacon Press, 2012).

7 Audre Lorde, *Zami: A New Spelling of My Name* (Freedom, CA: Crossing, 1982), 7. All subsequent references cited in text.

8 Sharon Patricia Holland, *The Erotic Life of Racism* (Durham: Duke University Press, 2011).

9 Mel Y. Chen, *Animacies: Biopolitics, Racial Mattering, and Queer Affect* (Durham: Duke University Press, 2012).

10 José Esteban Muñoz, *Disidentifications: Queers of Color and the Performance of Politics* (Minneapolis: University of Minnesota Press, 1999); Grace Kyung-won Hong, *The Ruptures of American Capital; Women of Color Feminism and the Culture of Immigrant Labor* (Minneapolis: University of Minnesota Press, 2006); Roderick Ferguson, *Aberrations in Black: Towards a Queer of Color Critique* (Minneapolis: University of Minnesota Press, 2003); and Garber, *Identity Poetics*.

11 Ferguson, *Aberrations in Black*, 4.

12 Holland, *The Erotic Life of Racism*; and Amber Jamilla Musser "Re-membering: Adding Lesbian Feminist Mother Poet to Black," *No Tea, No Shade* (Durham: Duke University Press, 2016), 346–61.

13 Clare Hemmings, *Why Stories Matter: The Political Grammar of Feminist Theory* (Durham: Duke University Press, 2011); Becky Thompson, "Multiracial Feminism: Recasting the Chronology of Second Wave Feminism," *Feminist Studies* vol. 28, no. 2 (2002): 337–60; Victoria Hesford, *Feeling Women's Liberation* (Durham: Duke University Press, 2013).

14 Holland, *The Erotic Life of Racism*, 66.

15 Lorde, "Uses of the Erotic," 56.

16  Alexis Pauline Gumbs, "We Can Learn To Mother Ourselves: The Queer Survival of Black Feminism 1968–1996" (PhD diss., Duke University, 2010), 51.

17  Cherríe Moraga, *Loving in the War Years: Lo Que Nunca Pasó Por Sus Labios* (Boston: South End Press, 2000), 42.

18  Melanie Klein, "Love, Guilt, and Reparation," in *Love, Guilt and Reparation: and Other Works 1921–1945*, Vol. 1 (New York: Simon and Schuster, 2002), 312–13.

19  David L. Eng, "Reparations and the Human," *Columbia Journal of Gender and Law* 21 (2011): 574.

20  Sandra Soto, *Reading Chican@ Like a Queer: The De-mastery of Desire* (Austin: University of Texas Press, 2010), 18.

21  Moraga, "For the Color of My Mother," *Loving in the War Years*, 52, 53 (italics in original).

22  Jack Halberstam, *Female Masculinity* (Durham: Duke University Press, 1998).

23  Ann Cvetkovich, *An Archive of Feeling: Trauma, Sexuality, and Lesbian Public Cultures* (Durham: Duke University Press, 2003).

24  Cherríe Moraga and Celia Herrera Rodriguez, *A Xicana Codex of Changing Consciousness: Writings, 2000–2010* (Durham: Duke University Press, 2011), 184.

25  Morgan Collado, http://xqsimagazine.com/2012/04/13/on-actually-keeping-queer-queer-a-response-to-cherrie-moraga/.

26  Muñoz, *Disidentifications*, 7.

27  Lyndon Gill, "In the Realm of Our Lorde: Eros and Poet Philosopher," *Feminist Studies* vol. 40, no. 1 (2014): 169–89; and Musser, "Re-membering Lorde."

# PART III

## *Reading Queerly*

# CHAPTER 8

# Camp Performance and the Case of Discotropic

*Nick Salvato*

## Dis. Go.

*Really, Mary?* I recall some pointed phrase like this one, accompanied by some relatedly pointed gesture like eye rolling, obtaining as my first, unvarnished response to the invitation to tarry once more with camp. After a half-century of self-aware writing about camp, preceded by at least as much everyday life, artistic, and critical discourse that has since been genealogically associated with the newer writing to constitute a camp tradition, I could be forgiven for wondering, "Whither, now, the theorizing of camp" (and for asking you to hear in that musing the anxiety, "Wither, now, the theorizing of camp?").[1] Indeed, the accumulation of perspectives on camp has produced some settled truths that, strictly speaking, no new writing needs to rehearse; of these truths, and as I have begun the new writing with bitchy reluctance that is itself camp, I will rehearse the most salient:

(1) Camp is a style of relating, a process of active reception and negotiation, typifying queer community formations of the early and mid-twentieth century, where it manifests as a survival strategy in the face of an inimical world, yet camp has also manifested in mainstream sociocultural formations.

(2) The camp enthusiast responds to an object, text, code, or convention, usually from a dominant and dominating order, with a combination of abiding attachment and parodic dismissal, which makes of camp a qualified mockery and ambivalent assassination.

(3) Camping on an object also crucially involves some commentary on systems of sex, gender, and sexuality.

Demonstrating these propositions and their imbrication, keen writing on camp has produced other compelling effects. First, this writing has tended to route its ruminations through specific case studies on which careful attention, thick description, and detailed interpretation are lavished; camp has proven so slippery a character that, seemingly, she will wriggle right out of view and grasp unless she is caught in one of her sustained unfoldings. Among other reasons, the absence of foregrounding such a focused case study has opened to contestation Susan Sontag's landmark 1964 essay, "Notes on 'Camp,'" which is nonetheless rightly nominated as a groundbreaking entry in the annals of camp criticism; a reader could plausibly come away from (re)engaging Sontag with the sense that, if perhaps she had dwelt more abidingly with, say, the Wildean epigrams whose camp brilliance fascinate her so palpably in the moment of writing this essay – rather than enacting the semi-flailing maneuver to throw a lot of potential camp items at the wall and to see what sticks – then the piece would age more immune to the critique that its surveying reach is too promiscuously surficial (even as some camp, including this performative essay, is promiscuous and surficial).[2] By contrast, a comparatively over-looked 1962 essay by filmmaker and performance artist Jack Smith, "The Perfect Filmic Appositeness of Maria Montez," also worth regarding as groundbreaking camp criticism, escapes the "moldiness" that it associates with Montez's B-movies – the signature quality that makes them available for camp appreciation – because the *closeness*, a simultaneous intimacy and attentiveness, with which Smith lingers over Montez's corpus also consti-tutes a *sharpness*, thereby persisting as a model for those who would conceptualize camp.[3] More recent writing on camp benefits similarly from highlighting case studies: for instance, Pamela Robertson Wojcik's exam-ination of screen star Mae West, José Esteban Muñoz's engagement with performance artist Carmelita Tropicana, Matthew Tinkcom's meditations on Andy Warhol's pop art, and Tanya González and Eliza Rodriguez y Gibson's uptake of television series *Ugly Betty*.[4]

Second, writing on camp soars when its queer poses and intimations are not strictly queer but attend to other markers of identity, community, and sociality – that is, when it is robustly intersectional. All of the pieces cited above evidence not only the value of the case study but also the necessity of thinking about sex, gender, and sexuality in their embeddedness with other elements of sociocultural schemes, whether in Smith's pointing to the coloniality and Orientalism marking Montez's films, Robertson's unpacking of the vexed status of race in West's performances, Tinkcom's attentiveness to class, and Muñoz, Gonzalez, and Rodriguez y Gibson's emphases on ethnic dimensions of feminist camp. Alongside these inter-sectional analyses, others that constitute landmarks in the theorizing of camp include Moe Meyer's introduction to the pivotal anthology *The Politics and Poetics of Camp*, which investigates race, class, and protest in the political performance art of Joan Jett Blakk; and Judith Butler's reading of *Paris Is Burning*, which comprehends the raced and classed experiences of the camping subjects in the film.[5]

This essay takes a cue from such writings named by also dwelling with a case study, chosen in part for illuminating ways in which understanding the queerness of its camp means also understanding its black and trans facets: director and choreographer niv Acosta's *Discotropic*, a performance piece recently presented at a number of venues and that I experienced at New York City's 2016 COIL festival. I have fastened onto *Discotropic* for two additional reasons – one political, one affective – that I believe ought to animate any further writing that we do on camp, which must build upon yet also push in different directions from camp's critical legacy.[6] Where politics are concerned (and I am mindful of various robustly challenged accusations of camp's putative apoliticism), I do not – cannot – at this historical juncture think that any more ink should be spilled over camp that does not spill blood; that is, if we still toil with camp, it had better be camp that we can declare progressive, and better yet radical. For this reason, looking to experimental work in live performance like *Discotropic* offers a useful way to understand what remains special – and in need of promoting – about camp as it gets newly animated. Indeed, today's live queer performance, distinguished from efforts in cinema, television, and allied media, is *the* richest site at which to recognize camp's progressive inflections. As for feeling, though much camp remains arch, brittle, ironic, or witty – all well-worn modifiers with which, rightly, to comprehend camp – new scholarship must, following the humanities' affective turn, investigate too the less expected moods and tonal colorations of camp, including the nervous, melancholic, and indifferent.[7] *Discotropic*'s version of camp opens a window onto just such less expected affective flavors and savors; like other contemporary experiments in camp performance, Acosta and his collaborators understand that for camp to evolve, maintain relevance, and pack a punch, it must acquire dimensions largely absent from the genealogy traceable from Wilde and West to Warhol and Tropicana. This understanding is slyly intimated in the very name of *Discotropic*, only written in the program and never voiced in the piece's presentation and thus available to be heard dually: (1) as "Disco-trah-pic," signaling the use of (post)disco camp to disrupt the positioning of the black performing body as tropical or exotic – and thus aligning with camp strategies familiar from the writings indexed above and the artistic practices that they salute; and (2) as "Disco-troh-pic," troping or turning aspects of the piece *away* from camp familiarities and into a disco of altered rhythms, textures, and affects.

## Nerves' Acosta

For reworking at COIL, *Discotropic*, formerly presented at such unlike
yet equally noteworthy locations as the Kimberly Project and the New
Museum, was staged in a yet more unlike and unorthodox – and thus, for
this piece, altogether fitting – venue: a large, high-ceilinged, post-industrial
basement space in the Westbeth Artists' Housing complex on Manhattan's
lower west side. As Westbeth's website explains of its layered history,
the thirteen-building complex was originally the site of Bell Laboratories
from 1868 to 1966 and thus the place where "the first talking movie,
the condenser microphone, the first TV broadcast, and the first binary
computer were demonstrated"; since 1970, the repurposed complex has
featured several hundred affordable "live-work spaces for artists of all
disciplines and their families," and today it also features "large and small
commercial spaces, performance and rehearsal spaces and . . . studios both
individual and communal."[8] To perform *Discotropic* at this historically and
architecturally complex location resonates with and, in a fashion, reacti-
vates the location's competing qualities in evocative ways: like most of the
former and current residents at Westbeth, Acosta and his collaborators
work outside mainstream norms and with modest resources; at the same
time, they are using camp to comment on a history of commercial mass
spectacle of just the sort associated with and made by companies like Bell.

   The essentially unaltered, underground, cavernous room selected for
*Discotropic*'s presentation – in the words of reviewer Cory Tamler, "read-
[ing] more as ruin than basement" – conjures the aura of paradoxically
lively decay that kitsch theorist Celeste Olalquiaga has identified as seminal
to many incarnations of mass modernity's "artificial kingdoms."[9] The
camp performer casts a simultaneously critical and ludic eye on such
constructs. And turning the screw further still in *Discotropic* at Westbeth,
Acosta and his collaborators take whatever is ludic about the critical
reinhabitation of a Bell basement and allow it to gain in complexity
through giving it over to other tonalities. How this maneuver may work
phenomenally on audiences, from the beginning of the *Discotropic* experience, is suggested obliquely in Tamler's account of the piece's preamble,
worth elaborating upon:

> We were led in small groups through Westbeth's basement hallways: white,
> with a thick black line well over my height that I later learned was the
> Hurricane Sandy floodline. As we entered the performance space, an usher
> gave us permission to wander all of it, except for the raised stage in the
> center. I wandered . . . The audience already present was gathered at the

mouth of one of [three] side chambers, looking in at a dancer in a rubbery cape and goggles, dragging his feet through fine black dust, an explorer feeling his way around an unfamiliar space. The other chambers were empty and I played explorer myself (so far as I noticed, I was the only one). I found them lined with nylon strings glowing in blacklight that also revealed marks and smears on the walls. Deep at the back of this chamber's throat was a video camera and, crouching, I saw my face dark and large in its screen, framed/backlit in purple by the doorway behind me leading back out into the main room. I gave a little wave and walked back out into the purple. ("Past Versions")

Tamler emphasizes the "play. . ." involved in her "explor[ation]" of the space and invites us to read it as parallel to and echoing the play of curiously attired dancer Justin Allen; yet this play is not merely playful for either performer or audience member.

If the basement is a "ruin," the ruination's predicates are both less and more recent and include the uncanny reminder of Hurricane Sandy's destructive force, inscribed in the floodline on the walls whose blackness literally directs us as we follow its path to consider the other meanings and stakes of blackness aswirl in *Discotropic.* Two of the side chambers, situated at the far end of the playing space, are outfitted, respectively, not just with camera and glowing strings or "fine black dust," but also with potted artificial plants and industrial junk, representing the more jocular and sinister sides – both underlined as creepy – of modern mass production and its legacies. As these trappings of *mise-en-scène* orient us to consider the labor undergirding such production, we are likewise oriented to read Allen's dancing as fraught and haunted. He is not just dragging his feet but tapping and shuffling them and, in the process, creating a circle from the fine black dust, connoting all at once some of the various, encircling sites of capitalist production at which the black body has been excruciated in industrial modernity: the plantation with its dirt; the mine with its coal; yet also, as the light flickeringly catches the dust and makes specks glow (mirroring the disturbingly glowing "marks and smears on the wall" of another chamber), the glittering stages and silver screens where the imperative to tap or shuffle may be highly constraining, not unlike the other historical directives that demand black laborers to "perform or else."[10] In turn, the enclosed feeling produced by Tamler's performance for the camera in the adjacent chamber prompts her to name that space a "throat," where her obliged "crouching" thus constitutes something like capture and consumption; having framed her performance thus, the "little wave" that she makes to the camera reads as hesitant, even shaky. *Uncanny, creepy, fraught, haunted, constraining, enclosed, hesitant, shaky*: these modifiers with which I have adorned my account of *Discotropic*'s prelude aim to indicate the predominant ethos of *unease* – not usually the primary ethos of camp – with which the gambit ushers audiences into the experience of the piece.

The unease is compounded by the deliberately ambivalent manner in which Allen's body is sexualized. Beneath the vinyl cape that Tamler mentions (evoking a world of bondage, yet one made awry through the weird juxtaposition of cape with goggles), Allen is shirtless and wears skintight black pleather short shorts. As his drawing of the dust circle closes, he begins to twerk and moves nearer and nearer to the audience that has been invited by ushers to look around the space – in this instance, thus situated uncomfortably to ogle Allen. The discomfort comes first from the emplotment of his dance in the brutal genealogy of laboring black bodies described above, then builds through additional choices: Allen's back is turned on the audience as he approaches it more closely, constituting a refusal to reciprocate our act of looking; and his twerking is deconstructed – conspicuously loose, slow, and thereby reflexively announcing itself as a move usually designed to incite desire yet altered here, in its stretching, to ask us to pause over what it means for desire to be incited thus. An operator of a handheld camera captures this part of Allen's performance, projected onto the back wall of what will be the main, elevated playing space, a large platform at whose back, stage left, a connected, secondary platform makes a runway to a small offstage area (at stage right, a spiral staircase leads up to an open space whose overhead positioning and audio equipment lend it the aura of a club's DJ booth). The large, shaky, and awkwardly angled projection of Allen's image amplifies the unease that his dancing produces. A further, simultaneous amplification of that unease is achieved as he is joined in the deconstructed twerking by the piece's three other black dancers, Acosta, Monstah Black, and Ashley Brockington. There is no seating for *Discotropic*'s audience, who must endeavor to avoid colliding with each other or the disarmingly close dancers, studiedly indifferent to our presence and movements as their own movements essentially push us around "our" part of the space, next to the side chambers and before the stage.

Once the performers take to that stage, *Discotropic* grows in strangeness – and campiness. One of its signature camp gestures (*assaults* might be more accurate) comes early in the piece from a monologue recited by Brockington as she crawls from back to front of the raised platform; so crucial is this monologue to Acosta's imagining of *Discotropic* that it takes center stage, as it were, in copy devised for COIL's website:

Reflecting on the role of black presence in sci-fi history, inspiration was drawn from ... actor Diahann Carroll [and] her part in the [1978] TV movie *Star Wars Holiday Special.* Cast by NBC at the behest of donors and audience members, who insisted that a black person appear on the show, Carroll appears only as a holographic fantasy – an illusion that distills the ways in which the black female body has been consumed in mass media: as alien, bodacious, and marginalized. Dominant science fiction narratives are rewritten through engagement with queer politics and Afrofuturism, claiming new imaginary territory rich in possibility.[11]

Brockington's monologue is the same one recited by Carroll in the special, which aired only once on network television and which has, in a semi-cultish way, circulated in a bootleg form on various platforms. It would not be an overstatement to describe *Star Wars Holiday Special* as an unmitigated disaster in aesthetic, political, and technical registers. In a book with the delicious title, *What Were They Thinking? The 100 Dumbest Events in Television History,* David Hofstede puts the special in the number one slot – and glosses this ranking with the assessment that the special constitutes "the worst two hours of television ever": a perhaps irresistible, if also in this case toxic, object for camp contemplation.[12] One thick slice of the toxicity is (half-)baked into the intertwined racism and sexism that palpate so goofily and clumsily in the segment in which Carroll, in her preposterous, creepy role as Mermeia Holographic, performs her monologue; Mermeia identifies herself as a perfect fantasy object and tells Itchy, Chewbacca's woefully named father, again and again and in a sultry whisper, how adorable she finds him.[13] In gleeful response, he squeals and grunts in his "language," which does not use sounds that we can recognize as words and thereby renders him essentially preverbal.

No special skill is required to comprehend the objectification of Carroll, marked by her race and gender, and the corresponding racialization of oversexed, primitivized Itchy, joining the parade of "racial 'others' [who] populate the film" *Star Wars* and who, as Adilifu Nama observes, "are all bizarre aliens of color."[14] By contrast, quite a lot of skill – and camp – inheres in *Discotropic*'s sly, subtle, and slippery reproduction of the monologue, fashioned at surprising odds with the crudeness and overtness of the source material. Brockington recites the monologue without changing a syllable – and why would Acosta make changes, as the monologue's words already strikingly contain as seeds within them (begging for flowering) the undoing of their own objectifying, exoticizing, and infantilizing logics. What remains to complete such camp exposure is its thickening and texturing through vocal, gestural, physical, and material choices. In contradistinction to Carroll, framed in a relentlessly static close-up, denied any significant mobility, and locking her eyes on the camera without much range of activity, Brockington makes a dramatically slithery crawl over *Discotropic*'s stage, across which she works – and in a final, puncturing coup, jerks – her costume's long silver train; in sync with these moves, which she inhabits with a defiant flair and coiled intensity, and each time that she intones the repeated line, "I find you . . . adorable," she makes pointed, long, ambiguously overdetermined eye contact with a different spectator (every one a spectator chosen purposefully for seeming to manifest markers of identity – like ability, age, gender, race – different from the others also chosen). Far more than a simple, oppositional turn of her gaze back at her audience, Brockington's effort is a multistranded, reflexive meditation on the precarious status of embodied relationality, its oscillation between subjective and objective nodes, and the uncertainty or changeability of its racialized and sexualized dimensions. The energy that drives this performance, as well as the energy that it inspires in its receivers, is – akin to what unfolds in *Discotropic*'s preamble – *nervous*, as is the laughter that erupts in weird and wobbly ways over the course of the monologue's recitation: not your mother's camp (that is, if your mother were Sontag), in which the laughter forges an easier and surer sense of collectivity, but camp nonetheless in its crossing of citation and defamiliarization with queer libidinousness and deranged style.

## Black and Blue

In the promotional material cited above, Acosta identifies *Discotropic*'s impulses not just as queer but also as indebted to the late twentieth-century artistic movement Afrofuturism, which opposed itself to commercial, especially cinematic, science fiction that pivoted between the (non) representation of blackness as a "structuring absence" and renderings of "the black body" – subject to "physical deformation," "physical stigma," or "sadistic victimization" – as "a site of representational trauma, the ultimate signifier of difference, alienness, and 'otherness'" (7). As "alternative sites of resistant black culture" and thus "viable sources for the creation of counternarratives that challenge not only the conventions of [science fiction] cinema but various racial discourses" embedded in that cinema, Afrofuturist projects accomplish complex temporal and historical work (9). Laura U. Marks theorizes this temporality and historicity in a compelling assessment of Afrofuturism's version of sci-fi:

> [In] the artistic and intellectual movements that have come to be called
> Afrofuturism, ... Black musicians, writers, and artists argue that since the
> great rupture of the Middle Passage, African diaspora people have been
> doing science fiction. People who have lived the legacy of slavery are time
> travelers ... [E]ver since Africans were kidnapped, forced onto slave ship
> holds and plantations, and forbidden to use their languages, their descend-
> ants have survived and created in this alienated, dislocated state. They have
> done so by assembling futures from fragments of the past, preferring to
> disdain the present that accords them less than human status or, at best,
> offers "inclusion" in a humanity not of their design, and using technology
> and art to invent when historical research fails to yield anything useful.[15]

Outfitted with a rich array of visual and sonic technics, the disco was one
fertile site for such work in "assembling futures from fragments of the
past." In turn, the disco's reimagining in and as the space of *Discotropic*
extends the Afrofuturist effort to perform creative assemblage; enmeshing
Afrofuturist and camp stylizations, the piece brings the Afrofuturist dimension of this enmeshment closer to the fore as it progresses, and makes of
Afrofuturism *itself* a fragment of the past (and the past's imagining of the
future) to be ingeniously glossed and reworked. Of the several short
movements that comprise the remainder of *Discotropic* after Brockington's
monologue, two merit attention for this mashup of Afrofuturism and
camp: a march set to the song, "Sunshower," and a dance that begins as
a solo for trans performer Monstah Black, then turns into a group number.

A 1976 disco hit for Dr. Buzzard's Original Savannah Band (since
sampled regularly by other, mostly hip-hop artists), "Sunshower" was, at
the time of its original release, culturally adjacent and artistically proximal
to experiments in Afrofuturism – a proximity transformed more closely
into identity through the song's reinvention in *Discotropic*.[16] As the four
performers, swaying their hands in gentle waves, make a very slow march
across the stage, they repeat in near monotone and dozens of times the
line, generated expressly for this piece (and ringing a change on one of
Afrofuturist icon Sun Ra's lyrics), "We travel the bass waves from planet
to planet." The procession ends in their still arrangement on the spiral
staircase, and as, at any given moment, three of them continue to intone
the line about musically coordinated planetary travel, each one of them
breaks out in a mini-solo and takes a turn singing snatches from "Sunshower" – with its emphasis on radiant love deserving glorification – over
the other, incanted line. The solos are aggressively flat, somberly rendered,
and accompanied by the blue, brooding guitar improvisations of Dion
Tygapaw in the DJ station. Thus a song formerly anchored in the lyrical

assertion that happy love might shower a subject with sun rather than rain is willfully dampened at the same time that it is conjugated sonically to the evocation of sci-fi, diasporic journeying. This dampening also contrasts stridently with the hot pink lighting that bathes the performers as well as a potted, artificial plant, placed at the top of the staircase and turned orange in the light's glow. Taken together, these different elements of performance produce an effect of melancholic camp; the performers wink queerly at the romantic, heteronormative notion that love could simply be sunnily bright, yet that winking is the heavy and weary winking of subjects who, to recall Marks's language, are also "doing science fiction," traveling time and space as a result of and as a *way* of "liv[ing] the legacy of slavery," an "alienated, dislocated" – which is, here, to say alien and disco-located – "state."

The solo for Monstah Black that follows this sequence does not extend its melancholic mood but rather shades into a form of camp that I would call indifferent. Black's moves are borrowed from a range of popular idioms, including disco, vogue, and breakdancing, yet he performs them in a deliberate semblance of simultaneous laziness and jerky automation – as if a futuristic, intelligent machine breaking down, aware of the breakdown, and unbothered by it. Black's listless expression communicates that he is simultaneously unbothered by a number of other "broken" elements of the performance: that the straps of the black overalls he has worn throughout the evening do not cover his sizeable breasts, which bounce conspicuously in this sequence; that the audience can stand close enough to the edge of the stage to see his beads of sweat multiply, despite the putative slackness of his moves' execution; that the silver-painted baseball cap he dons for the solo, covered with geometrically diverse metal pieces and little blue lights, is ridiculous (in notes that I composed to capture my impressions right after seeing the performance, I wrote that the hat is "evocative all at once of circuitry, lunchboxes, and miniature model cities, while not literally representing any of them: Bauhaus meets Grace Jones's closet"). When the other performers join him onstage to conclude *Discotropic*, their collective hisses, made to sound like noises from steam machinery, corroborate the impression that the dance is a form of automation. Yet they also make faux-orgasmic sounds and mock-exclamations of slang expressions that originate in black, queer subculture ("Yaaasss!" "Cunty!"), which complicate automation through its intertwining with animation and, further still, complicate the animation by scare-quoting it. The cumulative effect is to signal a knowingness – but a blasé knowingness – about the paradoxical dehumanizing of black subjectivity as automated and at the same time hyperanimated.[17] Once more, per Marks, if "historical research" into the roots of such dehumanization "fails to yield anything useful" for superseding it, there is nonetheless the capacity for moving in synchrony and solidarity, for "using technology and art to invent" a temporary respite from white hegemony and supremacy, for making the breathing room that comes from breathing, hissing, and exclaiming together, for darkening the room and then calling for the lights.[18]

## Conclusion: Ecstatic Corpus

Accompanying the COIL program for *Discotropic* and available for reading afterward – thus extending the life of the performance or, more nearly, constituting its afterlife – is a two-page story initiated by Acosta and written with his co-performers as a game of Exquisite Corpse, conducted via text message in the month leading up to the Westbeth presentation. The story swirls around a "glistenin'" thing that, like the dehumanized black subject whose figuration propels *Discotropic*, confounds the distinction between "object" and "being"; we come to learn of this thing, a queer "black phallic crystal" called the Cuntospire, that it is a "gravity dampener" making its way to the "gravity well" in the core of the planet JayJarr (alluding to the name of Jar Jar Binks, one of the most appallingly racist characters in the *Star Wars* franchise).[19] Thus producing a curious, stimulating condition between gravity and its obverse – call it levity – for the JayJarrs and visitors to their planet (including a Venusian named dipki), the Cuntospire inspires a response altogether fitting, given its exquisite imagining in relation to *Discotropic*: dance.

> What was this? This rhythm? Were the inhabitants ... dancing? The atmosphere throbbed unexpectedly, seesawing between gravity and non-gravity, and everyone's, including dipki's, body bounced and shook. As the atmosphere pulsed, dipki nodded to the beat. This reminded him of the raves he'd throw back on Venus in the space craters, the terrain whirling up around him. This new place suddenly felt like home. But still ... where WAS he exactly? He couldn't help himself! He let out a loud OOM HAHA OOM HAHA BOOM!

This capsule in the text-message-based – and high camp – tale works allegorically and utopically in the manner we expect from science fiction: rave-throwing dipki is a stand-in for Allen, who contributed this missive to the correspondence; Venus recalls Earth, its "space craters" the North American scene in which the raves were thrown; and the "new place" that feels "like home" does so not quite because it "remind[s]" dipki of his old "terrain" – which, after all, is the "alienated, dislocated state" that Marks describes – but because a more buoyant and liberating dislocation bubbles through the asymptotic approach to the transcendence of gravity, associated rather with the traumatic pull of history and the disenabling grip of racism. The nodding, bouncing, and shaking here are more infectious, more *ecstatic*, than any of the nervous, melancholic, and indifferent energies embodied in *Discotropic*; on changing JayJarr, even the atmosphere "throb[s]" with pleasure (the throbbing pleasure gets really queer when another character, Eckofuts, whose name emphatically *echoes* both the *futural* part of Afrofuturism and the *foot* of the dancer, "wrap[s] his thickum legs around the Cuntospire"). The ecstatic corpus – body, text – yielded by Exquisite Corpse is vivified by keen longing and opens onto a hope more immodest than any glimpsed in *Discotropic*; the "seesawing" and "whirling" of the story make a generous, generative postscript to the performance.

To zoom out from that allegorizing postscript's content to the structural relationship it bears to the piece whose composition, rehearsal, and executions prior to COIL precede and prompt it, I wonder whether that relationship might itself allegorize, however accidentally, something about camp. Like the queer theory of which its conceptualization forms a sliver, camp has been proclaimed dead more than once, rising phoenix-like each time. Yet as Caryl Flinn has demonstrated so compellingly, these belied assessments are not the only "deaths of camp"; a constitutive element of camp is its own reckoning with the deadly and deathly, its enlivening occupations of morbid preoccupation.[20] The question that could be raised every time camp itself is raised from the dead – and, once more, raises some dead – is whether the tendential accent in that latest camp iteration will be on raising or deadness, enlivening or morbidity, gravity or levity. The movement from unease and melancholy to hope and ecstasy, traceable in the interval between *Discotropic* and the sci-fi story attached to it, could inspire the fantasy that camp will likewise grow, if only incrementally, more joyous and aspirant.

Yet to overread in that way depends upon construing the product of Exquisite Corpse as what I have called *Discotropic*'s *extension, postscript,* and *afterlife*. From another perspective, the story precedes *Discotropic*, or at least the incarnation of the piece at COIL: the performance had been composed long before, but it wasn't presented publicly by the story's writers until after their texting game had concluded; and of course, given the story's enclosure in the program, I could have read it before rather than after the performance. Would I then have felt yanked back from a wording of "queer optimism" to a worlding of "cruel optimism"?²¹ The question of how to fantasize, speculate, overread, and overreach is irresolvable, logically; rhetorically, then, at least, Exquisite Corpse (or rather, the technology that enabled it) might have the last word. And that word would be, "Today." The printed version of the *Discotropic* collaborators' story is literally a snapshot of what appeared on Acosta's screen as the composition was unfolding; thus a log of that fiction-making activity as well as a presentation of the fiction, the text contains headnotes above entries that record the sending of messages at "12/8/15, 11:29 PM," "12/31/15, 10:03 PM," and so forth. The final such headnote reads "Today," and a deliberation informs its sharing. Acosta could have captured an image of what his screen displayed some day or days after the final installment of Exquisite Corpse was produced, at which point the software used in its making would have dated it differently. Instead, he wants us to see the story "end" (its final words are quite open-ended and give us a sense of activity on JayJarr *in medias res*) "Today," in part because *Discotropic* implicitly poses the question, "What exactly is 'today'?" Troubling any stable notion of linear time is common to camp, to the temporal turn in queer theory of which camp criticism comprises a subset, and to Afrofuturist cultural production, in all of which formations *Discotropic* ramifies. Today becomes yesterday. It comes tomorrow. It could be a tropic in a galaxy far away or a disco in our own backyard. If it matters, it is certainly black. If it feels real, it is probably blue. And if it feels right, it may just be pink.

## Notes

1  For writings constellated together to constitute a camp canon, see, for instance, Fabio Cleto, ed., *Camp: Queer Aesthetics and the Performing Subject* (Ann Arbor: University of Michigan Press, 1999). For speculation on camp's origins and tracing its evolutions, see David Bergman, ed., *Camp Grounds: Style and Homosexuality* (Amherst: University of Massachusetts Press, 1993).

2  Susan Sontag, "Notes on 'Camp,'" in *Against Interpretation and Other Essays* (New York: Dell, 1969), 277–93.

3  Jack Smith, "The Perfect Filmic Appositeness of Maria Montez," in *Wait for Me at the Bottom of the Pool: The Writings of Jack Smith*, ed. J. Hoberman and Edward Leffingwell (New York: Serpent's Tail, 1997), 25–36.

4  See Pamela Robertson Wojcik, *Guilty Pleasures: Feminist Camp from Mae West to Madonna* (Durham: Duke University Press, 1996); José Esteban Muñoz, *Disidentifications: Queers of Color and the Performance of Politics* (Minneapolis:

152      NICK SALVATO

University of Minnesota Press, 1999); Matthew Tinkcom, *Working Like a Homosexual: Camp, Capital, Cinema* (Durham: Duke University Press, 2002); and Tanya González and Eliza Rodriguez y Gibson, *Humor and Latina/o Camp in* Ugly Betty*: Funny Looking* (Lanham: Lexington Books, 2015).

5 See Moe Meyer, "Introduction: Reclaiming the Discourse of Camp," in *The Politics and Poetics of Camp*, ed. Moe Meyer (New York: Routledge, 1994), 3–9; and Judith Butler, "Gender Is Burning: Questions of Appropriation and Subversion," in *Bodies That Matter: On the Discursive Limits of Sex* (New York: Routledge, 1993), 81–98.

6 niv Acosta, *Discotropic*, Westbeth Artists' Housing, New York City, January 6–10, 2016.

7 For another illustrative example of contemporary camp that is likewise both politically progressive and tonally dissimilar to most twentieth-century camp, especially in its handling of sentimentality, see Taylor Mac, *The Lily's Revenge*, in *The Downtown Anthology: 6 Hit Plays from New York's Downtown Theaters*, ed. Morgan Gould and Erin Salvi (New York: Playscripts, Inc., 2015), 189–306.

8 "History," *Westbeth: Home to the Arts*, http://westbeth.org/wordpress/about/history.

9 Cory Tamler, "Past Versions of the Present Future in niv Acosta's *Discotropic*," *Culturebot: Maximum Performance*, January 20, 2016, www.culturebot.org/2016/01/25365/past-versions-of-the-present-future-in-niv-acostas-disco tropic; and Celeste Olalquiaga, *The Artificial Kingdom: On the Kitsch Experience* (Minneapolis: University of Minnesota Press, 2002).

10 I borrow this idea and its phrasing from Jon McKenzie, *Perform or Else: From Discipline to Performance* (New York: Routledge, 2001).

11 "*Discotropic*," *Performance Space 122*, January 2016, www.ps122.org/discotropic.

12 David Hofstede, *What Were They Thinking? The 100 Dumbest Events in Television History* (New York: Back Stage Books, 2004), 204.

13 Pat Proft, Leonard Ripps, Bruce Vilanch, Rod Warren, and Mitzie Welch, *Star Wars Holiday Special*, dir. Steven Binder and David Acomba, CBS (original air date: November 17, 1978).

14 Adilifu Nama, *Black Space: Imagining Race in Science Fiction Film* (Austin: University of Texas Press, 2008), 28.

15 Laura U. Marks, "Monad, Database, Remix: Manners of Unfolding in *The Last Angel of History*," *Black Camera* vol. 6, no. 2 (Spring 2015): 112–13.

16 Stony Browder, Jr. and Thomas Browder, "Sunshower," *Dr. Buzzard's Original Savannah Band* (RCA, 1976).

17 For a sophisticated account of this paradox, see Sianne Ngai, "Animatedness," *Ugly Feelings* (Cambridge, MA: Harvard University Press, 2005), 89–125.

18 For a conceptualization of the progressive, queer political potential in synchrony, see Elizabeth Freeman, "Synchronic / Anachronic," in *Time: A Vocabulary of the Present*, ed. Joel Burges and Amy J. Elias (New York: NYU Press, 2016), 129–43.

19 niv Acosta, Justin Allen, Monstah Black, and Ashley Brockington, Program insert (unpaginated), *Discotropic*, COIL, Westbeth Artists' Housing, New York City, January 6–10, 2016.
20 Caryl Flinn, "The Deaths of Camp," in *Camp: Queer Aesthetics and the Performing Subject*, 433–57.
21 See Michael D. Snediker, *Queer Optimism: Lyric Personhood and Other Felicitous Persuasions* (Minneapolis: University of Minnesota Press, 2008); and Lauren Berlant, *Cruel Optimism* (Durham: Duke University Press, 2011).

CHAPTER 9

# *Reading in Juxtaposition*
## *Comics*
### *andré carrington*

The visibility of sexuality as subject matter in popular graphic novels (like Julie Maroh's *Blue is the Warmest Color*) and the suggestive aesthetics of classic comic books provide sustained interest among queer-minded readers.[1] However, the forms in which these stories are told and the habits of reading they generate also present queer issues for literary studies. Comics readers populate a variety of knowledge communities, from art school sophisticates to rebellious youth. Important experiments in self-invention play out on the pages of alternative comix and zines, and the ascendancy of superhero comics has also given rise to touchstones for queer (dis)identification. The legacies of genre fiction, including science fiction, fantasy, and romance, attest to the edification of heteronormative ideals, but these, too, are subject to redefinition from one reading to the next.[2] Due to their unique systems of production and distribution, comics are among the most subcultural of print cultures.[3] They are neither wholly textual nor categorically nonverbal, which makes them especially apt for queering the conventions of interpretation.

This chapter assesses how comics have played an integral role in bring-ing matters of concern for queer studies to academic and public attention. It models the connections between comics and queer studies by troubling genealogies, following lines of inquiry that have been integral to the formation of queer knowledge practices, and breaking down the boundar-ies between disciplines. Instead of simply focusing on writers who identify themselves in queer terms or representations of sexuality and gender variation themselves, queer theory has transformed literary studies, in part, by convincing multiple audiences that "visual phenomena such as film, theater, and television are increasingly central to thinking what it is to do queer work, to be queer, to see queerly, and to think queerly."[4] Comics rehearse queer approaches to visual and print cultures without losing sight of the "variety of expectations and opportunities for readers to decipher meaning from both that which is visible and invisible in the text."[5]

Drawing on texts that have proven amenable to teaching queer lessons, this chapter outlines how queer comics turn the page in popular culture and literary studies.

## Comix vs. Comics: Queering Genealogies

Scott McCloud's *Understanding Comics* presents his definition of comics, "juxtaposed pictorial and other images in deliberate sequence intended to convey information and/or produce an aesthetic response in the viewer,"[6] to pursue the following goal:

> I felt that there was something lurking in comics ... something that had never been done. Some kind of hidden power! But whenever I tried to explain my feeling, I failed miserably ... If people failed to understand comics, it was because they defined what comics could be too narrowly! A proper definition, if we could find one, might give the lie to the stereotypes – and show that that potential of comics is limitless and exciting![7]

Critics may take exception to McCloud's definition, but he conceives it as a means to an end. Defining comics (and "art" more broadly) allows him to *explain his feelings* to unknowing interlocutors. His subjective definition imparts the flexibility necessary to include examples from a variety of cultural traditions into the category of comics. McCloud's intervention was inspired by his practice as a cartoonist and a desire for the art form's recognition. Whereas readers devoted to comics might identify with these motivations, others, like Samuel Delany, pursue the same objectives of countering disciplinary biases and broadening our critical horizons without the same investment in establishing a comprehensive approach to the medium.[8]

Delany's 1996 essay, "The Politics of Paraliterary Criticism," takes a queer approach to understanding comics. As an author experienced in many genres, Delany treats theoretical abstraction as counterproductive to the analysis of texts and their function in the world. As Chris Hatfield notes, "Delany, leery of the reductiveness of such formulas, argues for local and multiple *descriptions* of comics instead, functional descriptions that need not aim for the airtightness, nor the transcendent ontological authority, of 'definitions.'"[9] Delany's use of "descriptions" in the plural highlights their value as methodological tools adaptable to engagements with many different objects. "The Politics of Paraliterary Criticism" elevates description over definition at the *paradigmatic* level. In the aggregate, comics may be characterized through a variety of useful descriptive terms, but individual texts belie the notion that they tend to conform to qualities that can be specified in any single defining statement. Delany writes, "It is not the concept of category, as carried by the metaphors of family and of genre, that I object to. It is rather the imposition of family values ... the assumption that family or genre members must submit to these generational relations."[10] His recommendation to downplay resemblances between texts treats the unpredictability of comics as a compelling feature rather than a problem to be resolved.

"Queer comics" is too nebulous for a single literary history to provide researchers with a comprehensive guide to the contents it names.[11] We can, however, recount some formative encounters with queerness from the recent history of comics to provide an orientation to the primary texts that form the basis for English-language scholarship on the subject. For a cadre of cartoonists who have been working in the medium since the 1970s, the publication of comics with overtly homoerotic themes is a shared experience. Their work with the same outlets, such as Kitchen Sink Press and *Gay Comix*, provides ample evidence from which we could derive a consensus about the emergence of the first "generation" of gay and lesbian comics in the watershed of feminist activism.[12] While these artists were celebrated as "pioneers" at the first Queers & Comics conference at the Center for LGBTQ Studies in New York, in 2015, the intellectual histories of queer studies have been enriched by autonomous developments in comics that require more than a family reunion to commemorate.[13]

When comics attract scrutiny for their provocative content, they demonstrate how popular media reinscribes and subverts cultural mores. A moral panic instigated by psychologist Frederic Wertham made comics emblematic for debates regarding mass culture, media effects, and cultural policy.[14] From the 1950s onward, portrayals of sexuality in American comics courted controversy, alternately inviting charges of obscenity, posing a regulatory problem for institutions like schools and libraries vis-à-vis young readers, and appealing to the mature sensibilities of adults.[15] Some narratives introduce mixed messages into heteronormative scripts through sexually ambiguous characters and storylines, such as the pairing of adult male heroes with young sidekicks, and readers construe these relationships in markedly different ways.[16] As superheroes have become the mainstay of the industry, and comics have become central to popular entertainment, queer figures have undergone their own mainstreaming with marginal increases in the employment of queer talent and queer characters. Meanwhile, the "underground" has migrated to webcomics, crowdfunding, and other independent publishing venues. Each of these layers in the history of queer politics and culture tracks the careers of comics artists working over several decades.

The politics of representing sexuality pushed many queer comics to the margins. As Robert Triptow writes, "Gay cartooning denotes pornography to some minds. So for artists with marketable styles to work for a homosexual audience is a risky business."[17] This proviso refers to homophobia, but Triptow's remarks also highlight texts like Lee Marrs's *Pudge, Girl Blimp* and *Wimmen's Comix*, which speak to the connection between homoerotic imagery in comics and women's self-representation in arts and letters.[18] Pornography became a metonym for gay comics for the same reasons that comics by and for women acquired a reputation for subverting heterosexist norms: sexuality and gender are necessary but not sufficient factors in the politics of representation performed by queer comics. Authors and readers who were also mobilizing for feminist and gay liberation reasserted their prerogatives as co-owners of the medium to mitigate the impact of images that signified their identities solely in terms of their difference from straight men. Queer contestations and alliances ensued within comics just as they had in the formation of activist coalitions.

To wit: when feminist writers and artists confronted the pathologies ascribed to female sexuality and supplanted them with a discourse of affirmation in the 1970s, comics played a part. Women formed their own editorial collectives to break away from the male-dominated underground comix scene. They solicited work concerned with stylistic innovation, humor, reproductive and sexual health education, and erotic gratification, such as *It's Not Me Babe* and *Tits and Clits*. As Joyce Farmer recalled: "[we] wanted our comic to be entertaining, but more important, *Tits and Clits* was all about female sexuality and women's imaginative solutions to our unique challenges."[19] Jen Camper, Roberta Gregory, and Joan Hilty, who worked in the same milieu, credited the emergence of *Gay Comix* in 1980 to the momentum provided by politically conscious and sexually explicit feminist comics from the previous decade.[20]

Hillary Chute makes another compelling argument linking feminist and queer concerns in comics by acknowledging how a heterosexist double-standard structures the reception of sexually explicit imagery. Speaking of underground cartoonist Aline Kominsky-Crumb:

> Kominsky-Crumb's uninhibited representations of her own forceful sexuality in a light that is not always palatable, or favorable, make her a pioneering – if underrecognized – figure in the broad world of feminist visual culture. Yet there is virtually no academic criticism of her work and little more in mainstream literary and art journalism. Given that

Kominsky-Crumb has been writing the darker side of (her own) female
sexuality for almost four decades, it is no surprise that her work is neglected – her underwhelming reception contrasts markedly to that of her
husband, cartoonist Robert Crumb, who has been canonized exactly for
writing the darker side of (his own) tortured male sexuality.[21]

For Chute, women's comics redress a gap in our critical understanding of
gender and sexuality as well as their role in individuals' struggles for self-
determination. The same norms that create a permissive environment for
white cisgender heterosexual men in the arts marginalize other perspectives
on race, gender, sexuality, and practices of self-expression.

Gay men, including Rupert Kinnard and Howard Cruse, contend with
different aspects of the same "masculinist economy of knowledge production" (40). Kinnard, a Black gay disabled cartoonist who created the
Brown Bomber and Diva Touché Flambé under the pen name "Professor
I. B. Gettindowne," authored several strips in which his heroes face a
timely foil: the respectable "GWM" (Gay White Male). In one installment, GWM pleads for assimilation with the empty promise that rights
for his Black and gender-nonconforming counterparts would follow. The
comic ends with a threat: "You watch your step, Bomber, or you won't
even be given the right to wrap that 'do rag' around your head!"[22] His
words call attention to Brown Bomber's improvised, gendered, and racially
distinctive appearance: in place of the masks worn by superheroes, B. B.
wears "his sister's scarf" over half his face, with his eyes peering through
cut-out holes. Elsewhere, the Diva suggests B. B. exaggerates his affinity
with the flourishing of Black gay men's creative output in the 1990s. B. B.
celebrates his fellow BGMs for becoming "America's sweethearts," naming
"the late Joseph Beam, Essex Hemphill, Assoto Saint, Isaac Julien, Marlon
Riggs, and others." He appears in the next panel wearing sunglasses, a
goatee, a kufi emblazoned with the African continent, and a spear, all
stylistic signifiers for Black militancy at the time. From his early illustrations inspired by the aesthetics of Black exploitation cinema to his satire of
Black nationalist posturing, Kinnard's work treats images of Black and gay
identities with critical perspicacity and brotherly love.

Howard Cruse corroborates the link among underground, feminist, and
lesbian and gay comics by including them under the sensational cover of
*Gay Comix* #1. At Queers & Comics in 2015, he recalled, "once we
announced what we wanted to do Rand Holmes couldn't wait to volunteer
cover art for the first issue, which also included comix by my personal
inspirations: Roberta Gregory, Mary Wings, and Lee Marrs."[23] Holmes, a
Canadian who identified as straight, was a star within the underground

comix movement. His riotous cover illustration juxtaposed a bare-chested, hot-dog-eating male skater with a shocked onlooker hiding in a closet. Cruse edited the first four issues of *Gay Comix*, and his work spans a range of storytelling modes: from the upbeat, endearing comic strip *Barefootz* to *Stuck Rubber Baby*, a melancholy graphic novel set amid the civil rights activism and violent massive resistance that characterized the author's native Alabama.[24] Published in 1995, *Stuck Rubber Baby* complicated images of white gay men by restoring their presence within a history of local resistance and intracommunity conflict quite distant from the urban scenes of gay liberation.

Cruse also portrayed male couples in comics before such imagery became typical. In *Wendel*, a comic strip he published in the *Advocate* magazine, he pictured the intimacy of a gay couple while celebrating their sexual foibles and those of their outré peers. At a turning point in the series, the principal characters dream about a wedding ceremony while on a camping trip. The officiant is a talking bear, all the attendees are naked, and the customized vows include "promise not to nurse grudges or sulk unduly?" and "prevent forest fires whenever possible?"[25] From a time when legal marriage was not yet a practical consideration for queer activists, this vision of affirmation reimagines existing cultural forms in order to articulate a wholly idealistic agenda. At a later date, Samuel Delany's graphic novel *Bread & Wine*, illustrated by Mia Wolff, offers a contrasting example of an intimate relationship between men that answers the "antisocial turn" in queer studies with a queer definition of happiness. Ann Matsuuchi describes *Bread & Wine* as an example of "[José Esteban] Muñoz's hermeneutic construction of queer futurity" by highlighting the text's "attention to systematically unacknowledged moments of everyday life, highlighting the potentialities of spaces created by the movement of bodies and social forces."[26]

Influenced by feminism and Cultural Studies, queer studies retains its skepticism toward consumer culture without abandoning the social and psychic functions of fantasy. Some find the escapism of comic books off-putting and even naive, while others revel in their utopian possibilities. In the tradition of Constance Penley's *Close Encounters* and Henry Jenkins's *Textual Poachers*, Ramzi Fawaz's groundbreaking study *The New Mutants* illuminates the role of mass-produced entertainment in popularizing counterhegemonic notions of sexuality, citizenship, and spectatorship. Whereas superheroes had traditionally embodied fantasies of masculine power and patriotic ideals, postwar American comics reinvented these figures as vehicles for "the cosmopolitan worldviews of movements for international human rights, civil rights, and women's and gay liberation."[27] Tracking the shift from individualistic narratives focused on detectives, swashbucklers, and heroes with secret identities like Superman toward comic books about superhero teams as ersatz families in the 1960s, Fawaz emphasizes the collective dimension of what he terms "popular fantasy." The altered bodies of superheroes like the *Fantastic Four* "imaginatively crafted a new kind of citizen capable of engaging cosmopolitan political projects without an attachment to narratives of heterosexual normalization and bodily regimentation."[28] Proceeding to studies of the *X-Men* and the titular *New Mutants*, Fawaz examines the fictitious invention of "mutant" identity as both an allegory for sexuality and gender identity – subject to the pressures of assimilation and normativity – and also a trope for identity as a matter of political positionality.

Recent developments bear witness to the continuing proliferation of queer purposes as well as publics. At the height of the AIDS epidemic, artists like Ivan Velez, Jr. portrayed queer youth of color in comics for the Hetrick-Martin Institute, a school for LGBT students in New York.[29] Today, from Tumblr posts, to crowdfunding efforts exemplified by Spike Trotman's *Let's Kickstart a Comic*, to publications funded by community-based organizations like *Sexile/Sexilio* – in which Jaime Cortez recounts the story of Cuban exile and trans* activist Adela Vazquez in comics form – queer communities are still using graphic narratives to disseminate knowledge and pleasure.[30] The corporations that control much of comic book publishing and distribution undoubtedly recognize this demand; by green-lighting stories that reimagine legacy characters such as Batwoman and Iceman as lesbian or gay, they vindicate the long-held suspicions of some readers while inviting homophobic scrutiny and disappointed cynicism from others.[31] The continual evolution of comics in form and content demonstrates the depth and breadth of the root system that sustains queer interventions in the popular imagination.

## Queer Methods: From Memoir to Medicine

In "Queer and Now," Eve Sedgwick appraises how literary forms become objects of love, recounting her desire to internalize the "numinous and resistant power" of certain texts by apprehending their formal codes at a level of "visceral near-identification."[32] While Sedgwick cultivated this relationship with poetry and the novel, others pursued "the tools for a formalist apprehension of other less prestigious, more ubiquitous kinds of text: genre movies, advertising, comic strips."[33] She argues that this urgent, often personal affinity characterizes queer encounters with any given cultural form. Accordingly, Matt Brim and Amin Ghaziani write, "the most pervasive characteristic of queer theory may be its methodological use of self-narration/self-invention in the service of scholarship."[34]

Alison Bechdel showcases the productive role of self-narration as a method of thinking about queerness through her critically acclaimed life writing. Although she made a living for decades publishing the comic strip *Dykes to Watch Out For* in alternative and community-based periodicals, encounters with conventional literature are instrumental to Bechdel's construction of her persona across two graphic memoirs. In *Fun Home*, she discovers and names her sexuality and questions her relationship to her closeted father through reading. The memoir bespeaks an obsessive orientation toward symbolization as a characteristic of the author's personality, and it also compels the reader to indulge the repetition compulsion that grows out of Bechdel's formative experiences. Through meticulous attention to the dense visual and verbal composition of the text, Chute intuits a pattern through which "*Fun Home* enacts repetition at every level: in its preoccupation with individual images; in its narrative conceit of telling and showing a private story through 'great books'; in its re-creating of paper archives; in the author's creative process, in which she physically reinhabits scenes of the past in order to draw them; and in its overall narrative structure" (177). The unrepresentability of her father's death – leaving open the question of whether the cause was accident or suicide – and her ambivalence toward him as a closeted gay man and a forceful influence on her intellect are central to Bechdel's textual practice. She reconstructs the literary insights she originally learned from her father and embeds them in allusions that express their newfound significance. For critics interested in trauma, *Fun Home* exemplifies the archival impulse in literary studies discussed by Jacques Derrida and queered by Ann Cvetkovich.

The archival turn is just one direction Bechdel's queer act of remembrance facilitates. Her comics also partake in the queer method that Lisa Diedrich calls "graphic analysis."[35] *Are You My Mother?* has elements unfamiliar to its predecessor: scenes of the author/protagonist undergoing therapy, citations from psychoanalyst D. W. Winnicott that provide chapter titles, and illustrations for particular concepts in psychoanalysis. One reviewer finds the preponderance of these signposts throughout the text unproductive, characterizing the book as "an undistinguished edifice by a builder who forgot to remove the scaffolding."[36] Yet the visibility of this "scaffolding" reveals how Bechdel was "training herself to improvise" by constructing what psychoanalysis terms "transitional phenomena."

Critics like Diedrich and Heather Love suggest that Bechdel combines theory and practice. Both texts display the influence of Obsessive-Compulsive Disorder (a diagnosis that Bechdel speaks about openly) on her creative method, which Love describes as "forensic" in *Fun Home*. Diedrich writes: "Bechdel offers what I would describe as a meta-obsessive-compulsive documentation of the process of documentation itself; on this meta-level, psychoanalysis becomes useful to Bechdel's graphic analysis as a way to help her place the objects of her analysis into a new [transitional] setting and thus a new story of the self" (186). The new stories of the self that graphic narratives produce in the interest of reclaiming or subverting images of deviant sexuality might seem to fluctuate between two options: assimilation allows some to approximate normalcy, and resistance normalizes what was once deviant.[37] Queer studies has sought to dismantle the incentives that entice sexual minorities and other marginalized subjects to internalize the logic of deviance – even if they valorize it – that is tacitly associated with being "normal" in modern societies.

Rather than reducing the praxis of queer worldmaking to deviance, some scholars and activists embrace a "turn to ethics" that "explore[s] alternative possibilities that could not be subsumed under the imperative to resist."[38] Michel Foucault's *History of Sexuality, Vol. 3: The Care of the Self* laid a foundation for queer ethics by interrogating how modern, individualistic freedom, which claims to "liberate" sexuality from moralism, ends up submitting it to regulation. Janet Jakobsen explains:

> For Foucault, this freedom as autonomy requires self-discipline in which . . . the ideal of freedom induces us to produce ourselves through the norms of the human sciences. Those are the norms of autonomous individualism, including the discourse of sexuality. We become autonomous individuals by freeing ourselves from the imposition of the law, but we also give the law to ourselves.[39]

Prisons and psychiatry were laboratories for these social experiments, but Foucault emphasizes how disciplinary power permeates "free" societies. Notwithstanding, some practitioners of "the care of the self" articulate novel ways of being with sexuality, biopower, and madness. Queer modes of life writing, including comics, move beyond the resistance/assimilation binary by dedicating cultural resources to the art of being unwell and coping with debilitating circumstances. They construct parity between healthy and deviant imagery through juxtaposition and through their circulation as everyday objects rather than rarefied specimens.

As comics enter the nonfiction genres of journalism, memoir, and self-help, they transform the cultural politics of difference. For instance, Ellen Forney positions the artist as a stakeholder in the struggle to redefine the relationship between creativity and "madness." She uses graphic memoir to unpack her own relationship to the archetype of the "crazy tortured genius artist," representing the words and images she grappled with in the aftermath of her bipolar diagnosis.[40] She integrates sexuality into the flow of fantasies and realities transformed by diagnosis and treatment. Tegretol renders her unable to achieve an orgasm; cannabis alleviates the sexual side effects, but her psychiatrist advises against using it.[41] She considers placing a personal ad to seek out her ideal date, an "episode-free, 'high functioning' bipolar," thinking, "In my head, she looked like a high school friend's mother – elegant & comfortingly bland."[42] Forney represents a model application of the comics form to what Villarejo recognizes as a Foucauldian effort to "think the theory/practice doublet as an uneasy name for a real problematic."[43]

Forney's work not only illustrates – it educates and theorizes. It is an autoethnographic counterpart to what MK Czerwiec and Ian Williams call "graphic medicine," a collaborative effort to reconfigure the relation between medical science, the healthcare professions, and creative practice.[44] Building upon thinkers such as Martha Nussbaum and Rita Charon, graphic medicine integrates comics into the practice of providing care: "By visually bridging the chasm between medical professional and patient – literally putting them in the same panels – comics reveals them to be two sides of the same experience."[45] Czerwiec's *Taking Turns*, which reflects on her experiences caring for AIDS-diagnosed patients in the 1990s, exemplifies this mission. In the words of one doctor, "On Unit 371, it seems to me that the spirit is, 'this could be me.' Not just for the gay guys. People somehow get the empathy thing that we are all just people taking turns being sick. I may be the nurse or doctor today, but I could be the patient tomorrow."[46] By enlisting the subjects they represent in the production of their own narratives, comics creators like Bechdel, Forney, and Czerwiec queer the methods we use to apprehend culture.

## Juxtaposition: Gods & Monsters

The superhero's preponderance in comics has kept the notion of popular culture as modern myth alive. From Wertham's aspersions toward the "Ganymede-Zeus type of love relationship" between Batman and Robin to the violent, Orientalist spectacle of Frank Miller's *300*, sexuality has been a catalyst for this equation.[47] The connection between comics and other popular traditions comprises more than wish fulfillment, however. Eric Shanower's conspicuously homoerotic rendition of the Trojan War in his *Age of Bronze* series, for example, models an "ethos of intimacy and inclusivity."[48] Whereas unmistakably romantic portrayals of Achilles and Patroklus are a hallmark of adaptations of the *Iliad*, its repetition alongside other sexual episodes in *Age of Bronze* thematizes, "through sheer quantity alone, the preeminent place that love and sexual desire occupy in the literary and artistic tradition of the Trojan War."[49] As *readings* of prior literary constructions of sexuality, works like Shanower's contribute to contemporary interpretations of the relation between familiar and distant sexual cultures.

Modern comic books are among the most distinct textual media to emerge from the United States.[50] At a metatextual level, comics is an indisputably global medium: manga and bande dessinée emerged autonomously long before the United States existed, and they thrive within their respective language communities. The medium's versatility also facilitates a great deal of cultural cross-fertilization. Subcultural "crossover" has been a notable phenomenon, with independent breakthroughs like the Hernandez brothers' *Love and Rockets* capturing the attention of journalists and tastemakers.[51] Proving that comics can also cross moral and political boundaries, the pornographic "Tijuana Bibles" of the interwar era irreverently parodied figures like Popeye, Clark Gable, and Mussolini.[52]

More recently, Gengoroh Tagame, a thirty-year veteran of bondage-themed gay manga, published his first work for a general readership: the family-friendly graphic novel *My Brother's Husband*. Shortly before its debut, Tagame relayed how the same underlying motivations that previously inspired depictions of hypermasculine men in scenes of sexual humiliation led him to a story about a North American gay man visiting his late husband's straight brother and niece in Japan: "[T]he reasoning for my writing *My Brother's Husband* is fundamentally the same as why I started writing gay porn manga. I wanted to read it. It didn't exist. I had to write it."[53] Making fantasies legible is a common thread throughout the experiences of authors and audiences from marginalized backgrounds. When Tagame refers to writing, he is also literally referring to drawing. In his discussion of how he adapted the skillset he had used to tantalize readers with sexual fetishes associated with eating to the task of depicting a mundane family supper, he noted: "One thing I discovered in the process though, was that depicting really filthy anal sex and someone really getting into a delicious bowl of ramen, were from a drawing technique standpoint, the same. The key to both of these depictions is to 'make you feel the sensations' and to 'bring out the quality' of the activity." Emphasizing facial expressions, evoking empathy, and arousing specific visceral responses are among the shared features of Tagame's sensuous imagery. Regardless of language and subject matter, artists may queer their compositional methods to provoke distinct sensations or address different audiences.

The simultaneous but not necessarily complementary operation of pictorial and verbal registers influences the "uptake" of work in comics. While some convey queerness through the interaction of form and content, others maintain a degree of "inappropriateness," never quite fitting into a genre. Considered as a hybrid construction – a chimera – queer comics can disrupt culturally circumscribed interpretations by bringing together elements that are conventionally held apart. Craig Stroupe coins the term "irritating juxtapositions," citing the difficulty inherent in names like "media literacy" and "visual rhetoric," to indicate the novelty of the circumstances that make avant-garde art practices relevant to readers:

> These critical metaphors or oxymoronic neologisms produce ... interpretive dilemmas that both negate the norms represented by the opposed elements – in the case of "visual rhetoric," the conventional assumptions we make about how images work as opposed to how words do – as well as suggest positive alternatives ... such dilemmas represent a creative irritant, the grain of sand that ideally instigates a pearl.[54]

The "irritation" between sensory and/or linguistic registers becomes productively queer when their juxtaposition "echoes categorical instabilities or cultural conflicts that already inform an audience's historical situation and moment."[55]

To conclude this discussion of what queer studies and comics can learn from each other, we should appreciate how the impossibility of reducing the divergent traditions represented in contemporary queer comics to a single canon of texts provides the point of departure for future innovation. Lynda Barry invents the genre term "autobifictionalography" to describe her book *One Hundred Demons* (Chute 16). Chute uses Barry's work to demonstrate how "comics have come to reside productively on the fault line between 'high' and 'mass'" culture (99). This dynamic relies in part on Barry's publication of her comic strips in book form; Printed Matter, a New York-based nonprofit organization, took an interest in artists' books and viewed Barry's work in that vein. By bringing her work to the fine art world, Barry puts questions of form that comics have long considered to a different public: "The most salient aspect of *Naked Ladies* is its form; the book puts portraiture and prose fiction together, but does not match them in any precise denotative or illustrative way" (Chute 105). This incommensurable relation between graphic composition and narrative engenders the "irritating juxtaposition" that Stroupe identifies with formally similar works. The multiplicity of typefaces used in *One Hundred Demons*, sometimes within a single word, echoes the experimental poetry of Dada and Bauhaus (Chute 112–13). The mixed-media, cut-and-paste collage technique by which the text is assembled "evokes both artists' books and children's pop-up books, juxtaposing and rendering unstable, in this aspect as elsewhere, the discernable line between childhood and adulthood" (113). By dwelling on its childlike, "naive" appearance, Barry's work reiterates the "ordinariness of her trauma" as a common feature of girlhood (109).

While Chute highlights the value of innovations like Barry's in the context of culture writ large, queer studies might examine comics in the light of the marginalized literary heritage of women of color in particular. Barry's "autobifictionalography" hearkens back to another famous neologism: "biomythography," the term Audre Lorde coined for her life narrative *Zami: A New Spelling of My Name*. The resonance situates Barry's work within a lineage of women of color breaking through artistic conventions with unforeseen implications. In Melinda De Jesús's assessment, "Barry's cartoon explorations of Filipina American mestizaness juxtapose the binaries of liminality and mestiza consciousness in order to proffer alternative conceptions of being that contribute greatly to Filipina American visibility, agency, and decolonization."[56] By emphasizing the racial and national dimensions of the author's critical position as well as the way she is situated with respect to gender, sexuality, and the conventions of visual art, De Jesús recalls the often obscured foundations of queer creativity in bodies of knowledge articulated by racially and sexually marginal subjects. The common thread throughout Barry's work includes a "search for identity and belonging, the same themes dominating Filipino American writing from Carlos Bulosan and Ben Santos through Peter Bacho, Jessica Hagedorn, R. Zamora Linmark, M. Evelina Galang, and Brian Ascalon Roley."[57] Her protagonist, also named Lynda, models the hybridity of "autobifictionalography" as a representational strategy: anecdotal and ethnographic, visual and verbal, queer in its orientation to sexuality and queer of color, US/Third World feminist.[58]

De Jesús also addresses the way Barry engages a wholly different register of the senses – smell – through a reading of the "Common Scents" chapter in *One Hundred Demons*. Here, the protagonist reckons with her neighbors' revulsion at the smells of food in her home. In one scene, Lynda's grandmother (portrayed as visibly darker than Lynda) offers her some durian fruit, which couples an undesirable scent to a pleasant taste.[59] The young protagonist's curiosity in this scene rehearses the dilemma inherent in her mestiza identity: she is constantly tasked with accepting or rejecting the reassuring familiarity of her home and family, but her appearance affords her the privilege to blend in with her white peers. Disavowing the resources provided by her mestiza consciousness comes at a painful cost. De Jesús posits Barry's work as a reminder that "the too-often-unrecognised genealogy of queer theory's major concerns and methodologies leads to the work of thinkers like [Gloria] Anzaldúa and Lorde."[60] As a rejoinder to the "romanticized and celebratory nomadology" sometimes found in queer theories of liminality, and a more pluralistic alternative to hypotheses about the inherent queerness of the comics form, queer interpretations might emphasize the hybridity of comics as an *interface*.[61] Anzaldúa uses the term interfaces for "the very spaces and places where our multiple-surfaced, colored, racially gendered bodies intersect and interconnect."[62] The comics page could not represent queerness any better way.

Drawing comics into the articulation of queer cultural practices transforms the relationship between queerness and textuality. Working across the boundaries between media, professions, and audiences is an enriching task for authors and critics of all disciplinary orientations. We come to this work with a range of desires, and the versatility of words and images provides myriad ways for us to learn about ourselves and one another through reading.

## Notes

1 Julie Maroh's lesbian comic *Blue is the Warmest Color* may be her best-known work; see Noah Berlatsky, *Wonder Woman: Bondage and Feminism in the Marston/Peter Comics, 1941–1948* (New Brunswick: Rutgers University Press, 2015); Will Brooker, *Batman Unmasked: Analyzing a Cultural Icon* (London: Bloomsbury, 2001).

2 Andrea Wood, "Making the Invisible Visible: Lesbian Romance Comics for Women," *Feminist Studies* vol. 41, no. 2 (2015): 296–97.

3 J. Jack Halberstam, "What's That Smell? Queer Temporalities and Subcultural Lives," in *In a Queer Time and Place: Transgender Bodies, Subcultural Lives* (New York: NYU Press, 2005), 169–70.

168      ANDRÉ CARRINGTON

4 Amy Villarejo, "Queer Film and Performance: 'In Theory,'" *GLQ: A Journal of Lesbian and Gay Studies* vol. 7, no. 2 (2001): 314.
5 Wood, "Making the Invisible Visible," 332–3.
6 Scott McCloud, *Understanding Comics: The Invisible Art* (New York: Harper-Perennial, 1993), 20.
7 Ibid., 3.
8 Samuel Delany, "The Politics of Paraliterary Criticism," in *Shorter Views: Queer Thoughts and the Politics of the Paraliterary* (Middletown, CT: Wesleyan University Press, 2000), 226.
9 Chris Hatfield, "Indiscipline, or, The Condition of Comics Studies," *Transatlantica*, no. 1 (2010): 5.
10 Delany, "The Politics of Paraliterary Criticism," 268.
11 Given the breadth of McCloud's definition of the form and the qualifications that Delany introduces, I will refer to "cartoon," "comic," and "graphic" texts throughout this chapter in association with the diverse language used among the artists who create them. Where an author/artist explicitly *rejects* a given term to identify their work, I will not apply it.
12 Alex Dueben, "An Oral History of Wimmen's Comix Part 1," *The Comics Journal*, March 31, 2016, www.tcj.com/an-oral-history-of-wimmens-comix.
13 "About the Conference," Queers & Comics Conference, April 14–15, 2017, California College of the Arts, www.queersandcomics.cca.edu/about.
14 Bart Beaty, *Frederic Wertham and the Critique of Mass Culture* (Jackson: University Press of Mississippi, 2005).
15 Amy Kiste Nyberg, *Seal of Approval: The History of the Comics Code* (Jackson: University Press of Mississippi, 1998); Joshua Lambert, "The Prestige of Dirty Words and Pictures: Horace Liveright, Henry Roth, and the Graphic Novel," in *Unclean Lips: Obscenity, Jews, and American Culture* (New York: New York University Press, 2014), 63–98.
16 Neil Shyminsky, "'Gay' Sidekicks: Queer Anxiety and the Narrative Straightening of the Superhero," *Men and Masculinities* vol. 14, no. 3 (2011): 288–308.
17 Robert Triptow, *Gay Comics* (New York: Plume, 1989), 4.
18 Ibid., 16–18.
19 Dueben, "An Oral History of Wimmen's Comix Part 1."
20 Alex Dueben, "An Oral History of Wimmen's Comix Part 2," *The Comics Journal*, April 6, 2016, www.tcj.com/an-oral-history-of-wimmens-comix-part-2.
21 Hillary Chute, *Graphic Women: Life Narrative & Contemporary Comics* (New York: Columbia University Press, 2010), 40. Subsequent references appear in parentheses in text.
22 Rupert Kinnard, "The Whimsical History of Cathartic Comics, 1976–1996," Pioneers of Queer Men's Comics, Queers & Comics Conference, May 8, 2015, Graduate Center, City University of New York. Conference Presentation.
23 Howard Cruse, Pioneers of Queer Men's Comics, Queers & Comics Conference, May 8, 2015, Graduate Center, City University of New York. Conference Presentation.

24 Triptow, *Gay Comics*, 26.

25 Howard Cruse, *The Complete Wendel* (New York: Universe, 2011), 112–13.

26 Ann Matsuuchi, "'Happily Ever After': The Tragic Queer and Delany's Comic Book Fairy Tale," *African American Review* vol. 48, no. 3 (2015): 271–2.

27 Ramzi Fawaz, *The New Mutants: Superheroes and the Radical Imagination of American Comics* (New York: New York University Press, 2016), 4.

28 Ibid., 68.

29 Ivan Velez, Jr., *Tales from the Closet* (New York: Hetrick-Martin Institute, 1987).

30 Jaime Cortez, *Sexile/Sexilio* (Los Angeles: Institute for Gay Men's Health, 2004).

31 Lawrence Ferber, "Queering the Comics," *The Advocate*, July 18, 2006, 50; George Gustines, "Iceman Comes Out," *New York Times*, November 7, 2015, C3.

32 Eve Sedgwick, "Queer and Now," in *Tendencies* (Durham: Duke University Press, 1993), 4.

33 Ibid.

34 Matt Brim and Amin Ghaziani, "Introduction: Queer Methods," *Women's Studies Quarterly* vol. 44, nos. 3–4 (2016): 16.

35 Lisa Diedrich, "Graphic Analysis: Transitional Phenomena in Alison Bechdel's *Are You My Mother?*," *Configurations* vol. 22, no. 2 (2014): 184.

36 Dwight Garner, "Artist, Draw Thyself (and Your Mother and Therapist)," *New York Times*, May 2, 2012, C1.

37 Sander Gilman, *Difference and Pathology: Stereotypes of Sexuality, Race, and Madness* (Ithaca: Cornell University Press, 1985).

38 Janet Jakobsen, "Sex + Freedom = Regulation Why?" *Social Text* vols. 84–5, nos. 3–4 (2005): 287.

39 Ibid., 293.

40 Ellen Forney, *Marbles: Mania, Depression, Michelangelo, and Me* (New York: Gotham Books, 2012), 118.

41 Ibid., 175–84.

42 Ibid., 227.

43 Villarejo, "Queer Film and Performance," 315.

44 MK Czerwiec and Ian Williams, About Graphic Medicine, www.graphic medicine.org/about.

45 MK Czerwiec and Michelle Huang, "Hospice Comics: Representations of Patient and Family Experience of Illness and Death in Graphic Novels," *Journal of Medical Humanities* vol. 38, no. 2 (2017): 112.

46 MK Czerwiec, *Taking Turns: Stories from HIV/AIDS Care Unit 371* (University Park: Penn State University Press, 2017).

47 Frederic Wertham, *Seduction of the Innocent* (New York: Main Road Books, [1954] 2004), 190.

48 Chiara Sulprizio, "*Eros* Conquers All: Sex and Love in Eric Shanower's Age of *Bronze*," in *Classics and Comics*, ed. George Kovacs and C. W. Marshall (Oxford: Oxford University Press, 2014), 219.

49 Ibid., 214.
50 George Kovacs, "Comics and Classics: Establishing a Critical Frame," in *Classics and Comics*, 7.
51 Douglas Wolk, "Gilbert Hernandez: Spiraling Into the System," in *Contemporary Literary Criticism*, vol. 378, ed. Lawrence Trudeau (Detroit: Gale, 2015).
52 Jeet Heer, "Tijuana Bibles," in *Saint James Encyclopedia of Popular Culture*, ed. Sarah Pendergast and Tom Pendergast (Farmington Hills: St. James Press, 2000), 656–7.
53 Gengoroh Tagame, Keynote Address, Queers & Comics Conference, April 15, 2017, California College of the Arts, San Francisco. Conference Presentation.
54 Craig Stroupe, "The Rhetoric of Irritation: Inappropriateness as Visual/Literate Practice," in *Defining Visual Rhetorics*, ed. Charles Hill and Marguerite Helmers (Mahwah: Lawrence Erlbaum, 2004), 244.
55 Ibid., 251.
56 Melinda De Jesús, "Liminality and Mestiza Consciousness in Lynda Barry's *One Hundred Demons*," in *Multicultural Comics*, ed. Frederick Aldama (Austin: University of Texas Press, 2010), 74.
57 Ibid., 77.
58 Ibid., 76.
59 Ibid., 84.
60 Mikko Tuhkanen, "Queer Hybridity," in *Deleuze and Queer Theory*, ed. Chrysanthi Nigianni and Merl Storr (Edinburgh: Edinburgh University Press, 2010), 92–3.
61 Ibid., 94.
62 Ibid., 97.

# CHAPTER 10

# Reading for Transgression
## Queering Genres

### Rebekah Sheldon

"Destroy, destroy."

(Gilles Deleuze and Felix Guattari, *Anti-Oedipus*, 1972)

## Making Trouble after the End of Transgression

Donna Haraway's 2016 *Staying with the Trouble* begins with an analysis of the titular term *trouble*. "Trouble is an interesting word," Haraway writes. "It derives from a thirteenth-century French verb meaning 'to stir up,' 'to make cloudy,' 'to disturb.'"[1] Etymologically, trouble is a thing that mixes; troubled times are mixed up times, times of hazy import and unclear consequence. To make trouble is to stir up what has become overly rigid. It is a tactic for undermining stabilities and shaking foundations. Haraway argues that troubled times may need some of this disturbance, but they need something else too. They need small acts of making, building, connecting, and caring. In periods of eroding social and cultural norms, we must stay with the trouble that is already here, leaning into trouble's labyrinthine paths, mending broken connections, and fixing new structures to hold onto small areas of stability. Troubled times call on us to accept responsibility for the ways we make the world and not for the ways we hope to unmake it. "Staying with the trouble requires learning to be truly present . . . as mortal critters entwined in myriad unfinished configurations of places, times, matters, and meanings" (1).

Haraway's ethics of staying with the trouble gives potent expression to a widely felt shift in the practice of queer studies. While it is true that queer theory has always had an interest in the ethics of making, for example in the queer counterpublics articulated by Gayle Rubin, Michael Warner, and Lauren Berlant, such making is nonetheless still imagined as posed *against* stable, hegemonic cultural forms.[2] Recently, however, the urgency in queer studies has shifted away from positions that seek to disturb the norm,[3] and toward positions that advocate for ways to build a better shared world. That distinction may at first appear slippery since all critique aims to make the world more just by generating analytic frames within which to understand and respond to injustice. What makes staying with the trouble different is its emphasis on understanding damaging know-ledge structures in order to repair the damage they have caused. Repair engenders a different style of reading than critique, a point made early on by Eve Kosofsky Sedgwick in her discussion of reparative reading practice: "The reparatively positioned reader tries to organize the fragments and part-objects she encounters or creates."[4] Sedgwick may have in mind a psychological scene of fragmentation, but her formulation works remark-ably well as the basis for the multispecies thriving Haraway conjures in *Staying with the Trouble*. Both writers foreground the extensive damage done by institutions that were once the object of transgressive reading practices. In light of that damage, it is no longer enough to transgress; we must also repair what has been broken and create new institutions and practices for future flourishing.

In this chapter, I propose that to be after queer studies is to be after transgression. Reading for transgression was an important practice in queer studies, one that warranted queer studies' close connection to literary theories centered on the role of language in culture. Roland Barthes's seminal *The Pleasure of the Text* goes some way to demonstrating what it meant to read for transgression. In this slim and aphoristic volume, Barthes compares texts that produce pleasure to those that induce bliss. The text of pleasure, he writes, "is linked to a *comfortable* practice of reading," one whose comfort derives from its continuity with the surrounding culture and its norms.[5] By contrast, the text of bliss is one that "imposes a state of loss, the text that discomforts (perhaps to a state of a certain boredom), unsettles the reader's historical, cultural, psychological assumptions, the consistency of his tastes, values, memories, brings to a crisis his relation with language" (14). From the historical vantage given us after queer studies, it may seem counterintuitive at the least to associate a positive feeling like bliss with a negative one like loss. For Barthes, however, the positive affect of pleasure in fact perpetuates the status quo. Pleasure comes from fulfilled expectations and continuity with established modes of meaning making. By contrast, bliss derives from a violent renunciation of those expectations, driving the reader to crisis. Barthes' deconstructive move here is to insist that these are not alternative forms – either pleasure or bliss – but rather that bliss inheres in the pleasurable text. The resistant writer and the transgressive reader can disinter the text of bliss from out of the work of pleasure by poising them against each other and using one to cut into the other.

> Two edges are created: an obedient, conformist, plagiarizing edge (the language to be copied is in its canonical state, as it has been established by schooling, good usage, literature, culture), and another edge, mobile, blank (ready to assume any contours), which is never anything but the site of its effect: the place where the death of language is glimpsed. (6)

The death of language comes from the reader's recognition that meaning is always hinged on meaninglessness. Words and the meanings they carry are supported by letters that mean nothing in themselves. Barthes finds the text of bliss operating paradigmatically in fictions of sexual transgression (for example, here he is discussing language in the Marquis de Sade) but its erotic charge does not come from what the work represents but rather from the "the seam ... the fault, the flaw" (6) that emerges between culture's meaning-making structures and the meaningless materiality of language itself, the mobile, blank edge of language.

Language is the site of the binaries that classify and divide the world into the discrete categories of comfortable everyday usage: man/woman, human/animal, adult/child, straight/gay, speech/writing, meaning/nonsense, normal/pathological. Deconstruction argues that the dominant term in all binary oppositions is in fact reliant on the dominated category to maintain its sense. However, it is also in language that those categories may be destabilized and denaturalized. Cutting into the text of pleasure to expose its reliance on the meaninglessness of language is one way of destabilizing the "obedient, conformist" effect of language. That the effect of this destabilization is eroticism is no mistake. As Judith Butler argues in *The Psychic Life of Power*, under conditions of hegemonic heteronormativity, accomplished heterosexuality relies on "preempting the possibility of homosexual attachment."[6] The binary pairs man/woman and straight/gay thus limit the range of possible erotic attachments and so the explosion of the binary opens the floodgates of the self to diffuse erotic energies.

Cutting into language, destroying norms, blissing out on discomfort – all were embedded within a context in which the dominant culture took for itself the role of the proper and understood itself as the keeper of normalcy, morality, good taste, and health. Transgressive fictions, in moving to thwart these expectations, sought out their opposites – pathology, criminality, monstrous passions, marginal lives, bad taste, sickness, violence, and decadence.

## Reading after the End of Transgression

As we have seen in Barthes' discussion of bliss, transgression often inhabits the logical structures of heteronormative social life in order to expose them to danger. As such it is a practice of inhabitation that moves from inside the things it seeks to dismantle. Its reading practice is faithful and thorough, if ultimately driven by antipathy. By contrast, Sedgwick's reparative reader is paradigmatically choosy. Part of the purchase of reparative reading is in the license it gives readers to ignore or intentionally transform representations that might otherwise feel inimical to one's wellbeing. In *Staying with the Trouble*, Haraway might be understood as performing this kind of reparative reading with etymologies. In a longish footnote to the final sentence I quoted above, Haraway meditates on her choice of the word *critters* from the phrase "mortal critters."

> Critters is an American everyday idiom for varmints of all sorts. Scientists talk of their "critters" all the time; and so do ordinary people all over the U.S., but perhaps especially in the South. The taint of "creatures" and "creation" does not stick to "critters"; if you see a semiotic barnacle, scrape it off. In this book, "critters" refers promiscuously to microbes, plants, humans and nonhumans, and sometimes even to machines.

Haraway advises her readers not worry too much about the web of associations that have become affixed to *critters*, especially any that might either constrain or purport to be the truth of its meaning. Critters might be a term of endearment for nonhuman animals (the phrase "what a cute critter!" comes to mind), but that is neither the whole of its sense nor its singular truth. It can mean these things, but it doesn't have to mean them and meaning them in one place and time doesn't limit what it might mean in another place and time. Haraway's point – "If you see a semiotic barnacle, scrape it off" – speaks as much to her readers' own be-barnacled sensibilities as to the encrustations on the word itself. Indeed, the practice of semiotic barnacle scraping is one she demonstrates in the very next paragraph to explain her use of Cthulhu in her subtitle *Making Kin in the Chthuluscene*. Cthulhu may be the name of the infamous monster of H. P. Lovecraft's "Call of the Cthulhu" and thus of an emblem of his xenophobic worldview, but a small labor of scraping and displacement of the final *h* returns *chthonic* from the Greek *khthonios* meaning "of the earth" and widely used to refer to a range of earth deities.[7]

Thus despite its marginality to the main argument of the book, this footnote is in fact crucial to the forms of staying with the trouble that

Haraway advocates. What these acts of etymological analysis suggest is that the troubles of the present have occasioned for Haraway and for queer theorists more generally a transformed relation to meaning making. Here and now, Haraway tells us, *making* is the order of the day and whatever tools we have to hand will have to be made to work. And yet there is something deeply uncomfortable about semiotic barnacle scraping even when it is aligned with Sedgwick's reparative reading, a discomfort that has everything to do with those opening acts of etymology. In works of criticism, etymologies trace the semiotic barnacles that adhere to and cluster certain words together. The idea is that words tend to conserve even archaic meanings, which may be latently available in the word's contemporary usage. What makes it possible to make it otherwise? What tool strips Cthulhu of the xenophobia that clings to Lovecraft? What guarantees that the new meaning will stay fixed, with no shadow of what had been? And even if the answer is that the labor of barnacle scraping is ongoing, still there is something uncomfortable in the reduction of semiotic agency such scraping requires.

It is notable, then, that Haraway's barnacle scraping happens in the context of monsters, critters, and trouble. Monsters have always shown a marked capacity for meaning production, even for excesses of meaning. As Jeffrey Jerome Cohen notes in his "Monster Culture (Seven Theses)," the term *monster* is etymologically related to the Latin *monstrum*, to reveal. "Like the letters on the page," Cohen writes, "the monster signifies something other than itself, it is always a displacement."[8] Displacements of this kind – upwellings of meaning outside of authorial intentionality – have been the basis for transgressive queer readings that seek to showcase the toxic fascination with same-sex desire that explicitly homophobic discourse both disavows and also can't help but disclose. It is also what a barnacle-scraping, staying-with-the-trouble version of queer reading displaces in favor of making. For better or worse, however, meanings are slipperier than that. Whatever the state of the world and its various hegemons, transgressive queer practices of reading recognize the fathomless indeterminacy of language.

In what follows, I consider the case of the monster in the history of queer reading practices in order to trace the routes by which queer studies came to be "after queer studies" (in the sense of after transgression) and to show how that history may be read for the barnacles that affix to it despite itself. For monsters press ever more closely. Contemporary media is full of zombies and vampires. Alongside these familiar specters are other eldritch horrors and a new genre to name them: the New Weird with its host of occult, chthonic, and xenobiotic figures. Alluring as the vampire, but geomantic where the vampire is romantic, these creatures give figure and form to what Hannah Arendt named "the unnatural growth of the natural" in the age of climate change.[9] Like climate change itself, the monsters of the New Weird are reclusive, disinterested, and gently distressed by the effects they produce. The monsters of the New Weird retain their indifference because they are of another order. Their indifference is a potent reminder that human social organization is just one among many worldly and cosmic forces. Such a salutatory humbling of the human, however, elides the pointed question this chapter seeks to take up: What will we do when the monsters come back?

## Queer Monsters

"We have not yet broken our bizarre link with the undead." So wrote Ellis Hansen in his contribution to the iconic collection *Inside/Out: Lesbian Theories, Gay Theories*.[10] Published in 1991, the collection emerged from the overlay of AIDS and queer theory, a climate Diana Fuss in her "Introduction" characterized as one of "enthusiasm, passion, anguish, fear, fervor, and general fevered commotion" (v). Casting a critical eye across a hundred years of gay male abjection, Ellis Hanson argues that the long-standing figuration of the queer as a kind of infecting vampire merely changes aspects in the era of AIDS. "Sexually exotic, alien, unnatural, oral, anal, compulsive, violent, protean, polymorphic, polyvocal, polysemous, invisible, soulless, transient, superhumanly mobile, infectious, murderous, suicidal, and a threat to wife, children, home, and phallus" (325), the gothic horror of the vampire and the gay man comes from the specter of surplus liveliness in excess of reproduction.

The vampire figures prominently in the annals of queer theory. As a late gothic figuration, the vampire is a part of the same formation in the late nineteenth century that queer theory often takes as its object of criticism. Queer theory is tied to the concerns of the late nineteenth century, which, in Sedgwick's famous formulation, saw the installation of sexuality as the most centrally important fact of psychic and social life[11] and from which the contemporary conditions of misogyny, homophobia, and racism take their modern shape. The familiar Gothic monsters – Dracula, Franken-stein, Mr. Hyde, Dorian Grey – were forged in the crucible of those world-historical forces and their institutionally legitimating discourses. As J. Jack Halberstam has persuasively demonstrated, the vampire condensed specific historical anxieties about sexuality, race, class, and empire into one highly wrought and overdetermined figure: the monster whose body is transgressive both in its peculiar appetites and in its elastic, boundary-shattering form.[12] As in other Gothic figures of unnatural embodiment, the vampire signals many different conditions to the late Victorian reader. Pervert and seducer, the vampire not only crosses boundaries of nation, class, and species, he inverts them. Ostensibly the foreign element displaced into the domestic interior, the vampire in fact estranges the familiar; ostensibly the lecherous despoiler of purity, he becomes the desired object of female lusts; neither animal nor man, not alive but also not dead, the vampire undoes the fixity of taxonomic distinctions.

Most especially, the vampire turns inside out the pedagogy of reading by collapsing the distance between reader and read. The Gothic monster "creates a public who consumes monstrosity, who revels in it, and who then surveys its individual members for signs of deviance, monstrosity, excess or violence."[13] The erotic charge of reading about the vampire comes to adhere transitively to the reader's own acts of phobic discernment. And since the vampire is the overdetermined site of boundary violations, any number of anxieties might find expression therein. By the same token, however, consumption is inherently a crossing of boundaries, one that opens "fear of and desire for the possibly latent perversity lurking within the reader herself" (13). The figure of the vampire thematizes this perverse consumption as contamination by literalizing it. "The vampire is not lesbian, homosexual, or heterosexual; the vampire represents the productions of sexuality itself. The vampire, after all, creates more vampires by engaging in a sexual relation with his victims and he produces vampires who share his specific sexual predilections" (100). The vampire opens himself to be consumed and in opening himself consumes the consumer. So while the vampire may "produce a disciplinary effect" (13) by displacing the perverse self onto a figure of alterity, that procedure requires taking on some of the poison it hopes to extract. Though ostensibly sterile, the vampire reproduces through every open vein and eye.

The vampire, in other words, not only brings into focus the symptomatic anxieties of his age in a way that makes those symptoms readable, he also disturbs the causal relation between disease and diagnosis. Knowledge of the vampire infects the knower, converting him even as he angles toward extirpation. More to the point, the vampire who exemplifies phobic structures by eliciting horror and disgust also makes those phobic structures available for critical diagnosis. For both lay reader and queer critic, the disciplinary effect of monster stories comes from learning to read the symptoms. Yet there is nothing safe about becoming literate in monstrosity; the reader of monsters is always potentially suspect as a monstrous reader. As Sedgwick reminds us, this is what is at stake in that bit of common wisdom "it takes one to know one."[14] The knowing that shows what one is always also redounds on the speaker in a cycle of epistemological contagion. After all, it takes one to know that it takes one to know. Knowing, reading, consuming, transmitting, converting: knowledge work is always dangerously in touch with the other within. While Hanson may rue the "bizarre link to the undead," such a link is in fact neither especially bizarre nor undesired. The queer critic is the monster insofar as she rejects established categories by diagnosing their incoherencies and instabilities. Her transmission of knowledge poses its own vampiric danger to heteronormativity.

For paradigmatically, the knowledge that converts as it is consumed is knowledge of the unnatural. The vampire is not for nothing composed of transgressed boundaries. The first and most essential kind of dangerous knowledge furnished by the vampire and his monstrous readers is his embodied example that things might be otherwise than they appear to be. Indeed, that they already are. For the distinction between the natural and the unnatural only seems to be a binary like any other. That the natural and its cognates require the supplement of antonyms at all threatens their cogency at every turn. If nature is all that is, then nothing can be outside the order of the natural. Otherwise, the concept collapses in on itself. To speak the condemnation *contra naturum* (against nature) is to inadvertently underscore the provisional status of the natural and thus, ironically, to intimate the existence of another nature. Fearful, fascinating, and powerfully contaminating, the Gothic monster is the paradigmatic figure of this queer nature.

*Contra naturum* has long served as a legal, moral, and cultural condemnation for nonreproductive desire. To make the case for the inherency of sexual norms, popular and professional discourse has often had recourse to examples from the animal kingdom. In her essay, "Animal Transex," Myra Hird challenges this meaning-making practice.[15] She does so, however, not by turning away from nature but instead by looking at it more closely. Studying instances of animal queerness from sex-transitioning fish to the reproductive strategy of barnacles (whose females host hundreds of tiny male symbionts), Hird concludes that there is little in nature to support the normative legal, moral, and cultural meanings that have been ascribed to it. On the contrary, she argues, not only is queerness *natural*, it has much to teach us about what queerness could be. Indeed she argues that the ethological evidence makes humans the odd ones out in a natural world overflowing with apparent perversities of nature. Hird's move to turn our attention to nature does indeed seek to undo the assumed equation of nature with innocent plenitude, itself read as presumptively heteronormative.[16] In this sense, it is still a transgressive reading practice. Instead of seeking to infect – that is, to understand in order to dismantle – the dominant paradigm that keeps nature fixed to heteropatriarchy, Hird brings a new archive to bear on it.

In taking a lesson from nature, Hird reads for instances of transgression in order to show that the unnatural is in fact natural. For that reason, however, her work also unbraids the set of assumptions that make transgression itself understandable. Studying nonhuman animals makes clear that "trans as nontransgressive" is the conclusion to which nature itself leads us. Her essay's turn away from the antinormative makes it part of a broader shift. As opposed to the ambitions of queer theory in its inaugural moments, which sought to demonstrate the historical co-constitution of large-scale social forms in order to denaturalize them, contemporary queer studies reach for examples of natural transgression in order to demobilize the notion of the unnatural and the transgressive. The more monstrous to naive notions of natural law, the better. Rather than seeking to disable norms, Hird works to generate new practices from the lifeworlds and ways of being that are going on all around us – from the barnacle on up. These are our hopeful monsters.

## Hopeful Monsters

If the queer practice of reading for transgression was tethered to a critical project of *undoing* – messing up binaries, destabilizing rigid forms – then contemporary queer studies no longer reads to transgress. From the perspective of the present, maintaining organization over time is an accomplishment. Rather than breaching boundaries or showing how they were always already breached, queer theory has turned to practices of doing, making, caring, building, fostering, and speculating. In short, queer studies in its contemporary mode seeks to generate new ways of knowing, feeling, and being, what Anna Lowenhaupt Tsing et al. call "the arts of living on a damaged planet."[17]

Recent works in queer theory have conscripted a host of monsters to help with this task. In her *Bodily Natures*, for example, Stacy Alaimo reads with Greg Bear's *Darwin* series, which narrates the effect on American culture of a generation of mutant human children.[18] Bear's children have new physical characteristics: most notably, they communicate through special pheromones and facial colorations. They inspire disgust and violence, but the hope they offer for social justice is not in what they reveal but instead in what they possess, their bodily natures and the hope for new modes of communication. Nicole Seymour in her *Strange Natures: Futurity, Empathy, and the Queer Ecological Imagination* takes up the radiation-poisoned conjoined twins in Shelley Jackson's *Half Life* in order to "model ethical approaches to the problem of environmental health and justice in the Atomic Age."[19] In "Little Monsters: Race, Sovereignty, and Queer Inhumanism in *Beasts of the Southern Wild*," Tavia Nyong'o's subtle and incisive contribution to the *GLQ* issue on Queer Inhumanisms, the wild and the monsters it harbors emerge "out of our drive toward new and more cogent myths for our present, less governed and more anarchic modes of living and creating" in the doom of the Anthropocene.[20] Yet the hope they offer "runs the knife edge between affirming . . . resilience and consolidating . . . abandonment" (265).

Indeed, many of the hopeful monsters of recent queer theorizing might as easily be taken as reasons for despair: Heather Davis's dead dolphin, killed by swallowing a pink plastic dildo, might well fall under this heading,[21] as would the garbage heap of Nigel Clark and Myra Hird's *O-zone* essay "Deep Shit." Taking mass extinction as the exigency for their analysis, Hird and Clark posit what they call "the evil twin" of this late capitalist eco-decadence.[22] The dump isn't just a collection of used-up human goods. It is the kind of chemical soup that microbial life has been especially adept at adapting as metabolism. We don't know what kinds of unwilled inhuman proliferation, what sort of monsters of waste, these soups might make, but it is unlikely to be simply dead, inert, or passive. As they write:

> But what if there is a flip side to the anonymous eclipse of so many species or strains? Not a lightness to the darkness and occlusion of the unregistered extinction event, but something more in the nature of an evil twin. What if, without trying, without knowing, without even the possibility of our finding out, we humans were increasing the sum total of biological diversity on Earth? (46)

These framings are deeply ambivalent about these chthonic upwellings. Hird and Clark's article is, after all, titled "Deep Shit" for a reason. Their monstrous garbage dump is less a hopeful monster than a simply indifferent one. Indifferent to us, that is. For us, though, getting intimate with shit may simply be the condition of life in the Anthropocene. As they maintain, "what finally becomes of our defecations is up to the swarms of miniscule beings that ultimately engendered our existence" (51).

It's important to note the differences from the earlier discussion of Gothic monsters. Halberstam is clear that Gothic monsters must be treated with ambivalence. In recuperating them, we are always reading against the grain of their disciplinary effects. In all the stories I have discussed in the previous section, catastrophe is an unavoidable condition of everyday life. The blueprints these hopeful monsters offer are therefore tuned to modulation rather than transgression. They teach us how to navigate instability and how to foster precarious survivals and local thriving. If they read against the grain at all, it is only insofar as they refuse to treat environmental calamity as a disgusting impurity, a breach of a prior innocence. Instead, the emphasis is on the possibilities for resilience found in nature's animacy. As in Sedgwick's description of reparative practices they set out "the task of building a common world" from out of the "heterogeneous parts" of the existing order.[23] In this sense, they work through advocacy rather than criticism.

In the conclusion of *Staying with the Trouble*, Haraway moves this one step further by folding criticism directly into storytelling. Taking seriously Ursula Le Guin's notion of stories as "carrier bags" in which to collect the stuff of survival, Haraway calls for storytelling as a practice of world making. Set in a speculative near future after the collapse of many life forms and forms of life, Haraway's tales track five generations of symbiont clones, the Camilles. Transgenically linked to the species they are dedicated to protect, the children have features that facilitate communication and understanding with that species. Camille 1, holobiont to the monarch butterfly, was genetically patterned to smell milkweed on the wind and digest it without harm, which allowed her to travel on the monarch's migratory paths and to sense the same dangers in the way that butterflies would. Camille 2 had her forebears' genetic traits and also chose to have butterfly antennae grafted onto her chin. These traits helped the Camilles to become "apt students of their own human-butterfly worldings" alongside their education in many forms of struggle. Camille 2, for example, lived with the Zapatistas to learn their strategies of non-violent struggle, while Camille 3 read works of twentieth-century fantasy and science fiction. In charting these paths, Haraway hopes that the story of the Camilles will inspire the reader to their own acts of "recuperative terraforming before the apocalypse" (213).

There is little ambiguity here. If it is not yet possible to link sympoetically with endangered species, there are still utopian fantasies and revolutionary struggles that might provide "a pilot project, a model, a work and play object, for composing collective projects" (136). But do they return a reading practice? Bruno Latour has argued that "what performs a critique cannot also compose" (475). What of the converse? Are such compositions themselves acts of criticism? Haraway's choice to conclude *Staying with the Trouble* with the Camille Stories intimates that myths do something different than readings can do. If we construe our task in this way, and if we see stories as composing the best models for living in the Anthropocene, why pursue the work of criticism at all? To ask a familiar question, what's queer about this – as a method, an object, or an argument about nature? And what is the status of the story in this paradigm? A carrier bag, after all, sounds suspiciously like a womb, with all the ascriptions of passivity and receptivity that have adhered to feminized metaphors at least since Plato. What does it mean to want stories that mean only one thing? If there is no ambiguity, in other words, perhaps it is because that ambiguity has been scraped off.

It's worth recalling one of the foundational assertions of queer theory from Sedgwick's much-cited essay "Queer and Now." She argues that the privilege of queer reading is in its perverse will to find those places where "the meanings don't line up tidily with each other."[24] She doesn't want to judge them or to rectify them but rather to fall in love with their stubbornly profligate polysemy. It is in contemplating the dusty corners and overblown conventions of texts – the startling detail, the odd repetition, the unnecessary flourish, the overdone scene, the apparently meaningless triviality – that Sedgwick built a new paradigm to explain the operations of homophobia. In converting fascination to exposition, her queer reading holds on to the ambivalence of loving the thing that hurts. Reading for transgression is always such a practice of ambivalence. It requires us to recognize the duplicity of stories, which always mean more (or less) than we intend. It reminds us that even the best constructed models may nonetheless disclose the monsters that lurk at their, and our, hearts.

## Monsters beyond Our Control

This is the lesson of N. K. Jemisin's Broken Earth trilogy, which offers a paradigmatic hopeful monster in the person of Alabaster. At the conclusion of the first novel, Syenite realizes that Alabaster has not merely escaped from the earthquake that signaled the start of another destructive season of failed crops and dust-clouded skies; he was its maker. And far from regretting what he has done, he has come instead to ask Syenite for her help in finishing the job.

Syen and Alabaster are Orogenes, biologically capable of sensing kinetic energy in geological strata and redirecting it in accordance with their will. Orogenes are necessary because they quell the myriad instabilities of the Earth, brought about long ago by the failed attempt to fully control the Earth's vitality and redirect it for human purpose. Orogenes are powerful, but in their world's age such skills make their bearers objects of repugnance. They are kept under strict surveillance, guarded, bred, and overseen; their lives and deaths controlled by the Imperial forces that offer protection from mass violence and kill those who refuse it. In the world Jemisin builds, colonial oppression filters through environmental exploitation, resource extraction, and capitalist wealth expropriation to show how all of them find expression in everyday experiences of phobic violence. The Orogenes's geosense serves as both the justification for their domination and the novel's hope for an evolutionary fix to the problem of anthropogenic environmental change, for they alone can restore the Earth's lost stability. But to realize that hope, they must first destroy the existing order.

> [Alabaster] reaches forth with all the fine control that the world has brainwashed and brutalized out of him, and all the sensitivity that his masters had bred into him through generations of rape and coercion and highly unnatural selection . . .
>
> He reaches deep and takes hold of the humming tapping bustling reverberating rippling vastness of the city . . .
>
> He takes all that, the strata and the magma and the people and the power, in his imaginary hands. Everything. He holds it. He is not alone. The earth is with him.
>
> Then he breaks it.[25]

The non-Orogene majority of the Stillness will suffer as a result of Alabaster's actions and it is this ability to cause suffering and do harm that makes the Orogenes into monsters in the eyes of the majority. Revenge, however, is not Alabaster's motive. Like a physician resetting a badly healed bone, Alabaster breaks the world in order to restore it. His decision sets in motion the circumstances that just might lead to the restoration of order and prepares the way for a better, truer healing. What the novel first proffers as a profound act of destruction in fact serves the end of reparation. In this, however, Alabaster is opposed to the Earth itself. One of the series most startling revelations is that while the Earth may be a victim of human exploitation, it is not insensate matter, passive except for its useful energies and materials. But neither is it a ready collaborator in the effort to create multispecies worlding, as in Haraway's Cthuluscene. It is sentient, it is angry, and it has a plan of its own to bring about the end of life on Earth.

By the third volume in the series, Alabaster has died and Syenite has taken up his purpose. Unaware of her mother's plan, Syen's daughter Nassun also quests; her goal is total worldly destruction. Earth, civilization, humanity – all she judges irremediably guilty. During her quest, however, she learns the histories that have brought the Earth to its present state and she begins to understand its rage and violence.

> For the world has taken so much from her. She had a brother once. And a father, and a mother whom she also understands but wishes she did not. And a home, and dreams. The people of the Stillness have long since robbed her of childhood and any hope of a real future, and because of this she is so angry that she cannot think beyond THIS MUST STOP and I WILL STOP IT –
>
> – so does she not resonate with the Evil Earth's wrath, herself?[26]

Identifying with the Earth's wrath, she realizes the intertwining histories that have embittered and deformed everyone she knows might nonetheless be made to bear different futures. And so in her final showdown with her mother, she chooses reparation over sacred violence in the hope that another world is possible. Aligning her will with her mother's, she restores the Earth's balance and saves the world. She proves herself a helpful monster after all.

Cohen concludes "Monster Culture (Seven Theses)" with the motto "monsters are our children" (20). By this he means two things: First, that monsters are the product of our cultural imaginaries and thus index back to the cultures that produce them. Monsters are our children in the sense that they come from us and so we may read ourselves in them: "the monster exists only to be read" (4). But there is a second valence to Cohen's analogy of monsters and children. Our child monsters may also be our own monstrous children, like and unlike, self and not-self, arising from somewhere hidden and outside of our control, and so full of eldritch knowledge "and a discourse all the more sacred as it arises from the Outside" (20). The idea that stories will have only one meaning and the related idea that it is possible to scrape off semiotic barnacles not only makes use of children for the story but makes the stories themselves into children: familiar, innocent, hopeful. In scripting monsters as helpers, *hope* became *help*. Our monsters lost the difference, the agency, and the agenda that made them monstrous to begin with. Nassun's actions in the final book of Jemisin's Broken Earth trilogy are a potent reminder that the future is not wholly under the control of the present; although Nassun redeems her legacy of righteous rage by choosing to repair what she did not break, her rage reminds us that not all of our monstrous children may be so willing to do the work of taking up their parents' tasks.

## Conclusion

This chapter began with trouble and ended with hope. That I intended for *trouble* to carry a positive valence and *hope* a negative one speaks most incisively to my own continued commitment to the Gothic terms of a monstrous queer reading practice. If this preference of mine seems counterintuitive, perhaps that speaks to the necessity, in a time of everyday catastrophe, for the hopeful constructions of myth and the sharp-edged tools of barnacle scraping. Perhaps, in other words, ignoring ambivalence and ambiguity serves the strategic purpose of destroying systems of oppression to rebuild toward a more equal distribution of life possibilities. That might be true. In that case, I would urge holding onto the memory of trouble's troublesome tendency to stir up and make cloudy, to awaken forces that disrupt preexisting models and conjure meanings at crosspurposes with the stories from which they arise. These worrisome effects of trouble are indeed my own hopeful monsters.

## Notes

1 Donna Haraway, *Staying with the Trouble: Making Kin in the Chthuluscene* (Durham: Duke University Press, 2016), 1. All subsequent references appear parenthetically in the text.
2 See Michael Warner, *The Trouble with Normal: Sex, Politics, and the Ethics of Queer Life* (Cambridge, MA: Harvard University Press, 2000); and Michael Warner and Lauren Berlant, "Sex in Public," *Critical Inquiry* vol. 24, no. 2 (Winter 1998): 547–66.
3 See Robyn Weigman and Elizabeth A. Wilson, eds., *Queer Theory without Antinormativity*, Special issue of *differences* vol. 26, no. 1 (May 2015).
4 Eve Kosofsky Sedgwick, *Touching Feeling: Affect, Pedagogy, Performativity* (Durham: Duke University Press, 2003), 146. Interestingly, Sedgwick anticipates that readers will object to reparative reading based on its preference for the aesthetic and its "frankly ameliorative" politics (144). A critique of "merely reformist" politics (144) only makes sense if the institutions to be reformed appear inexorable. To ameliorate catastrophe, however, an aesthetic judgment may be the best possible heuristic.

5 Roland Barthes, *The Pleasure of the Text*, trans. Richard Miller (New York: Hill and Wang, 1975), 14 (italics in original). All subsequent references appear parenthetically in the text.

6 Judith Butler, *The Psychic Life of Power: Theories in Subjection* (Stanford: Stanford University Press, 1997), 135.

7 H. P. Lovecraft, "Call of the Cthulhu," in *H. P. Lovecraft: Tales* (New York: Library of America, 2005), 167–97.

8 Jeffrey Jerome Cohen, "Monster Culture (Seven Thesis)," in *Monster Theory: Reading Culture*, ed. Jeffrey Jerome Cohen (Minneapolis: University of Minnesota Press, 1996), 4. All subsequent references appear parenthetically in the text.

9 Hannah Arendt, *The Human Condition*, 2nd ed. (Chicago: University of Chicago Press, 1958), 47.

10 Ellis Hanson, "Undead," in *Inside Out: Lesbian Theories, Gay Theories*, ed. Diana Fuss (New York: Routledge, 1991), 324–41. All subsequent references appear parenthetically in the text.

11 See in this context Sedgwick's famous dating of the homo/hetero bind to the Oscar Wilde indecency trials in 1895. Eve Kosofsky Sedgwick, *Between Men: English Literature and Male Homosocial Desire* (New York: Columbia University Press, 1985), 216–17.

12 More specifically, Halberstam argues that "multiple otherness is subsumed by the unitary otherness of sexuality" (7–8). Read as sexuality, the vampire's overdetermination nonetheless evokes the many anxieties of class, of race, of foreignness that are also condensed into this figure. My thanks to E. L. McCallum for making this point to me.

13 J. Jack Halberstam, *Skin Shows: Gothic Horror and the Technology of Monsters* (Durham: Duke University Press, 1995), 12. All subsequent references appear parenthetically in the text.

14 Eve Kosofsky Sedgwick, *Epistemology of the Closet* (Berkeley: University of California Press, 1990), 222, 225.

15 Myra Hird, "Animal Trans," *Australian Feminist Studies* vol. 21, no. 49 (2006): 35–48.

16 Helen Merrick well expresses this point. She writes, "The (ab)use of the concepts of the 'natural' and 'unnatural' in regulating queer sexualities stems from the fact that 'natural' s invariably associated with 'procreative'" (219). See Helen Merrick, "Queering Nature: Close Encounters with the Alien in Ecofeminist Science Fiction," in *Queer Universes: Sexualities in Science Fiction*, ed. Wendy Gay Pearson, Veronica Hollinger, and Joan Gordon (Liverpool: Liverpool University Press, 2008), 216–32.

17 Anna Lowenhaupt Tsing et al., eds., *Arts of Living on a Damaged Planet: Ghosts and Monsters of the Anthropocene* (Minneapolis: University of Minnesota Press, 2017).

18 Stacy Alaimo, *Bodily Natures: Science, Environment, and the Material Self* (Bloomington: Indiana University Press, 2010).

19  Nicole Seymour, *Strange Natures: Futurity, Empathy, and the Queer Ecological Imagination* (Urbana-Champaign: University of Illinois Press, 2015), 151.

20  Tavia Nyong'o, "Little Monsters: Race, Sovereignty, and Queer Inhumanisms in *Beast of the Southern Wild*," *GLQ: A Journal of Gay and Lesbian Studies* vol. 21, no. 2 (2015): 265. All subsequent references appear parenthetically in the text.

21  Heather Davis, "Toxic Progeny: The Plastisphere and Other Queer Futures," *PhiloSOPHIA* vol. 5, no. 2 (2015): 232–50.

22  Myra Hird and Nigel Clark, "Deep Shit," *O-Zone: A Journal of Object-Oriented Studies* vol. 1, no. 1 (2014): 44–52. All subsequent references appear parenthetically in the text.

23  Bruno Latour, "An Attempt at a Compositionist Manifesto," *New Literary History* vol. 41 (2010): 474. All subsequent references appear parenthetically in the text.

24  Eve Kosofsky Sedgwick, *Tendencies* (Durham: Duke University Press, 1993), 3.

25  N. K. Jemisin, *The Fifth Season* (New York: Orbit, 2015), 7.

26  N. K. Jemisin, *The Stone Sky* (New York: Orbit, 2017), 248.

# CHAPTER 11

# Sovereignty

## A Mercy

### Sharon Patricia Holland

"The animal looks at us, and we are naked before it.
Thinking perhaps begins there."

(Jacques Derrida, *The Animal that Therefore I Am*, 2009)

"Where else but in this disorganized world would such an encounter
be possible?"

(Toni Morrison, *A Mercy*, 2008)

In *The Dreaded Comparison: Human and Animal Slavery*, about which
Alice Walker said "this powerful book ... will take a lifetime to forget,"
Marjorie Spiegel brings to bear a series of always awful and sometimes
artful proofs about the relationship between the suffering of nonhuman
animals and the situation of the enslaved.[1] At one point in her critique,
Spiegel turns to Sterling Brown's 1968 essay, "Negro Character as Seen by
White Authors." While noting the post-emancipation shift in the attitude
of whites toward their black counterparts, Brown uses the image of the
"docile mastiff" turned rabid "mad dog" to draw readers' attention to the
stereotyping of blackness as bestial. Spiegel then observes, "in seeing
comparisons of blacks to animals that were so prevalent in the period
literature of his study, Brown accepted and, through his response, subse-
quently strengthened the negative views about animals held by the racist
authors ... Brown's indignation at these offensive books blinded him to
the fellow victims of their propaganda" (37). Spiegel's assessment pulls in
two directions. The first is more obvious: that stereotypes of animals are
universally held. The second is more opaque: that blackness' normative
gaze upon the animal therefore prohibits ethical relation. In an encounter
with the animal, enslaved experience can justify dropping the bottom out
of the question of blackness' ethical commitment to the animal other. This
is a fundamental problem this essay seeks to engage. In the work for "after
queer" that I want to do here, it is perhaps fitting that my inquiry is
not about blackness' relationship with white others/othering, but about

blackness' relationship with racialized others. Much of the work of queer critique has been focused on what is forgotten in whiteness' imagining of queer thresholds. I for one am tired of caring about the other outside, and in particular a human other outside whose concern for our collective theorizing is marginal at best. My "after queer" takes indigenous intellectual tradition seriously and sees the founding of nation, so often invoked as a holy temporal past tense when all was right and good, as another instance of nonnormative identity formation, rather than its solidification.

In the course of her examination of animal and human suffering – and this is an important detail because no moment of comparison in this book opens the possibility of shared pleasure, only pain – Speigel makes the obligatory liberal nod toward the condition and sentiment of the "Native American":

> Notably, traditional, culturally-intact Native Americans and many other aboriginal peoples hunted out of real necessity, with respect for, and in harmony with, the balance of nature. Theirs was not a profane act, nor an unconscious attempt to symbolically conquer chaos ... Harmony and respect were central to an entire world-view, a view of the universe, with which the very lives of Native Americans were imbued, from birth until death, and, in their philosophy, from death until rebirth. (64)

Now that's a mouthful.

This type of conceptualization of Indian life is not uncommon and Phil Deloria painstakingly documents how US culture arrived at such overwhelming and overarching collective sentiment about "Native Americans."[2] How might we think through these historicized and culturally produced entanglements about blacks' and Indians' relationship to the animal? I say historicized because views of Indian life and animals are sedimented in a kind of archaic – Deloria's word – historicization of an 'Indian time' before settler colonialism, a kind of anti-temporality where subjects and their relations are locked in static rapport. By comparison, views of black life and animals solidified during slavery, as Spiegel's book relentlessly catalogues, and the possibility for blackness to relate to animal being is constantly foreclosed by the threat of falling into becoming already the animal other. As Megan Glick aptly notes, "[t]o imagine a state of literally becoming-animal is to imagine a state of dehumanization so profound as to be too dehumanizing to talk about."[3]

Spiegel's frontloading of negative black relation to the animal via Brown's work leads her to end her observations with several quotes in support of her comparative argument; three of these are pulled from

Frederick Douglass and the most famous African-American vegetarian/
fruitarian, Dick Gregory. Spiegel doesn't discuss, but brings into evidence
in the penultimate section of her book, the most oft-quoted line of
Douglass's section on "The Treatment of Animals" from "The Present
and Future of the Colored Race in America" (1863):

> There is no denying that slavery had a direct and positive tendency to
> produce coarseness and brutality in the treatment of animals, especially
> those most useful to agricultural industry. Not only the slave, but the horse,
> the ox and the mule shared the general feeling of indifference to the right
> naturally engendered by the state of slavery. The master blamed the
> overseer, the overseer the slave, and the slave the horses, oxen and mules,
> and violence fell upon the animals as a consequence. (107)

The line of descent that Douglass draws here perhaps has allowed black
studies to decenter the place of the animal in the question of black being.
When we get to the phrase "violence fell upon the animals," we are led to
believe that the chief perpetrators of violence toward the animal are enslaved
subjects; their violence toward animals is *naturalized* and even more sedimented because it is a black subject who speaks from the vantage point of
veracity's best ally: experience. Violence from black beings toward animal
beings is naturalized under a totalizing system of descending degradation.
But the important kernel here is in the following line: "Not only the slave,
but the horse, the ox and the mule shared the general feeling of indifference
to the right naturally engendered by the state of slavery." change to read:
The capacity for same-feeling or shared feeling is opened up by Douglass's
remarks, upending his certain ordering of things. A decade later in 1873,
Douglass conceptualizes human/animal relations thus: "one of the greatest
pleasures connected with agricultural life may be found in the pleasant
relations capable of subsisting between the farmer and his four-legged
companions" and later he urges "and to do this, there is but one rule, and
that is, uniform sympathy and kindness"[4], In fact, Douglass's animal-
forward reflection upon agrarian life represents the chief tension of the
present animal studies quandary: what is the balance between sameness and
difference, civilizing mission and gentle hegemony? This is the same question that pops up in Animal Studies across a range of (inter)disciplinary
homes: What *is* that fine distinction between hum/animal? In almost every
debate at the axis of human/animal, I have yet to see an engagement with
the consequence of slavery or the words of the formerly enslaved on
this issue.

In the comparative framework I draw here, black relation to the animal
is rendered as a blind spot, impossible because of the machinations of

slavery, while Indian relation to the animal is naturalized, as part of a cultural matrix, universalized to the point of becoming the great Indian chain of being. Thinking through these relations among Indian, Black and nonhuman animal raises the question: Is it possible to upend an ongoing tradition about human freedom with a line of thought created by others, already othered, or precariously human? What are the queer possibilities of thinking outside our human script? How might these possibilities recast how we think about queer in a particular way?

Years ago I wrote an article about Afro-Native literature and the importance of thinking through issues of sovereignty and emancipation.[5] I now pick up the loose thread of that argument to explicate further the relationship of these stereotypical views of black/Indian relation to the nonhuman animal. In historical accounts, at least, it seems as if "freedom" and "self-determination" are a task that Indian and black peoples are not up to accomplishing on their own. Moreover, this fitness for self-government/ self-governance is dependent not upon the relations among humans, but mired in one's relationship to the nonhuman animal, making the present-day "question of the animal" absolutely beholden to the articulation of aspects of sovereignty and freedom constitutive of indigenous and black life, respectively.[6] Since sovereignty and self-governance are articulated through a host of normative relations (family, race, nation, and time), a queer aperture is vital to untangling what matters and when to our collective struggle for freedom.

Scholarship on sovereignty and dispossession occur across a range of tribal homes – from Robert Warrior (Osage) to Phil Deloria (Standing Rock Sioux), from Jodi Byrd (Chickasaw) to Kehaulani Kauanui (Native Hawai'ian), and Aileen Moreton-Robinson (Quandamooka First Nation) to Jean O'Brien (Ojibwe).[7] Each recognizes the intense interplay between emerging state and established nations, a will-to-possession that is both geographical and performative, a shadow play of enormous consequence that confuses contact with conquest. Our popular understandings of sovereignty flatten the middle ground to the black-and-white thinking of *before* and *after*. Dispossession, in the performative sense, looks a lot like Joseph Roachs's paradigmatic surrogacy; the pilfering of nonwhite cultures and the taking – through violence or by other means – of the body provide the opportunity for reflection upon what whiteness really is, as a culture *and* a concept. Such rumination reminds me of Hortense Spillers's early reading of Harriet Jacobs's *Incidents*, where she notes that the black female body can be stolen and inhabited at *any time* – a terrorizing temporality – by her white mistress.[8] Such dispossession of land, culture, and body creates instabilities across a range of inhabitations and identities, making identity a serious problem for whiteness. One such inhabitation that remains relatively underexplored is that of nonhuman animal life. It is to this slippage between and among hum/animal/blackness that I now turn my attention.

Taking one more glance at Spiegel, in the same chapter on "Hunting" where she gives praise – specious though it might be – to a monolithic indigenous lifeway, she also states rather offhandedly "hunters may pay up to $50,000 to legally kill an endangered polar bear in Canada, purchasing a hunting license from a Native American tribe that peddles them for cash." So much for the peace, love, and coconuts argument about native culture which ends the chapter. Here, the beautiful fiction of Indian essence falls away when it comes into direct contact with sovereignty's self-determination. When it comes time to self-determine, the indigenous body is a mere peddler, a black market capitalist. So too does black life falter in the wake of emancipation, as Spiegel quotes Brown's opinion that "in freedom they are beasts" (156). The twin images of the sovereign and the beast are brought to bear here in a stunning kaleidoscopic interplay.

Drawing on the crosscurrents of work in Black Atlantic thought on the human, political theory's musings on power and biology, and Cartesian philosophy's worrying about the hum/animal distinction, I bring such thinking together with work in Native American and Indigenous Studies on dispossession. All of these discourses should be informing one another, since questions of self-possession and determination constitute the stuff of colonization.[9] Jodi Byrd observes: "This notion of becoming savage is what I call the transit of empire, a site through which the United States with ties to Enlightenment and Victorian colonialism propagates itself through a paradigmatic 'Indianness' tied now to the global ascendency of liberalism."[10] For Byrd, in this "paradigmatic Indianness" Indian peoples represent the "already known," the been-there done-that of US empire so that they serve a "mythological function" which shores up the liberal project of multicultural inclusion that relies upon our continued obfuscation of what happened "back then." Temporally, this is the site of impossible reckoning, as US sovereignty is predicated on a constant absenting. This is a story about "land, labor, journey and displacement" (33). This connection among black, Indian, and I would add a nonhuman animal, a connection about "land, labor, journey and displacement," plays out in Toni Morrison's *A Mercy* (2008) – a peculiar, pithy, but dense homage to relations among peoples in the fledgling nation (circa 1690), the time that "race" forgot. *A Mercy* appears to invoke a temporality fecund with possibility, and I hope that my brief reading toward the end of this essay demonstrates its utility for the queerness of all relations in early settler time. But first a bit on sovereignty and freedom.

## Beasts of Burden

After the 1871 Congressional decision to suspend treaty-making practices with indigenous groups, the United States entered into a colonial power relationship with native peoples, at least in the eyes of Kevin Bruyneel's *The Third Space of Sovereignty*. In the period between 1871 and the political movements of the 1960s that brought forth moments like the American Indian Chicago Conference (AICC), this colonial relationship worsened. Thinking through Bruyneel's arguments (and by extension Deloria's) about the necessary and mythic disappearance of the "Indian" into an archaic past, and the attempt to hollow out the black/indigenous other for use by the fledgling nation state, I map how sovereignty can be understood alongside self-determination and emancipation, nodes which find the Indian *and* black other deteriorating into a naturalized state – to a beast, who cannot govern itself nor be tamed by others.

In *The Beast and the Sovereign*, Jacques Derrida notes:

> Here, whenever we speak of the beast and the sovereign, we shall have in view an analogy between two current representations (current and therefore problematical, suspect, to be interrogated) between this type of animality or living being that is called the "beast" or that is represented as bestiality, on the one hand, and on the other a sovereignty that is most often represented as human or divine, in truth anthropo-theological.[11]

Thus, the *condition* of sovereignty depends upon the nonhuman animal, or to echo Derrida, "a type of animality" (14), making ideas of animal being intrinsically bound to the ability of the sovereign to self-determine not only his/her own fate, but that of others. Derrida paints the landscape of interaction between beast and sovereign with the stuff of fairy tales – the big bad wolf, among others – demonstrating that the "archaic" or the "unheimlich" is in play during this scripted interaction. To be sovereign – the ability to govern (self-govern), to think oneself competent enough to self-govern – is to be civilized, a mission demonstrated in one's ability to either tame or determine the conditions under which animal life matters – and, if I were inclined to be thinking more necropolitically, the conditions under which the animal always already dies.[12]

To solidify what I mean by this archaic past, I turn to Bruyneel's apt description of the catch-22 that some indigenous peoples find themselves in relation to – and this is perhaps another mouthful – "the modern American liberal democratic settler-state." In his assessment of the Mille Lacs Band's response to then Minnesota Governor Jesse Ventura's challenge to native sovereignty, Bruyneel notes:

> there are two prevalent American sentiments about indigenous people's political status. The first sentiment is that indigenous tribes and nations claim a form of sovereignty that is unclear because it is not easily located inside or outside of the United States ... The spatial logic is quite simple: if the tribe is "part of the United States," it is not sovereign, but if it is to be sovereign, it cannot be part of and thus make demands on the United States. The second sentiment is that the treaty-secured rights of indigenous tribes stem from an archaic political time that cannot assume a modern form ... [In sum] Chippewa sovereignty is not permitted to develop into a modern form and engage in practices commensurate with present-day American political life.[13]

In many ways, the primary problem is temporal; the secondary problem is geographic. I am intrigued by the "political status" Bruyneel alludes to here, and especially his appeal to "American political life." The Animal Studies debate is steeped in discourse of the political, and in fact comes out of an historically grounded moment – the advent of post-World War II technologies like the prison camp or the CAFO – but it has little or nothing at all to say about how understandings of sovereignty and emancipation in its US context might change the landscape and focus of Animal Studies work. This is a serious frustration for me as a scholar, who always reads at the intersection of queer, feminist, and critical race studies. For Animal Studies scholars, politics *is* consumed with the distinction of hum/animal, yet it cannot see the ways in which this hum/animal relationship is etched upon discourses of freedom and sovereignty in relation to black and indigenous lives. From my vantage point, it appears that sovereignty – as a political effect – came to die in the Americas. That Euro-American struggle for independence keeps working itself over through the effigy of *that king*; and yet, as these notions of freedom morphed (in a postdemocratic epoch) into *modes* of governmentality, the question of sovereignty and its afterlife in the Americas should be of particular concern to Animal Studies scholars and advocates.

Assessments of what black "freedom" at the time of emancipation and beyond would look like travel along the lines of the racist to the truly celebratory. While the state of black persons in the US is neither colonial nor postcolonial, this neither/nor boundary, this inability for blackness to settle into its progress is reflective of the same states of injury and redress outlined by postcolonial theorists. Once formal campaigns – to repatriate blacks to Liberia for example – ceased, the black body, like its Indian counterpart circa 1871, was cast in a web of constant attempts at domestication; no longer what Bruyneel calls a "foreign concern," Indianness (and I would add blackness here as well) became a domestic problem to be solved through attempts at veritable eradication (148). But present life demonstrates the absolute failure of this effort to domesticate; the civilizing project is always one of genocidal intent. I want to turn now to Morrison's *A Mercy* to demonstrate ways in which this attempt to answer the question of black freedom and Indian sovereignty is *managed* by Morrison. I also want to draw our attention to how the novel clears the way for such domesticating through the figure of the nonhuman animal and human association with it.

## The "Quiet of Animals Sated at Last"

We are a nation obsessed with origins – if one were to listen to the hue and cry from different quarters of this country's tea party revolutionaries we would think that our origins certainly do not reflect the diversity of persons who pepper this small portion of the globe we call home. In *A Mercy*, the notion of "origin" is always already that: a notion – usually vague and unimpressive as a foundational idea of something. When we wish in our present tense for "how things were," we reset the clock on the past, populate it with those whom we imagine reflect our core values as a nation and then repackage that thing called history for more popular consumption. Anyone who wants to get back to that mythical and happy nation that our founding fathers authored hasn't had the pleasure of reading the tedious diary entries of Cotton and Increase Mather, or delighted in the musings of one Michael Wigglesworth, or contemplated Thomas Jefferson's more self-reflexive chapter called "Manners" in *Notes on the State of Virginia* on the devastating psychic havoc that centuries of slavery can wreak upon kin, home, and ultimately nation, or ventured to read William Apess's (Pequot) stunning manifesto, or had a look at David Walker's *Appeal*. If you note that these origin stories are cisgendered male crafted, this is also my point. Stories of origin and sovereigns rarely come to us in female-bodied form. When we start to have conversations about who belongs where and when and why I am reminded that except for certain tender mercies like acts of friendship, salvation, and sustenance none of us do "belong."

Diversity in this nation is not new. In fact, it is, plainly put, "a mercy" – if a mercy can be understood to encompass all of the acts between human

196 SHARON PATRICIA HOLLAND

beings that comprise the nature of diversity itself. In these times, our very biodiversity is dependent upon "a mercy" – acts of acknowledgement, kindness, and bravery pull human beings from the arc of hatred and isolation into the bandwidth of compassion and consideration of the other. Those same acts in turn must also pull nonanimal human beings from the brink of extinction. A mercy is a pause in the temporal; it is a shift in relations across the board – human, nonhuman animal. A mercy might be a kind of queer temporality, a sort of sordid relationality that acknowledges the twin impact of settler and enslaved economies. A mercy, according to the OED can be a blessing or a relief. In many ways a mercy is an ethical commitment. In his brief essay on "The Name of the Dog, or Natural Rights," Emmanuel Levinas observes, "with the appearance of the human – and this is my entire philosophy – there is something more than my life, and that is the life of the other."[14] In the Cartesian tradition that Levinas follows, it is important that the animal is distinct from the human. For some philosophers this difference is speech, for Levinas, it is the face. The "face" holds the possibility for recognition, for exchange, for mercy. Animals are thought to be incapable of such reciprocal gazing.

In her astute review of Morrison's novel, Elizabeth McHenry writes that the book is "a story about a world in which acts of mercy prove ambiguous, and the lines between cruelty and compassion are murky at best."[15] Indeed, somewhere between the ambiguous and the murky, "cruelty and compassion," the ethical commitment floats, awaiting our attention, our action. A Mercy tells the story of how Jacob Vaark, an orphaned immigrant from Amsterdam with a small, but steadily growing farm in New England, acquires Florens, Lina, and Sorrow – one surrendered, one left over, the other sold cheaply. The central action of the novel revolves around Florens's sexual obsession with and journey to find the "blacksmith" who has knowledge of healing herbs that might bring Jacob's wife, Rebekka, back from the brink of a smallpox death.

The opening of the novel is decidedly animal. Florens is the first character we meet and, in classic Morrison fashion, she comes to us out of the ether in the middle of recounting a difficult experience, boldly enjoying our ability as readers to be shocked into the time of the novel:

> Don't be afraid. My telling can't hurt you in spite of what I have done and I promise to lie quietly in the dark ... I will never again unfold my limbs to rise up and bare teeth. I explain. You can think what I tell you a confession, if you like, but one full of curiosities familiar only in dreams and during those moments when a dog's profile plays in the steam of a kettle.[16]

There goes that dog again and the madness of teeth bared, limbs unfolding. In the classic definition of "bared," the process is not a revelation but an unconcealment – the removal of a covering from something. But this is no secret being exposed; this act is making known what is always already there. Think Heidegger here. Think Agamben. Think too precarious life, of some sort or another.[17] I want to leave abruptly Florens's opening (to us) for other moments in the novel where this attachment to the animal is reiterated and becomes central to the novel's metaphorical and representational terrain.

The indigenous character in the novel and the oldest of the three indentured women on the farm, Lina "had been purchased outright and deliberately" (40). In the only section dedicated to her story, Lina worries about the festive mood that overtakes the farm at the building of Jacob Vaark's "double-storied, fenced and gated [house] like the one he saw on his travels" (51), noting how: "Killing trees in that number without asking their permission, of course his efforts would stir up malfortune" (51). This is the first indication that Lina is different from Sorrow and Florens, the two orphan girls that Vaark rescues one at a time. Morrison positions Lina to read literally the threat that black freedom poses to the territory and eventually the farm that they all inhabit. Upon meeting the unnamed blacksmith hired to work on the gates to Vaark's mansion, Lina recounts:

> Learning from Mistress that he was a free man doubled her anxiety. He had rights, then, and privileges, like Sir. He could marry, own things, travel, sell his own labor. She should have seen the danger immediately because his arrogance was clear. When mistress returned, rubbing her hands on her apron, he removed his hat once more, then did something Lina had never seen an African do: he looked directly at Mistress, lowering his glance, for he was very tall, never blinking those eyes slanted and yellow as a ram's. (53)

Again, it is the animal who lets us know the human's condition. Contemplating the blacksmiths' relative freedom, Lina tells us "In the town [she] had been taken to, after the conflagration had wiped away her village, that kind of boldness from any African was legitimate cause for a whip" (53). It is interesting that we find out about Lina's peoplelessness at the precise moment that she describes punishment for an exercise of free will, or because we are talking about a gaze here, punishment for the face-to-face practice of ethical commitment to the other – a practice that implies a question to be answered.

Morrison has Lina not only repudiate this commitment in racialized terms, but also states her relationship to such commitment through a discourse of homelessness. I would like to argue that this state of dispossession (if possession marks the "free," as in the paragraph above) is pivotal to our understanding of who Lina is in the novel. She becomes a character for us in the midst of marking her own kinless and placeless state while simultaneously reiterating established hierarchies of belonging in the eye-to-eye encounter between the blacksmith and "Mistress." In this moment of encounter – two face-to-face and one a third party – the blacksmith creates with his skilled eye – "a ram's eye" – an impossible ordering. His move to engage the Mistress in ethical relation is not only thoroughly undermined by his "ram's eye," but also by Lina's reiteration of a racialized ordering. The importance of the animal in negotiations of sovereignty and freedom is *how* we come to know that the blacksmith's act of self-determination is a sham. Without that "ram's eye," Lina's sentiment here would be backed by a terribly fallible oppressive system, but the question of the *animality* of the blacksmith allows that subterranean life-world to float to the surface.

Unlike Florens and the blacksmith, Lina is also vexed by the animal, as just a few pages from the scene above, she tells us of the disease that took her "family and all the others." Morrison writes:

> At first they fought off the crows, she and two young boys, but they were no match for the birds or the smell, and when the wolves arrived, all three scrambled as high into a beech tree as they could. They stayed there all night listening to gnawing, baying, growling, fighting and worst of all the quiet of animals sated at last. (54)

But here we have a contradiction, as Lina's kinless state and cultural solitude is cast in doubt by the presence of the "two young boys." Who are they to the girl who would become Lina? One could make the banal observation that her ideas of "family" might be bounded by female rather than male succession, but this move seems too easy, even "romantic," at best.

In many ways, the novel is about the awful "quiet of animals sated at last." Remaking herself through bricolage from contact in the Americas, Lina was "relying on memory and her own resources, she cobbled together neglected rites, merged Europe medicine with native, scripture with lore, and recalled or invented the hidden meaning of things. Found, in other words, a way to be in the world ... She cawed with birds, chatted with plants, spoke to squirrels, sang to the cow and opened her mouth to rain" (57). A seventeenth-century Temple Grandin, she becomes the quintessential American by being dispossessed of the narrative of her past – in her state of relative cultural collapse, she turns to the animal and communicates. Such communication does not signal meaning-making so much as it signals a becoming-animal that serves as the rationale for the novel's treatment of Lina as a medium. Whenever we move back in time, the world becomes thick with nonhuman animals. Moreover, the unmooring of Lina and her subsequent remaking prepares her for the following, at least according to Sorrow: "that Lina ruled and decided everything Sir and Mistress did not. Her eye was everywhere even when she was nowhere" (144). This eye reminds one of the ram's eye, but is disembodied and becomes the lens of management, a panopticon Foucault would be proud of. For Sorrow, Lina is the doer, the decider as she has the power to take the first, but not the second child of Sorrow and abandon it in the waters of a nearby creek. Lina's reach is *biblical*. Lina becomes a New World subject, seemingly able to manage bare life. Her relationship to Sorrow and Florens is articulated in biopolitical terms and my interest here is how – and queerly so – Lina accomplishes such power in the wake of having lost or relinquished her kin. Her power-not-power is perplexing. Being *sovereign* entails power over life and death and its manageability as well as encompasses a certain kind of geographical reach necessary to make the very idea of the capacity to rule possible. Lina might have some of the former in regard to the black captives around her – and even this power is subverted in the text – but she does not have what I would call a geopositive possessiveness integral to making sovereign practice work; at least not in its strictly euro-philosophical iteration. Lina's positionality and her becoming-animal creates several problems, including how to interpret the ethical life of the novel itself? In the next section I turn to a traditional philosophical ground in meanings of ethical relation/commitment to understand not only Jacob Vaark's turn toward having human chattel, but how nonhuman animality animates this trajectory at every turn.

### Ethical Lessons?

To think through some of the novel's challenges to what I am thinking of as "the ethical commitment," consider Jacob's rescue of the raccoon. This scene is the first "human" act of the story, but by involving an animal it demonstrates the ways in which saving the animal is always at the threshold of saving/rescuing the human being (from itself):

> Jacob urged the mare to a faster pace. He dismounted twice, the second time to free the bloody hindleg of a young raccoon stuck in a tree break. Regina [the horse] munched trail-side grass while he tried to be as gentle as

> possible, avoiding the claws and teeth of the frightened animal. Once he
> succeeded, the raccoon limped off, perhaps to the mother forced to aban-
> don it or more likely into other claws. (12)

Between two animals – the mare and the raccoon – and two iterations of a
"claw" – one belonging to the raccoon and another one to an unknown
predator – Jacob commits his first act of mercy. It is 1682 and he is
traveling via the "old Lenape Trail" on his way to D'Ortega's plantation in
Maryland.

Jacob's act of dislodging the injured raccoon is meant to tell us who he
is – the work with the animal steers us into future work with the human.
Jacob's accepting the girl Florens in exchange for an unpaid debt also
appears to be "a mercy" of signature meaning. I would argue that a mercy
toward nonhuman animals so informs what we would call human mercy
that we must consider them to be on par with one another – human acts
scripted by human/nonhuman animal distinction. Yet we find that acts of
kindness, as in the case of the raccoon that arguably is freed for "death," are
not always ethical acts. If the ethical commitment of the human is to the
other – or, as Levinas reminds us, "something more than my life" – then
what is Jacob's face-to-face commitment to Florens? We learn at the end of
the novel that "A Mercy" is this solitary act – all of the others in the novel
are just reverberations of the same, like a ripple on a pond.

Morrison provides some answer to the conundrum of this second act of
mercy in Jacob's attitude toward trading in human cargo, noting "Flesh
was not his commodity." But we are introduced to Jacob's disdain for slave
trading, not because of his absolute abhorrence of the thing itself – the
trade in "flesh" – but because of the people with whom he associates such
trade. He sees Maryland as a "palatinate [that] was Romish to the core.
Priests strode openly in its towns; their temples menaced its squares; their
sinister missions cropped up at the edge of native villages.... He was
offended by the lax, flashy cunning of the Papists" (15). Jacob is not
repulsed by slavery so much as he is unnerved by Catholicism: "there
was something beyond Catholic in [D'Ortega], something sordid and
overripe" (27). We have more descriptions of D'Ortega and his plantation's inhabitants – "a sloven man" (19); "their narrow grasp of the English
language" (20); "the foolish, incomprehensible talk" (22); and "curdled
arrogant fop" (29). Morrison seemingly sets the tension in the novel in
religious difference, rather than racial difference.

Along with racial and religious difference, however, there is sexual
difference – or difference in culturally articulated sexual practice – that
appears in this first scene of contact. The sexual tension in this encounter

with D'Ortega abounds and, if anything, D'Ortega's Catholicism indicates a nature almost too human, past its expiration point ("over-ripe"), and a concerted loss of a masculinity clearly needed for self-governance or at least the demonstrated capacity for sovereignty. Jacob's travel southward and his disdain for slavery conjures old gendered paradigms of the region's degenerate masculinity, interpreted in one spectacular instance through Harriet Jacobs's writing about the sexual exploitation of the enslaved "Luke" at the hands of his masters.[18] This old trope leads Jacob to an unquestioned place at the table of white supremacy's ruling order. He becomes the man who purchases human flesh, not to save it from a system, or itself, but to save it from the wrong type of sovereign rule. Here, to be sovereign is to *not* be queer, but to shore up such precarious masculinity as that which rests upon what an *other* is *not*; both Jacob and Lina will have to participate in managing animals and blackness, even in the context of "freeing" them as an ultimate expression of *king* sovereignty's purpose.

If the opening scene of Vaark's travel south holds open the possibility of his interspecies compassionate practice, a scene between (human) beings takes place between Jacob and Florens's mother:

> "Please Senhor. Not me. Take her. Take my daughter."
>
> Jacob looked up at her, away from the child's feet, his mouth still open with laughter, and was struck by the terror in her eyes. His laugh creaking to a close, he shook his head, thinking, God help me if this is not the most wretched business.
>
> "Why yes. Of course," said D'Ortega, shaking off his earlier embarrassment and trying to re-establish his dignity. "I'll send her to you. Immediately." His eyes widened as did his condescending smile, though he still seemed highly agitated.
>
> "My answer is firm," said Jacob, thinking, I've got to get away from this substitute for a man. But thinking also, perhaps Rebekka would welcome a child around the place. This one here, swimming in horrible shoes, appeared to be about the same age as Patrician, and *if she got kicked in the head by a mare*, the loss would not rock Rebekka so. (31; emphasis added)

But what brings Vaark to this point? I offer that the differences here could all be parsed through the article that moves us forward through acts of "mercy" throughout the text. Instead of "the" mercy – where "the" refers to something known to the listener – we have "a" mercy, an act more indeterminate and unspecified. What brings Jacob face to face with the mother about to give up her child is a turning point in the tension between Vaark and D'Ortega:

Jacob raised his eyes to D'Ortega's, noticing the cowardice of unarmed gentry confronted with a commoner. Out here in the wilderness dependent upon paid guards nowhere in sight this Sunday. He felt like laughing . . . Where else could rank tremble before courage? Jacob turned away, letting his exposed unarmed back convey his scorn. It was a curious moment. Along with his contempt, he felt a wave of exhilaration. Potent. Steady. (29)

Immediately after this moment, Jacob passes the cookhouse, sees the woman in the doorway and is offered the child. Like Faulkner's Thomas Sutpen in *Absalom, Absalom*, his visit to "the big house" produces an articulation of class difference so profound that it sets him to laughing, until he comes face to face with the woman. With the ethical commitment before him, Jacob can be persuaded to take the girl as an afterthought in a series of relations grounded in inequality: "[he] realized, not for the first time, that only things, not bloodlines or character separated them" (31).

A mercy here is a singular but mysterious act, known only to the interlocutors; as readers we are called to witness *it*, look for it even, but its siting cannot be adequately determined by us. In any event, this mercy's significance is not reciprocated by Jacob; he does not think of that moment literally in kind or in relationship to Florens's mother, but rather as evidence of his elevated stature in the world. This elevation causes him to have fantasies of building "a house that size on his own property" (31), again like Faulkner's "Sutpen's 100," and his design. Later in the same section, we learn that Jacob "did what was necessary: secured a wife, someone to help her, planted, fathered" (39). In Faulkner's text, Sutpen remarks "I had a design. To accomplish it I should require money, a house, a plantation, slaves, a family – incidentally, of course, a wife."[19] While Morrison writes that "Jacob sneered at wealth dependent on a captured workforce that required more force to maintain" and that he would not be "trading his conscience for coin" (32), we have to return to the earlier scene of Florens's exchange to gain proper perspective upon this act of mercy.

Remember this: "This one here, swimming in horrible shoes, appeared to be about the same age as Patrician, *and if she got kicked in the head by a mare*, the loss would not rock Rebekka so" (31; emphasis added). Earlier, the death of their fifth child in this same manner has rocked his otherwise "capable" (23) wife, Rebekka and so the substitute child – the enslaved – is valued, is exchanged because Jacob believes the "loss would not rock [her] so." Florens's potential "death by mare" is figured two times, as the first mare (Regina – who has a name, though Florens's mother does not) carries Vaark to the D'Ortega plantation, bringing about her separation from her mother and the second mare, having already killed the "five-year-old" Patrician is conjured here to produce a second value for Florens. The capriciousness of the animal is utilized by Morrison to mark Florens's situation in Jacob's eyes. The proximity to the animal makes her status as chattel even more cogent. The exchange of child for slave/child, the possible end of Vaark's bloodline, and the presence of the mare produce a situation which has all the makings of political philosophy's version of sovereignty. This mode of sovereign power percolates *before* Lina's loss of kin and kind, setting the stage for two modes of sovereignty to develop in the novel: one which denies indigenous claims through deterritorialization and another that produces a new Jacob Vaark, with all the *right* tools for sovereign power. Thus, rather than religious difference, or what comes before the age of racialization, the novel principally depicts the way in which the twin trajectories of indigenous sovereignty and European practices of sovereign power (un)couple so that sovereignty itself is reimagined as a space where only white men fear to tread.

A pernicious sovereignty cloaks itself as an act of mercy, while ushering in a crushing will-to-power that manifests itself later as Jacob Vaark's coming enterprise. Moreover, I contend that animal life is crucial to this cloaking, transforming kin and kind in a series of hum/animal postures. It would be a mistake to read only those explicit correlations between animal and black/indigenous humans as scenes that legitimate human denigration. By negotiating the meaning of nonhuman animal life to practices defined not by kin and kind, but commerce, a certain kind of sovereignty becomes operationalized and legitimated. A mercy allows Jacob Vaark to break through to sovereign power precisely because he has found the appropriate rhetorics for its reproduction. To care not for black and indigenous sovereignty here is not solely a matter of lapsed ethical commitment, but a profound change in human relations mediated by animal life. To ignore this animal life is to confound our ability to see how one kind of sovereignty overdetermines and insinuates itself *as* a new world order, one marking queer, cisgendered woman, black, and indigenous lives as always already outside.

In the end we realize that "a mercy" is not an act of God, but a deeply human endeavor: "It was a mercy. Offered by a human" (195). One could argue that the only human endeavor that matters is the ethical commitment to the other, who can be seen because of the commitment to "more than one's own life." It is clear that Florens's mother sees, recognizes, and inhabits this space called "a mercy"; it is also clear that Vaark's own vision is skewed by the way in which Florens is exchanged for so many things in the beginning of this novel – an exchange mediated by the persistent referencing to the animal. In the end, *A Mercy* rests on human, animal, gender, sex, class, and so much more.

The focus on the "human" in the novel is constantly interrupted by the gaze of the nonhuman other, which calls for sharper focus on the doers and the done to and demands a clearer perceptiveness about what freedom and sovereignty mean in the context of this new world order, whose logocentrism necessarily and repeatedly puts (hu)man at odds with animal. In *Homo Sacer*, Agamben sets forth the terrible possibilities of "supreme power," noting that "in the last analysis, [it is] nothing other than *the capacity to constitute oneself and others as life that may be killed but not sacrificed*" (101; original emphasis).[20] The sovereign's political embodiment as sacred life extends both the right to power and its unaccountability, as sovereignty can be detected in the act of getting away with (murder). This actualization is remarked upon by Agamben and Derrida as dependent upon the condition of the human/animal distinction, while the boundary between them is constantly called into crisis by "human" action. What I am searching for here is a way for us to understand how much discourses of sovereignty, self-determination, and freedom are caught in the double temporal bind of a past that cannot be reconciled with a future and an animality that must be managed and reckoned with as a threshold moment for both indigenous and black peoples. This query leads to other questions about what self-determination actually is; is it management ("politics supposes livestock" – Derrida), is it a civilizing mission, or is it forty acres and a mule, repatriation, or reparation? What exactly is that condition of sovereignty? Perhaps such questions are better left to the animal, who ultimately lives at the mercy of human beings.

## Notes

1 Marjorie Spiegel, *The Dreaded Comparison: Human and Animal Slavery* (New York: Mirror Books, 1996). All subsequent references appear parenthetically in the text.
2 See Philip J. Deloria, *Playing Indian* (New Haven: Yale University Press, 1998), and *Indians in Unexpected Places* (Lawrence: University Press of Kansas, 2004).
3 Megan H. Glick, "Animal Instincts: Race, Criminality, and the Reversal of the' Human,'" *American Quarterly* vol. 65, no. 3 (September 2013): 642. All subsequent references appear parenthetically in the text.
4 Frederick Douglass, "Agriculture and Black Progress: An Address Delivered in Nashville, Tennessee, 18 September, 1873," The Frederick Douglass Papers, Vol. 4 (New Haven: Yale University Press, 1991), 388.

5 See Sharon P. Holland, "'If You Know I Have a History, You Will Respect Me': A Perspective on Afro-Native Literature," *Callaloo* vol. 17, no. 1 (1994): 334–50.

6 For indigeneity, it is literally self-government, as free nations. For blackness, it is self-governance. I alternate to highlight the political differences.

7 Each scholar invoked here adds another entry point for a complex discussion of sovereignty in US indigenous intellectual tradition. Robert Warrior published the first book, *Tribal Secrets: Recovering American Indian Intellectual Traditions* (Minneapolis: University of Minnesota Press, 1995), that offers a cogent starting point for understanding the key moments in a thoroughgoing intellectual history. Jean M. O'Brien's path-breaking book, *Dispossession by Degrees: Indian Land and Identity in Natick, Massachusetts, 1650–1790* (Lincoln: University of Nebraska Press, 1997), works through a plethora of public records and "scattered evidence" (126) to arrive at a new methodology for understanding how, when and why Indian peoples became dispossessed of their land. This work certainly laid the methodological ground for Tiya Miles's *Ties that Bind: The Story of an Afro-Cherokee Family in Slavery and Freedom* (Berkeley: University of California Press, 2005). In this story of "Doll," Miles demonstrates the complex merging of whiteness, blackness, emancipation, sovereignty, and freedom, demonstrating that no story of emancipation can be entirely told without the presence of indigenous peoples. Jodi A. Byrd's *The Transit of Empire: Indigenous Critiques of Colonialism* (Minneapolis: University of Minnesota Press, 2011) tracks the confluence of natural events and human endeavor to understand the *interpolation* of indigeneity in the making of multiracial society. She manages to deftly articulate when and where nativeness challenges and then necessarily is obfuscated in order for the work of the emerging nation to move forward. In a collection of essays written over two decades, Aileen Moreton-Robinson (*The White Possessive: Property, Power and Indigenous Sovereignty* [Minneapolis: University of Minnesota Press, 2015]) attempts to redirect indigenous studies away from a model of articulating culture toward a model of understanding racialization. Hers is the most pointed and provocative exploration of indigenous sovereignties. "So too with Joanne Barker's edited collection, Sovereignty Matters: Locations of Contestation and Possibility in Indigenous Struggles for Self-Determination (Lincoln: University of Nebraska Press, 2005)."

8 Where mainstream queer temporality always already sees this space as playful – in my work and in the wider work of black/indigenous studies, dominant modes of thinking about the temporal (and I include queer studies in that) forget about the terror, while Jacobs and Hartman, Mathews, and Deloria and others have been reminding us of the terror of time stretched beyond recognition.

9 In *The Erotic Life of Racism*, I spend quite some time detailing how queer studies work, which often traffics at the intersection of race and feminism, doesn't always do its due diligence when it comes to mapping and understanding the various genealogies and trajectories of black feminist thought.

10 Jodi A. Byrd, *The Transit of Empire: Indigenous Critiques of Colonialism* (Minneapolis: University of Minnesota Press, 2011), 10. All subsequent references appear parenthetically in the text.

11 Jacques Derrida, *The Beast and the Sovereign*, Vol. 1 (Chicago: University of Chicago Press, 2009), 14. All subsequent references appear parenthetically in the text.

12 I am riffing from the title of Achille Mbembe's essay, "Necropolitics," trans. Libby Meintjes, *Public Culture* vol. 15, no. 1 (2003): 11–40.

13 Kevin Bruyneel, *The Third Space of Sovereignty: The Postcolonial Politics of U.S.-Indigenous Relations* (Minneapolis: University of Minnesota Press, 2007), xiv. All subsequent references appear parenthetically in the text.

14 Emmanuel Levinas, "The Name of the Dog, or Natural Rights," in *Animal Philosphy*, ed. Peter Atterton and Matthew Calarco (New York: Bloomsbury Academic, 2004), 50.

15 Elizabeth McHenry, "Into Other Claws," *The Women's Review of Books* vol. 26, no. 4 (2009): 16–17.

16 Toni Morrison, *A Mercy* (New York: Vintage, 2008), 3. All subsequent references appear parenthetically in the text.

17 In Heidegger's work on unconcealment, the open terrain of worlding emerges in the form of consciousness. To be open is to be in charge, to be fully human. The animal, not able to world, sits in concealment, always. For Agamben, who reads Heidegger's work as too prescriptive, the animal worlds alongside human beings, making and marking its precarity – there for the taking – as part of a (human) imaginary that *it* does not share with human beings. Agamben asks, what would happen if we let the animal be? What would happen if *overcoming* were not the endpoint of all "human" endeavor? See Gorgio Agamben, *The Open: Man and Animal* (Stanford: Stanford University Press, 2004).

18 See Harriet Jacobs, *Incidents in the Life of a Slave Girl* (1861) for her description of the enslavement of Luke.

19 William Faulkner, *Absalom, Absalom!* (New York: Vintage, 1990), 212.

20 Giorgio Agamben, *Homo Sacer: Sovereign Power and Bare Life*, trans. Daniel Heller-Roazen (Stanford: Stanford University Press, 1998), 101.

# Index